Young Working-Class Men in Transition

Young Working-Class Men in Transition uses a unique blend of concepts from the sociologies of youth and masculinity combined with Bourdieusian social theory to investigate British young working-class men's transition to adulthood. Indeed, utilising data from biographical interviews as well as an ethnographic observation of social media activity, this volume provides novel insights by following young men across a seven-year time period. Against the grain of prominent popular discourses that position young working-class men as in 'crisis' or as adhering to negative forms of traditional masculinity, this book consequently documents subtle yet positive shifts in the performance of masculinity among this generation.

Underpinned by a commitment to a much more expansive array of emotionality than has previously been revealed in such studies, young men are shown to be engaged in school, open to so-called 'women's work' in the service sector, and committed to relatively egalitarian divisions of labour in the family home. Despite this, class inequalities inflect their transition to adulthood, with the 'toxicity' neoliberalism – rather than toxic masculinity – being core to this reality.

Problematising how working-class masculinity is often represented, *Young Working-Class Men in Transition* both demonstrates and challenges the portrayal of working-class masculinity as a repository of homophobia, sexism and anti-feminine acting. It will appeal to students and researchers interested in fields such as youth studies, masculinity studies, gender studies, sociology of education and sociology of work.

Steven Roberts is Associate Professor in Sociology, School of Social Sciences, Faculty of Arts, Monash University, Australia.

Critical Studies of Men and Masculinities

Rapid transitions related to men and masculinities are occurring across the Western world: Men are living and working within post-industrial capitalist societies; the decline of homophobia in some cultural contexts has led to profound changes in the social dynamics of men; and the internet is transforming social lives, particularly for young people. Ways to understand the dynamics of men are diversifying even as social issues related to men and masculinities persist in a range of spheres at an international level. New theoretical developments have also occurred as empirical studies shed new light on familiar topics.

The **Critical Studies of Men and Masculinities** series will be an important hub for innovative and theoretically rich empirical research that develops a critical understanding of men and masculinities within contemporary societies. This series welcomes research monographs examining important social issues related to boys, men and masculinities, including issues related to class, sexuality, age, 'race', individualization, and gender relations in a range of social contexts (e.g. education, society, work, family, sport and media). Books advancing new or innovative theories to understand masculinities will be particularly welcomed, and the series will be a venue for cutting-edge empirical research. Edited books will be accepted if they address a key gap in knowledge and provide a compelling rationale for their inclusion. We welcome relevant scholarship from any country.

Mark McCormack, University of Roehampton.
Eric Anderson, University of Winchester.
Nick Rumens, Middlesex University.

Books:

Inclusive Masculinities in Contemporary Football: Men in the Beautiful Game
Rory Magrath

Young Working Class Men in Transition
Steven Roberts

Global economic restructuring has rippled through the class and gender landscapes, disrupting old norms and creating new opportunities in its wake. But we've heard little about the particularly gendered experiences of working class boys and men. Until now. Steven Roberts has listened attentively and drawn a complex and resonant portrait. Carefully researched, artfully discussed, this is for the 21st century what Paul Willis's book was for the 20th.
Professor Michael Kimmel, Executive Director, Center for the Study of Men and Masculinities, Stony Brook University, New York

In this book, Steve Roberts sensitively captures the experiences of working class young men and the impact of social and economic transformations. He expertly challenges pre-occupations with stereotypes of traditional men, by recognising the complex non-uniform ways young masculinities are being lived out in contemporary society. This ground-breaking book has been long over-due for those working in the fields of gender, work and young people.
Dr Chris Haywood, Reader in Critical Masculinity Studies, Newcastle University, UK

This engrossing and thought-provoking monograph sets out to challenge many of the orthodoxies surrounding the representation of working class masculinities in academic research. The longitudinal nature of the study upon which the book is based, including fascinating insights gleaned from social media ethnography, allows for a nuanced picture of the everyday lives of working class young men to emerge, one which is suggestive of change and transformation in many respects. Set against a backdrop of increasing precarity and powerlessness amongst working class youth, Roberts' book is a passionate call to take seriously 'the missing middle' in youth research.
Professor Sue Heath, Co-Director, Morgan Centre for Research into Everyday Lives, University of Manchester, UK

With this book Roberts presents an impressive account of young working-class men's lives. Impressive because of its sensitivity and attention to nuances in the empirical data; because of the theoretical ground it covers; and not least because of the intervention it poses by insisting on a positive story about young working-class masculinities. The book is essential reading for everyone interested in young people, gender relations and the potentials for social change.
Dr Signe Ravn, Australian Research Council DECRA Fellow, University of Melbourne, Australia

Young Working-Class Men in Transition

Steven Roberts

LONDON AND NEW YORK

First published 2018 by Routledge

2 Park Square, Milton Park, Abingdon, Oxfordshire OX14 4RN
52 Vanderbilt Avenue, New York, NY 10017

Routledge is an imprint of the Taylor & Francis Group, an informa business

First issued in paperback 2019

Copyright © 2018 Steven Roberts

The right of Steven Roberts to be identified as author of this work has been asserted by him in accordance with sections 77 and 78 of the Copyright, Designs and Patents Act 1988.

All rights reserved. No part of this book may be reprinted or reproduced or utilised in any form or by any electronic, mechanical, or other means, now known or hereafter invented, including photocopying and recording, or in any information storage or retrieval system, without permission in writing from the publishers.

Notice:
Product or corporate names may be trademarks or registered trademarks, and are used only for identification and explanation without intent to infringe.

British Library Cataloguing in Publication Data
A catalogue record for this book is available from the British Library

Library of Congress Cataloging in Publication Data
A catalog record has been requested for this book

ISBN: 978-1-138-21718-8 (hbk)
ISBN: 978-0-367-47372-3 (pbk)

Typeset in Times New Roman
by Taylor & Francis Books

For Cansu, Olivia and Aydin

Contents

List of illustrations x
Foreword xi
Preface xiii
Acknowledgments xv

1 Youth transitions, young men and social change 1

2 Dominant representations of working-class masculinity: The so-called 'crisis of masculinity' and the academic response 17

3 Making sense of men: Outlining a framework for the study of contemporary masculinities 41

4 The study context and methods 78

5 Looking back and looking forward at age 18–24: Educational histories and aspirations 84

6 Young working-class men navigating the precarious world of work: Identity in and out of the labour market 120

7 Contemporary working-class masculinities and the domestic sphere: The diminishing significance of 'the man of the house' 150

8 Emotional disclosure online and offline: Changes and continuities in forms of intimate expression among working-class men 180

9 Conclusion: Changing the tune, but not changing the record: working-class masculinity in transition 210

Index 222

Illustrations

Figure

1.1 'The generational decline of masculinity and femininity' 2

Table

4.1 Sample details at first interview 80

Foreword

We are delighted to publish *Young Working Class Men in Transition* in our book series, *Critical Studies of Men and Masculinities*. In conceiving of the series, we wanted to showcase empirical research that developed concepts and theories that advanced our understanding of men and the social dynamics of their lives. Our first monograph challenged conventional thinking of football as a bastion of homophobia and hyper-masculinity by documenting the attitudes toward gay people and homosocial behaviors of young men about to enter the professional leagues of football in the UK. In this second book in the series, Dr. Steve Roberts again compels academics to reconsider fundamental assumptions about the lives of men by focusing on the experiences of working-class millennial men.

Just as one foundational component of critical masculinities studies examined the role of sport in the production of men's gender, a second tenet has been the importance of class in structuring the way the social world is experienced. With a lineage that traces back to Willis's classic book *Learning to Labour*, through the work of Mairtin Mac an Ghaill, Linda McDowell, and Anoop Nayak, it has long been understood that work and forms of labour are central to how masculinity is practiced and embodied. By focusing on the transitions from education to work of working class men from the south east of England, the book provides a vital contribution to understanding how profound shifts in capitalism and globalization intersect with social progress made by women and sexual minorities. Pulling together a variety of concepts in a novel and compelling way, *Young Working Class Men in Transition* provides an all-too-rare sensitive and thought-provoking examination of the form and function of contemporary masculinity in the lives of young working-class men in the United Kingdom.

The book offers such a powerful exploration of the lives of working class young men and how they transition from education to work because it foregrounds the words of the participants and recognizes the diverse, complex and highly differentiated accounts of their social worlds. Whereas research on masculinities can too-easily homogenize working class men, Steve Roberts engages with an array of theoretical resources that enables recognition of the importance of class and gender without erasing the diversity of experiences of his participants.

We are confident that readers will be as engaged as they are impressed by Roberts' ability to blend a range of sociological theories to muster his arguments. His understanding of gender is closely engaged with the work of Raewyn Connell and Eric Anderson; Pierre Bourdieu's framework of class enables an understanding of its presence in a range of social domains; and a carefully-argued account of generation helps combat simplistic arguments of generational inequality. In so doing, Roberts demonstrates how social change has seen a flattening of hierarchies within masculinities even as class continues to be an important structure in participants' lives.

Roberts also manages to recognize the 'both/and' nature of the social world. Embracing research that documents the profound shift in young men's lives in the West since the 1980s, he demonstrates how class bears down heavily on young men, inflecting their behaviors well beyond the school gate and ensuring their employment trajectories remain turbulent. This reality is nuanced by the recognition that young men's gendered displays shift in positive directions as they transition to adulthood. An important finding to this work is that a great majority of data shows how older traditional codes of masculinity no longer have the same stranglehold on young men's lives today. Roberts makes this exceptionally clear.

Thus, *Young Working Class Men in Transition*, is an essential reading and a perfectly-timed contribution to the debate on young people, gender relations and the potentials for social change.

Mark McCormack, *University of Roehampton*
Eric Anderson, *University of Winchester*
Nick Rumens, *Middlesex University*

Preface

Taking working-class men's transitions from youth to adulthood as its core empirical focus, this book concerns social and economic changes, and the attendant possibilities for the performance of masculinity that have emerged as legitimate for contemporary working-class young men. The book stresses how masculinity has become modified and redefined by and for some, such that we might call it 'softened'. In presenting this material, I am not attempting to deny or apologise for the toxic components of masculinity that exist, that constrain the possibilities for identity for a not insignificant amount of men, that threaten the physical and emotional safety of people of any and all gender identities. The book is not related to or part of off or online activism that unhelpfully emphasises #NotAllMen as a rebuttal to anything that links men and masculinity to crime, aggression and toxicity. Instead, the purpose – having collected the data and observed first hand just how different the young men's lives, ideas and performances of masculinity were relative to representations in the literature – is to disrupt the stereotype of the working-class young man. Disrupting this stereotype does not mean neglecting or de-prioritising feminist aims for greater equality; rather it shows that at least some strides have been made in this respect. The job is not done, of course, but to my mind the field of sociology does a disservice to itself, to young men, and ultimately to everyone else if we are not willing to make clear how adherence to the old archetype of masculinity has become somewhat attenuated. To do otherwise runs the risk of reinforcing and reifying the older negative forms of masculinity and *narrows* the real and discursive possibilities for change. For those reasons we must not, as per Nicola Ingram, 'shut down the possibilities of nuanced, conflicted and complex identities'.[1]

Instead, it is my firm view that through documenting – but also critically exploring – positive developments in young men's gender performances, through showcasing the alternatives that are widely taken up by many men, including those men who are stereotypically situated as being incapable of escaping traditional demands of masculinity, we can aid the amelioration of the effects of the toxic or 'hegemonic' versions of masculinity. We must not *minimise* the role that discourses of orthodox or toxic masculinity have in producing the very real damage caused by men, but we must make efforts to *minoritise* those who engage in harmful practices, those harmful ways of being a man, and fully declare when we observe such practices to be undergoing change and losing their stranglehold on the majority of men. We might stand a better chance of facilitating genuine progress towards gender equality if we are prepared to give new generations a chance of knowing that those problematic ways of being a man are not 'normal', are not required, are not ordinary or for the majority.

In the words of Lynn Segal, in the opening to her classic text on masculinities, '*it is possible to steer a course between defeatist pessimism and fatuous optimism. Such, at any rate, is the project of this book*'.[2]

Notes

1 N. Ingram (2017). 'I'm not just one type of person': Aspirational working-class Belfast boys and complex embodied performances of educationally successful masculinities, in G. Stahl, J. Nelson, & D. Wallace (Eds.), *Masculinity and Aspiration in an Era of Neoliberal Education*. London: Routledge, pp. 71–88, at p. 72.
2 L. Segal (2007). *Slow Motion* (second edition). London: Palgrave, p. xxxvi.

Acknowledgments

Many people have variously shaped my thinking, inspired me, listened to me, told me to pipe down, believed in me and helped me, practically and intellectually, while doing this research. It feels nigh on impossible to rank those contributions; save one. The study's participants stand out. Their testimonies have been essential to the entire endeavour and are a source of immense value. Both their willingness to share their stories, and the *content* of their stories, bust all kinds of myths that build up around working-class men's lives. I hope to have done their accounts justice, to have suitably acknowledged that the story of working-class men is not deficit, nor misplaced teary-eyed nostalgia for a time 'when men were men'; theirs is a story of hard work, adaptation, promise, positivity, partnership, egalitarianism.

Heartfelt thanks are due to many others: Eric Anderson and Mark McCormack for their support in contracting and producing the book, and for stimulating my thinking and supporting my writing in various ways over the years; Elena Chiu at Routledge for unparalleled patience; Alison Neale for her incredible attention to detail in the copy editing; Sarah Vickerstaff for supervising the PhD, which originated the book's core ideas a decade ago; Derek Kirton and Matthew Bond for assisting the PhD supervision; all those who read and commented on drafts of my work over the years or even just sat and listened to me talk about it, and often, unwittingly, helped me shape it, including, Anika Haverig, Patrick Brown, Marcus Maloney, Karla Elliott and Cathy Waite; Simon Breeze for decades of friendship and for inspiring me, first, to go to university and, second, for making a PhD seem possible; Sarah Evans for her limitless and generous insight and for being the ultimate role model doctoral candidate and all round amazing chum; Alexandra Caruso for helping compile the literature used in the project, and to Brittany Ralph and Elsie Foeken for countless hours of meticulous attention to detail in proofing the final draft (and to all three for being such thought-provoking, incredibly smart honours students!); Sam Atkins and Paige Roger for their tireless efforts transcribing interview material and for watching the puppies!; Alan France, Rob MacDonald, Alison Fuller, Rachel Brooks for their invaluable advice and being unofficial, amazing mentors at various times; Signe Ravn, for being my buddy on the far side of the world, for being ever willing to collaborate and to listen, think, critique, support. Countless others, too, asked questions and offered comments at various conferences where the material has been aired over ten years – an immeasurable contribution.

Beyond the working environment, my daughter, Olivia, and my wife, Cansu, have lit up my life and given me purpose, direction and motivation. Cansu was also a life saver in a sleepless 48 hours in the build-up to submission in our joint efforts to compile missing references and furiously edit down. And then my dear Mum, who has suffered at the hands of masculinity at its most horrific and toxic. She taught me the importance of being a human being, over and above 'how to be a man', and has been the greatest influence of all. Love you all x

1 Youth transitions, young men and social change

Introduction

Whilst preparing this book, Donald Trump was elected as 45th President of the United States. Occupying what is widely considered the world's highest and most powerful seat of public office is a man who publicly and unabashedly espouses a very traditional and indeed toxic version of masculinity; this includes, among other things, promoting gendered divisions of domestic labour, passing off sexism and bragging about sexual aggressiveness and sexual assault as simply male-to-male 'locker room' banter, and talking (indeed, presiding) in ways that highlight the significance of stoicism, power, dominance and entitlement. Given this most high-profile of examples, and the fact that many men (and indeed women) voted for him despite and in some cases because of his performance of masculinity, the following claim may, to some, seem a controversial statement: The set of behaviours and characteristics that underpinned the relatively monolithic, culturally idealised version of manliness in western societies for most of the 20th century is waning (Anderson, 2009; McCormack, 2012; Roberts, 2013). Contrary to the example set by Donald Trump, this is particularly the case among younger groups of men, who in a wide array of settings and contexts have been shown to be redefining what it is to be masculine (McCormack, 2012), in a multitude of ways (Anderson & McCormack, 2016). Indeed, in the UK young men are increasingly disassociating with the idea that they might be 'completely masculine'. This is made abundantly clear in Figure 1.1, which details a 2016 nationally representative UK survey documenting how people score themselves on a six-point gender continuum, with the polar ends being 'completely masculine' and 'completely feminine'.

The percentage of people considering themselves completely masculine/feminine rises sharply as the age groups get older. In the same survey, a full 42% of men under 24 said they felt that masculinity has negative connotations, some 31 percentage points higher than men over 65, and 15 percentage points higher than comparably aged women.

If and how such attitudinal change translates into the lives of contemporary British young men is this book's central concern. More specifically,

2 Youth transitions, young men and social change

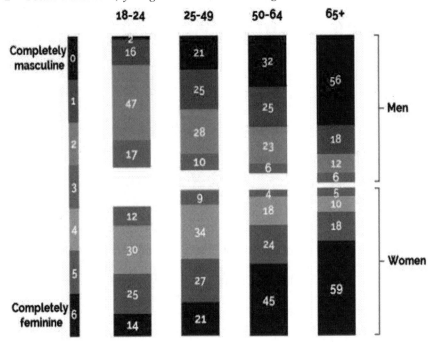

Figure 1.1 'The generational decline of masculinity and femininity'
Note: Figures in %.
Source: YouGov, May 2016.

drawing on a longitudinal qualitative study covering a seven-year period with young men of working-class origins from Kent, in the South-East of England, this book provides a detailed account of how masculinity informs working-class young men's transition to adulthood. I also critically explore if, how and in what ways working-class young masculinity is itself in a state of transition, but also how individuals' performances and perceptions of masculinity shift or remain static over time. Analysis of an extensive, in-depth dataset, collected from multiple face-to-face interviews in person and on *Skype*, *Facebook Messenger* and *WhatsApp* communications, and a *Facebook* ethnography, provides a rich contribution to a research area that lacks a focus on the changing nature and structure of employment and how this impacts on men's sense of themselves as men and on their gendered expectations (McDowell, 2014). The ambition from the outset was to shed further light on the idea that 'new forms of masculinity more in tune with the dominant attributes of a service-based economy … have yet to find any expression' (McDowell, 2003: 226) and, in doing so, to contribute to debates and theories which focus on social change as it applies to young adults and also the flattening of hierarchies within masculinities.

Prioritising the stories of the young men in their own words, the following pages adhere to Diane Reay's call to 'develop more accurate, and necessarily complex and highly differentiated, representations' (Reay, 2004: 1020) of working-class life. Combining theoretical resources derived from masculinities scholars Raewyn Connell (1987, 1995, 2000, 2005) and Eric Anderson (2005, 2009, 2011), with the utility offered by Pierre Bourdieu's array of 'research tools', the analysis provides insights into complex processes of change and continuity in respect of gender and class power relations, but also experiences of vulnerability, emotion and the very practical business of how young men draw (or are unable to draw) on various economic, social and cultural resources to negotiate the transition to adulthood in contemporary times.

In short, against the grain of large chunks of academic literature and the prominent popular discourses that position young working-class men as in 'crisis' or as adhering to a form of traditional masculinity that is negative, pernicious and also increasingly redundant, this book paints a picture of some positive social changes; of working-class young men whose journey through their transitions to adulthood demonstrate at the very least some subtle shifts in their performance of masculinity. The large bulk of the data presented herein illustrates breaks from the past such that the older traditional codes of requisite manliness no longer have the same stranglehold on young men's lives that they might once have done – that is, those older traditional codes of masculinity are no longer so surely 'hegemonic' (Connell, 1995; see Chapter 3), appearing to lack the support and the cultural ascendancy they have maintained for so long. We have by no means reached a gender utopia; there is still a masculinity at play that serves to legitimate the unequal relations of the gender order (Connell, 1995), but its hegemony, and attendant effects, appears to be observably fracturing, at least at the level of attitudes and identities. Working-class young men are much more than the representation abundantly apparent in Mac an Ghaill's (1994: 56) now classic text which posited that working-class boys perform a symbolic display of masculinity through 'the three F's – fighting, fucking and football'; indeed, they should not automatically be thought to conform to the narrow set of expressions often defined as orthodox masculinity (Anderson, 2005) – i.e. explicitly homophobic, avowedly anti-feminist and misogynistic, alongside a strong predilection for anti-feminine acting (see Ingram, 2018).

The shifts I document in this book are worthy of serious scholarly attention if we are concerned with promoting models of masculinity that do not rely so centrally on the subordination of others, such as women or gay men, or 'less than appropriately manly' men. As Messerschmidt (2016: 33) notes, scholars must 'distinguish masculinities that legitimate a hierarchical relationship between men and women, between masculinity and femininity and among masculinities, from those that do not'. This is essential if we are to 'facilitate the discovery and identification of "positive masculinities", or those that actually may help to legitimate an egalitarian relationship' (Messerschmidt, 2016: 34).

This book is not simply a 'good news story'. Neither is it a story about an exceptional bunch of young men, going against the grain. This book is about the form and function of contemporary masculinity in the lives of working-class men. There is far more to be done in the fight for gender equality, but this task entails opening up for scrutiny the *productive possibilities* of and for masculinity, and necessitates that we acknowledge positive social change where it occurs, as well as training our eye to what remains in need of change, how this occurs and why it remains fixed. To help achieve this aim, this book's focus is a group of (heterosexually identifying) young men who are *not exceptional*, either in their attitudes or in their social status. They are not 'the front line troops of patriarchy' (Connell, 1995: 79) associated with hegemonic masculinity.

As budding partners, fathers, workers and potentially breadwinners they might well be considered what Connell refers to as 'complicit' masculinities (see Chapter 3) – masculinities that characterise those men who are not especially powerful nor influence the dominant cultural symbols of manhood (Aboim, 2010: 3) – and their complicity or otherwise is a key feature of the analysis that follows. The subjects of this book are *also* marginalised on the basis of their working-class status; yet, they are not the most marginalised, most spectacular or most dispossessed members of the working class, as is the focus for many scholars, but instead are what I have previously termed the 'missing middle' of youth studies – those working-class men who, by virtue of being neither disengaged from school/work nor on a route to a 'typically successful' adulthood characterised by a degree and a professional occupation, are often ignored in social policy and research on youth transitions (Roberts, 2011).

Why might the transition to adulthood figure so prominently in discussions of men and masculinity? I take this up in more detail below, but in short, this is captured by the words of Robert MacDonald (2011: 427), who astutely notes that:

> the youth phase allows a privileged vantage point from which to observe broader processes of social change and, as such, to answer questions of wider relevance for sociology. If new social trends emerge it is feasible that they will be seen here first or most obviously, amongst the coming, new generation of young adults.

The findings outlined in this book then, through a focus on youth, are an important part of producing a better and more rounded understanding of what it is to grow up a young working-class man. The book illuminates what Messerschmidt (2016: 33) calls 'the various forms of mundane, run of the mill, nonhegemonic masculinities', resisting the temptation to presume working-class masculinity as a unitary and problematic discourse and/or identity category, and evidencing a shift, in many regards, towards what Anderson (2009) refers to as 'inclusive masculinities' (detailed in Chapter 3).

There is much more to be said about men and masculinity/ies, and the discussion will be further elaborated in Chapters 2 and 3. The plan for the remainder of this first chapter, however, is to make clear what studying transitions offers research on young adults, but also what 'transition' means and what it involves. The next section, then, sketches out some important details about the study of youth and its relationship with theories of social change, briefly highlighting also how youth sociology has come to more generally shape my approach to the sociological analysis contained within.

Youth transitions and social change

What comes to mind when we think about 'youth'? Even in an everyday sense it is likely to conjure a wide array of images and ideas. However, it's probable that for many people 'youth' is associated with young people and is likely considered an experience or phase that is located somewhere and somehow between 'childhood' and 'adulthood'. Sociologists of youth have been keen to emphasise that youth is a social construction (Wyn & White, 1997); growing up, and the various associated expectations or markers which come to mind that signal that one has become or is becoming an adult, is a contingent process, shaped by historical and geographical contexts. Youth is not a fixed process with a specific duration or content according to one's biological age. The experience of youth is diverse, and for many does not exist at all. This is evident if we consider the 168 million under-15s who form the global child labour force (ILO, 2015), but also in the fact that child labour was typical in industrialised countries until the late 1800s. In such circumstances, there is and was no period that might be considered 'youth' between the end of childhood and the start of adulthood.

Even accepting this mutability, youth, in lay thinking, is often considered to be a period of *becoming*, of being not quite adult. Sociologists problematise this deficit approach to understanding young people's lives, finding characterisations of young people as simply 'less than adult' to be patronising and dismissive of a period of life that is formative and highly impactful both in the here and now, and also upon one's future life as an adult (Wyn & White, 1997; Furlong & Cartmel, 2007; France, 2007). However, youth scholars do still adopt youth as a *relational* concept, sitting in contrast with, but only having meaning in relation to, the concept of adulthood. For sociologists, youth is perhaps best thought of as being a period characterised by both semi-dependency and semi-independency (Coles, 1995; Antonucci et al., 2014).

Analysing the experience and consequences of youth has for the most part been considered through the lens of what Ken Roberts (2003) calls the 'conventional transitions paradigm'. This approach has, for much of the last 50 years, been occupied with young people's experiences of and outcomes in three key, interrelated transitions: from school to work; from living with one's parents to independent living; and from family of origin to starting one's own family. Using this approach, examining the nature, direction and stability of these youth transitions has formed the central focus in understanding the links between social origins, routes and destinations, with an emphasis on how transitions to adulthood are inflected by dimensions of difference – especially class, but also gender and ethnicity (Roberts, 2009).

As noted, the transitions approach has been central to youth sociology for at least half a century; within this period the economic, political and social context in which young people make their transitions to adulthood has, of course, changed. The immediate post-war period is often heralded as a 'golden age' (Vickerstaff, 2003), when young people's transitions to adulthood were seen as collectively experienced as a linear, smooth and 'one step' process into the labour market and beyond (Ashton & Field, 1976; France & Roberts, 2017), with young men making 'mass transitions from the classroom to the factories and building sites, while young women followed pathways leading straight from school to shops, offices and factories' (Furlong & Cartmel, 1997: 12). This characterisation has been critiqued as being a 'rose tinted', naively nostalgic reflection, casually and falsely perpetuating the idea of an unproblematic past (see Vickerstaff, 2003; Goodwin & O'Connor, 2005, 2015). Nonetheless, things have changed and contemporary young people's transitions to adulthood in Britain, and across the industrialised world, have been profoundly affected by social and economic transformation.

The experience of education, employment, housing and starting a family for contemporary young people has been radically re-structured compared to their parents' generation. Institutionalised requirements for elongated engagement with the education system and an associated necessity to continually enhance one's education profile, an increasingly precarious youth labour market, the rise of service economies and the concomitant decline and/ or outsourcing of heavy industry and manufacturing, and a decreasing likelihood of young people being able to afford to buy – or often even rent – a home of their own have all resulted in 'a set of movements which are less predictable and involve frequent breaks, backtracking and the blending of statuses' (Furlong et al., 2003: 25).

Such changes are often seen as having particular implications for young men, especially those from lower socioeconomic backgrounds (McDowell, 2000, 2003; McDowell et al., 2014; discussed at greater length in Chapter 2). Lagging behind young women in education attainment and university participation (Hillman & Robinson, 2016), young men experience heightened risk of unemployment (McGuiness et al., 2017), and are likely to remain living in the parental home for longer (ONS, 2016) (yet men remain disproportionately represented in positions of economic and political power – see UN Women, 2017; Grant Thornton, 2016). Simultaneously, concerns abound about the disappearance of 'traditionally male' jobs and the potential implications of the rise of low-pay, low-level, seemingly feminised, service sector employment (McDowell, 2000; Nixon, 2009, 2017). The decline of the manufacturing sector, in particular, is often taken as a sharp indicator of this diminishment of 'men's jobs': in 1971 more than 33% of employment in the UK was in manufacturing, a figure that had halved to just over 16.5% by 2001. Contrastingly during the same period employment in business and miscellaneous services more than doubled from around 10% to almost 23% (Bradley & Hickman, 2004). Over the decade to 2011, manufacturing jobs declined from 2001 levels by a further 33% (Berry, 2015). The growing service sector brought with it increasing shares of 'non-standard work' such as part-time and/or flexible work and then, more recently, greater proportions of precarious employment. Indeed, since 1995, non-standard work, including temporary or agency work and zero-hour contracts,[1] has accounted for all UK net jobs growth (OECD, 2015). Ultimately, as Gunter and Watt (2009: 527) attest, 'the service-sector jobs that young men and women can realistically obtain ... are routine, subservient, low-paid and often insecure'.

These changes are especially important because paid work was for previous generations identified as being crucial for constructing men's identity, especially in relation to traditional notions that men should be providers and 'breadwinners' and that women ought be homemakers (Pease, 2002; Wilott & Griffin, 1996; Connell, 1995; Morgan, 1992; Cockburn, 1983); indeed, McDowell (2000: 289) describes 'the socially-valued attributes of masculinity' as being 'so dependent upon economic participation'. The consequences of these changes upon such men are central themes explored in this book; sociology's implicit – and oftentimes explicit – assumption that young men, unlike their fathers' generation, struggle to construct a socially esteemed masculinity under these conditions is something that must be empirically explored rather than simply accepted.

These new patterns, outlined above, have more broadly resulted in youth transitions being variously described, among other things, as 'complex', 'protracted', 'uncertain', 'fragmented', and also 'risky' (see Bradford, 2012; Furlong & Cartmel, 2007; France, 2007; Chisholm & du Bois-Reymond, 1993). Any of these, but in particular the notions of risk and uncertainty, have strong resonance with an important sociological theory presented by Ulrich Beck – the 'risk society' thesis (Beck, 1992; Beck & Beck-Gernsheim, 2002). Beyond noting that 'young people today have to negotiate a set of risks which were largely unknown to their parents' (Furlong & Cartmel, 2007: 1), Beck proposes that people must personally negotiate their social biographies, with structural forces such as class and gender no longer offering tangible, guiding communal reference points. This is a process Beck calls individualisation, where individuals are not just 'ever more free of structure; in fact they have to redefine structure' (Beck et al., 1994: 177). In this formulation, young people are *freed* from determined trajectories and simultaneously, paradoxically, *forced* 'to piece together their own biographies and fit in the components they need as best they can choose' (Beck-Gernsheim, 1998: 57). This capacity to self-formulate plans is a key necessity for but also derives from life in what Beck calls *reflexive modernity*, where 'the more societies are modernised, the more agents (subjects) acquire the ability to reflect on the social conditions of their existence and to change them accordingly' (Beck et al., 1994: 174).

While the extent of the relevance of Beck's theorising for youth sociology has been the subject of fierce critical debate (e.g. Woodman, 2009, 2010; Roberts, 2010, 2012; Threadgold, 2011), Beck's writings have also been praised and, perhaps most importantly, used as an impetus for youth (and other) sociologists to conduct empirical work that traces *both continuity and change* with respect to disadvantages, risks and inequalities. Indeed, Woodman (2010, 2012) gestures that we ought to read Beck's work as an *invitation* to understand how inequality is remade in new times. This seems to have been the approach taken by many youth scholars. Most notably this can be viewed in the influential work of Australian academic Johanna Wyn (2004: 17), who contends that young people 'are now navigators of their own biographies and careers', and that there now exists a 'new adulthood' (Cuervo & Wyn, 2011), meaning that young people's lives cannot simply be measured or even compared against the transitional experiences of their parents' and grandparents' generations; the transitions paradigm, for Wyn, overlooks the generationally distinctive possibilities for 'growing up' (Wyn & Woodman, 2006; see also Woodman & Wyn, 2015). Beck's approach has also arguably been foundational, even if only implicitly, for critiques of the transitions paradigm, notably from those who claim that the transitions perspective ignores the significance of youth cultures and lifestyles (e.g. Redhead, 1993; Miles, 2000; Bennett & Kahn-Harris, 2004). In both cases there have been calls to better prioritise young people's subjectivities and to move beyond seeing 'young people as troubled victims of economic and social restructuring without enough recourse to the active ways in which young people negotiate such circumstances in the course of their everyday lives' (Miles, 2000: 10), and to give greater emphasis to the existence of multiplicity, temporality and fluidity of expressions and other resources that allow for individuals to create their own identities in contemporary society (Bennett, 1999, 2011).

Others, too, have taken social and cultural changes as their starting point to present an idea of youth as being completely changed. Arnett (2004), for example, contends that there is now a new life stage between youth and adulthood: what he calls 'emerging adulthood'. Central to Arnett's influential claim is that young people are now capable of demonstrating their individual agency in delaying their transition and enjoying a period of freedom and independence beyond adolescence before they commit themselves to adulthood responsibility; they see themselves, says Arnett (2000), as being on the threshold of making long-term decisions and commitments. A seeming oversight in this formulation is that those with the capacity to enjoy this period (which might include having lived in an independent household for some years, having finished education and been employed for at least a year, or having done some travelling or other self-developing activities) are often shown to have very different social characteristics (particularly social class and qualification level) from those who do not (Bynner, 2005: Coles, 1995;

Furlong & Cartmel, 2007; Roberts, 2010). Arnett (2006: 115), though, contends robustly that the significance of structural factors in the lives of 'emerging adults' should be viewed as a hypothesis to be investigated rather than a starting assumption, because 'we may find that they are more important in some areas of life than in others, and more important for some individuals than others'. This seems to be a fair statement, and while I find Arnett's (and others noted above) emphasis on agency and subjectivity to be a little lopsided, to advocate for open-mindedness in empirical investigation seems a worthy sociological instinct.

Proceeding in this way is not necessarily easy, though. We can start by adopting a reflexive approach to better uncover any creeping personally held confirmation bias, or 'the tendency that people have to accept evidence that supports their own viewpoint and discount that which does not' (McCormack, 2012: 130). My inclination, instinct, or 'viewpoint' is one informed by the strand of research in youth studies that has been keen to note structural factors as retaining continued influence. For example, I have previously been very critical of how Beck relegates social class to being an outmoded, now-less-relevant or 'zombie' analytical category (Roberts, 2010), and have also argued Beck and his advocates (e.g. Woodman, 2009, 2012) somewhat frustratingly (even if sometimes inadvertently) marginalise class analysis in youth sociology (France & Roberts, 2017). My previous empirical research has also found Arnett's (2006) contention that emerging adulthood represents the 'apex of freedom' to be ill conceived (see Haverig & Roberts, 2011). I feel strongly also, as MacDonald (2011) notes, that there is a tendency in youth sociology to focus on the seemingly new, with any stress on the consistent and unchanging often seen as somehow signifying a less than optimally vibrant research field (see Woodman, 2013). Some of the earliest youth sociology literature I recall reading as I embarked on my own university education included Furlong and Cartmel's (1997) protestations about Beck's (and others, such as Giddens, 1991, and Bauman, 2000) overemphasis on individual reflexivity, but also more empirical arguments that explicate the continuing influence of social structures on young people's transitions to adulthood. Jones's (2002) explanation, for instance, of how the extended transition to adulthood of 'new times' has a pronounced and increasingly polarised class gradient, with middle-class youth tending towards a 'slow track' through extended periods of education and enjoying extensive familial support, while working-class young people in all advanced societies are more likely to take the 'fast track': over represented among early labour market entrants, early parenthood and early home leaving. Similarly, and relevant to the present study, other strong influences were Chisholm and du Bois-Reymond's (1993) arguments pointing to the continuation of the effects of gender relations upon youth transitions and the living out of what du Bois-Reymond (1998) refers to as 'gender specific normal biographies'.

So, in engaging with the question of how much freedom young people have in making their transitions – a question that is core to perennial debates in the youth literature – I have tended towards emphasising structure. However, I was determined to approach the research project presented in this book, a project that focuses on change and continuities among young working-class men, with an open-mindedness that prioritises the words and the meaning-making of the participants, and a reluctance to categorise their experiences *a priori*. In many ways, youth-related research demands this type of approach if it is to fulfil '[t]he great promise of youth studies [which] is not so much its ability to trace social change, or highlight patterns of continuity, but to show how the two are intertwined' (Woodman, 2013: 13). Because 'the examination of young people's lives provides a unique window on processes of social and economic change' (Furlong, 2012: 5), giving critical attention to how the construction of a socially esteemed masculinity mutually informs the negotiation of the transition to adulthood among young men from working-class backgrounds is an important part of this promise. A youth transitions-focused approach also avoids the privileging of solely the theme of men's formal employment (Mac an Ghaill & Haywood, 2014; Walker & Roberts, 2017), and allows for a deeper consideration of how young men construct and perform their masculinity in relation to their roles as friends, partners, parents, consumers, and more generally as 'emerging adults', and how this interacts with and is informed by the changing nature of contemporary working lives.

Book Outline and Chapter Synopsis

A key issue taken up in the empirical chapters is to critically consider 'the extent to which individuals are constrained by their structural contexts and how far they can build alternative identities despite their stigma' (Heward, 1996: 41). However, another crucial dimension the book tackles is the implications that arise from being able to break free from the constraints of traditional models of masculinity; as Scoats (2017: 340) suggests, we need to know whether inclusive behaviours are becoming a robust feature of adulthood.

Before getting to the rich material that informs my major argument, however, Chapters 2 and 3 address a few theoretical issues. First, social and economic changes are often used as the foundation for the idea that masculinity is in crisis. Chapter 2 critically evaluates this notion of crisis and explores how the research literature tackles such theorising. In addition, though, the chapter explores how some key literature has effectively problematised the crisis rhetoric but simultaneously, perhaps inadvertently, positioned working-class young men as remaining rather static in their gender performances.

Chapter 3 thoroughly details the core theoretical apparatus considered and used for analysis of the data. The chapter provides a comprehensive account of Connell's Hegemonic Masculinity Theory, and, as part of my critical engagement with her work, also proceeds to fully outline the foundations of Anderson's Inclusive Masculinity Theory. Useful as these foundational ideas of masculinity studies are, I also explain here how my study is supplemented by social generation theory as recently applied by scholars of youth sociology, and, more so, some appreciation of Bourdieusian social theory. The latter, especially Bourdieu's concept of habitus, provides some flexibility to ensure that the participants' lives can be understood beyond simply a lens attuned to the performance and production of masculinity, to account for how transitions are managed and negotiated, and come to be marked by class inequalities.

Before getting to the empirical findings, Chapter 4 provides a very short overview of the methods adopted for the study, introduces the sample, and offers some historical and contextual insights into the study's locale.

I then offer rich and detailed accounts of the data, divided into four themes. First, Chapter 5 centres on the participants' retrospective accounts of schooling and a consideration of aspirations for educational engagement as an adult. This chapter emphasises the presence of a middle-ground orientation, disrupting the dominant narrative around boys being either disaffected with or highly engaged in school. Their relative compliance despite limited reward is theorised as a working-class norm, one that continues through to at least some form of post-compulsory education. With the prospect of university, however, comes perceptions of significant risk. I argue here that it is better to think of these risks as being the determining factors for low rates of higher education participation among working-class young men, over and above some kind of cultural incongruity or aspirational deficit.

Chapter 6 analyses the participants' experiences of paid work, using longitudinal data to offer insights into changing attitudes but also the dynamic – and often very precarious – nature of labour market trajectories for working-class young men. I highlight that there are fewer penalties for deviation from the 'old script' of masculinity, and even some benefits for young men, their friends, colleagues, families and partners. Simultaneously, there are still limits, especially in relation to the world of work where a precarious existence seems to be the best that such young men can hope for. While traditional masculinity had seemingly guaranteed something – status, a wage, etc. – for older generations of men, it is now redundant. Yet, the necessary version of masculinity today, one that demands tolerance, subservience, docility and emotional labour as part of face-to-face interactions, offers little more than the possibility for accessing low-level jobs – it permits staying afloat and is not some kind of anecdote to unemployment, underemployment, or low-pay, low-skill work. I also consider here the array of alternative activities that the participants invest in that might bring about status and esteem. For the most part these are about the achievement of dignity and occur in relation to hobbies, charity fundraising, or work on the body. Such status is also found, though, in childrearing, and this is one feature of Chapter 7.

The focus in Chapter 7 is, first, the participants' articulation of support for equal shares of domestic responsibility in their late teens and early twenties. Seeing this as not incompatible with manliness, they instead position sharing a domestic workload as the right, or even natural, thing to do. Supporting these claims, in their interviews seven years later, often partnered and living with female partners and sometimes children, there is a strong culture of engagement in the domestic sphere. While perhaps not quite as equal as the men first explain, I show how it is young working-class men who are demonstrating more progressive or egalitarian attitudes – and that these attitudes are product of the working-class habitus for the contemporary generation.

Chapter 8 turns to the nature of intimacy and expressions of emotion. Despite the denial of such issues as important to working-class young men, the chapter, through a consideration of discursive practices in respect of friendship, discussions about loved ones and an analysis of *Facebook* activity, shows a much more complex pattern than some have suggested. Here, I illustrate a changing relationship with and a de-centring of homophobic language, an unequivocal embrace of male-to-male tactility and emotional interaction (akin to Anderson 2009, and McCormack, 2012). There is also, though, plenty of evidence of the typical heterosexism associated with orthodox or hegemonic masculinity. This is not a uniformly prioritised way of thinking, and for some it sits beneath the surface and can co-exist with progressive attitudes and respectful dispositions that seem entirely at odds with the traces of misogyny. The intent, context and effect of these discursive activities and physical practices is considered.

Finally, I conclude in Chapter 9 by summing up what these data mean for how we understand contemporary working-class masculinity, paying special attention to how these transformations have occurred and where there remains a need for considerably more progress. I also make some suggestions regarding future research endeavours, the potential of the book's evidence and the new ways of thinking it demands, and its implications for public and social policy. Some recommendations in respect to these issues close the book.

Note

1 Zero-hour contracts, also sometimes known as casual contracts, ensure that an individual can be hired but with no guarantee of a minimum number of hours. The worker is not obliged to accept any hours offered.

References

Aboim, S. (2010). *Plural Masculinities: The Remaking of the Self in Private Life*. London: Ashgate.
Anderson, E. (2005). Orthodox and inclusive masculinity: Competing masculinities among heterosexual men in a feminized terrain. *Sociological Perspectives*, 48(3), 337–355.
Anderson, E. (2009). *Inclusive masculinity: The changing nature of masculinities*. New York: Routledge.
Anderson, E. (2011). Masculinities and sexualities in sport and physical cultures: Three decades of evolving research. *Journal of Homosexuality*, 58(5), 565–578.
Anderson, E., & McCormack, M. (2016). Inclusive Masculinity Theory: Overview, reflection and refinement. *Journal of Gender Studies*, 1–15.

Antonucci, L., Hamilton, M., & Roberts, S. (2014). *Young People and Social Policy in Europe*. Basingstoke: Palgrave Macmillan.

Arnett, J.J. (2000). Emerging adulthood: A theory of development from the late teens through the twenties. *American Psychologist*, 55(5), 469.

Arnett, J.J. (2004). *Emerging adulthood: The winding road from the late teens through the twenties*. New York: Oxford University Press.

Arnett, J.J. (2006). Emerging adulthood: Understanding the new way of coming of age, in J.J. Arnett, & J.L. Tanner, *Emerging Adults in America: Coming of Age in the 21st Century*. American Psychological Association, pp. 3–19.

Ashton, D., & Field, D. (1976). *Young workers: From school to work*. London: Hutchinson.

Bauman, R. (2000). Language, identity, performance. *Pragmatics. Quarterly Publication of the International Pragmatics Association (IPrA)*, 10(1), 1–5.

Beck, U. (1992). From industrial society to the risk society: Questions of survival, social structure and ecological enlightenment. *Theory, Culture & Society*, 9(1), 97–123.

Beck, U., & Beck-Gernsheim, E. (2002). *Individualisation*. Sage: London.

Beck, U., Giddens, A., & Lash, S. (1994). *Reflexive Modernisation: Politics, Tradition and Aesthetics in the Modern Social Order*. Cambridge: Polity.

Beck-Gernsheim, E. (1998). On the Way to a Post-familial Family from a Community of Need to Elective Affinities. *Theory Culture and Society*, 15(3–4), 56–57.

Bennett, A. (1999). Subcultures or neo-tribes? Rethinking the relationship between youth, style and musical taste. *Sociology*, 33(3), 599–617.

Bennett, A. (2011). The post-subcultural turn: Some reflections 10 years on. *Journal of Youth Studies*, 14(5), 493–506.

Bennett, A., & Kahn-Harris, K. (2004). *After Subcultures*. Macmillan Education.

Berry, C. (2015). The final nail in the coffin: Crisis, manufacturing decline, and why it matters, in J. Green, C. Hay, & P. Taylor-Gooby (Eds.), *The British Growth Crisis*. Basingstoke: Palgrave.

Bradford, S. (2012). *Sociology, youth and youth work practice*. Palgrave Macmillan.

Bradley, H., & Hickman, P. (2004). Changing Fortunes of Young People in Contemporary Labour Markets. *Youth in Society: Contemporary Theory, Policy and Practice*.

Bynner, J. (2005). Rethinking the youth phase of the life-course: The case for emerging adulthood? *Journal of Youth Studies*, 8(4), 367–384.

Chisholm, L., & du Bois-Reymond, M.D. (1993). Youth transitions, gender and social change. *Sociology*, 27(2), 259–279.

Cockburn, C. (1983). *Brothers*. London: Pluto.

Coles, B. (1995). *Youth and social policy*. London: UCL Press

Connell, R.W. (1987). *Gender and power*. London: John Wiley & Sons.

Connell, R.W. (1995). *Masculinities*. Cambridge: Polity Press.

Connell, R.W. (2000). *The men and the boys*. Berkeley, CA: University of California Press.

Connell, R.W. (2005). *Masculinities* (2nd edn). Berkeley, CA: University of California Press.

Connell, R.W. (2016). Masculinity politics on a world scale, in B.K. Scott, S.E. Cayleff, A. Donadey, & I. Lara (Eds.), *Women in Culture: An Intersectional Anthology for Gender and Women's Studies* (second edition). Wiley Blackwell, pp. 234–238.

Cuervo, H., & Wyn, J. (2011). *Rethinking youth transitions in Australia: A historical and multidimensional approach*. Melbourne: Youth Research Centre, Melbourne Graduate School of Education, University of Melbourne.

Du Bois-Reymond, M. (1998). 'I don't want to commit myself yet': Young people's life concepts. *Journal of Youth Studies*, 1(1), 63–79.

France, A. (2007). *Understanding youth in late modernity*. London: McGraw-Hill Education (UK).

France A., & Roberts, S. (2017). *Youth and social class*. Basingstoke: Palgrave.

Furlong, A. (2012). *Youth studies: An introduction*. London: Routledge.

Furlong, A., & Cartmel, F. (1997). Risk and uncertainty in the youth transition. *Young*, 5(1), 3–20.

Furlong, A., & Cartmel, F. (2007). *Young people and social change*. London: McGraw-Hill Education (UK).

Furlong, A., Cartmel, F., Biggart, A., Sweeting, H., & West, P. (2003). *Youth transitions: Patterns of vulnerability and processes of social inclusion*. Edinburgh: Scottish Executive Social Research.

Giddens, A. (1991). *Modernity and Self-identity: Self and Society in the Late Modern Age*. Cambridge: Polity.

Goodwin, J., & O'Connor, H. (2005). Exploring complex transitions: Looking back at the 'Golden Age' of from school to work. *Sociology*, 39(2), 201–220.

Goodwin, J. & O'Connor, H. (2015). *Norbert Elias's Lost Research: Revisiting the Young Worker Project. Rethinking Classical Sociology*. Farnham: Ashgate.

Grant Thornton (2016). *Women in business: Turning promise into practice* [online]. www.grantthornton.global/en/insights/articles/women-in-business-2016/ accessed October 2017.

Gunter, A., & Watt, P. (2009). Grafting, going to college and working on road: Youth transitions and cultures in an East London neighbourhood. *Journal of Youth Studies*, 12(5), 515–529.

Haverig, A., & Roberts, S. (2011). The New Zealand OE as governance through freedom: Rethinking 'the apex of freedom'. *Journal of Youth Studies*, 14(5), 587–603.

Heward, C. (1996). Masculinities and families. *Understanding Masculinities*, 35–49.

Hillman, N., & Robinson, N. (2016). *Boys to Men: The underachievement of young men in higher education – and how to start tackling it*. HEPI Report 84. Oxford: Higher Education Policy Institute.

ILO (International Labour Organization) (2015). *World Report on Child Labour 2015*. Geneva: ILO.

Ingram, N. (2017). 'I'm not just one type of person': Aspirational working-class Belfast boys and complex embodied performances of educationally successful masculinities, in G. Stahl, J. Nelson, & D. Wallace (Eds.), *Masculinity and aspiration in an era of neoliberal education*. London: Routledge, pp. 71–88.

Ingram, N. (2018). *Working-Class Boys and Educational Success*. Basingstoke: Palgrave.

Jones, G. (2002). *The youth divide: Diverging paths to adulthood*. York: York Publishing Services for the Joseph Rowntree Foundation.

Mac an Ghaill, M. (1994). *The Making of Men: Masculinities, Sexualities and Schooling*. Buckingham: Open University Press.

Mac an Ghaill, M., & Haywood, C. (2014). Pakistani and Bangladeshi young men: Re-racialization, class and masculinity within the neo-liberal school. *British Journal of Sociology of Education*, 35(5), 753–776.

MacDonald, R. (2011). Youth transitions, unemployment and underemployment: Plus ça change, plus c'est la même chose? *Journal of Sociology*, 47(4), 427–444.

McCormack, M. (2012). *The declining significance of homophobia*. Oxford: Oxford University Press.

McCormack, M. (2014). The intersection of youth masculinities, decreasing homophobia and class: An ethnography. *The British Journal of Sociology*, 65(1), 130–149.

McDowell, L. (2000). The trouble with men? Young people, gender transformations and the crisis of masculinity. *International Journal of Urban and Regional Research*, 24(1), 201–209.

McDowell, L. (2003). *Redundant masculinities?: Employment change and white working class youth*. London: John Wiley.

McDowell, L., Rootham, E., & Hardgrove, A. (2014). Precarious work, protest masculinity and communal regulation: South Asian young men in Luton, UK. *Work, Employment and Society*, 28(6), 847–864.

McGuiness, F., Powell, A., & Brown, J. (2017). *People claiming unemployment benefits by constituency*, briefing paper Number 8209. London: House of Commons Library.

Messerschmidt, J. (2016). *Masculinities in the Making: From the Local to the Global*. New York: Rowman & Littlefield.

Miles, S. (2000). *Youth lifestyles in a changing world*. McGraw-Hill Education (UK).

Morgan, D. (1992). *Discovering Men*. London: Routledge.

Nixon, D. (2009). 'I Can't Put a Smiley Face On': Working-Class Masculinity, Emotional Labour and Service Work in the 'New Economy'. *Gender, Work & Organization*, 16(3), 300–322.

Nixon, D. (2017). Yearning to Labour? Working-class Men in Post-industrial Britain, in C. Walker, & S. Roberts (Eds.), *Masculinity, Labour, and Neoliberalism: Working-Class Men in Perspective*. Springer.

OECD (Organisation for Economic Co-operation and Development) (2015). *In It Together: Why Less Inequality Benefits All*. Paris: OECD Publishing.

ONS (Office for National Statistics) (2016). *Families and Household in the UK: 2016* [online]. www.ons.gov.uk/peoplepopulationandcommunity/birthsdeathsandmarriages/families/bulletins/familiesandhouseholds/2016

Pease, B. (2002). *Men and gender relations*. Melbourne: Tertiary Press.

Reay, D. (2004). 'It's all becoming a habitus': Beyond the habitual use of habitus in educational research. *British Journal of Sociology of Education*, 25(4), 431–444.

Redhead, S. (Ed.). (1993). *Rave off: Politics and deviance in contemporary youth culture* (Vol. 1). Avebury.

Roberts, K. (2003). Change and continuity in youth transitions in Eastern Europe: Lessons for Western sociology. *Sociological Review*, 51(4), 484–505.

Roberts, K. (2009). Opportunity structures then and now. *Journal of Education and Work*, 22(5), 355–368.

Roberts, S. (2010). Misrepresenting 'choice biographies'?: A reply to Woodman. *Journal of Youth Studies*, 13(1), 137–149.

Roberts, S. (2011). Beyond 'NEET' and 'tidy' pathways: Considering the 'missing middle' of youth transition studies. *Journal of Youth Studies*, 14(1), 21–39.

Roberts, S. (2012). One step forward, one step Beck: A contribution to the ongoing conceptual debate in youth studies. *Journal of Youth Studies*, 15(3), 389–401.

Roberts, S. (2013). Boys will be boys … won't they? Change and continuities in contemporary young working-class masculinities. *Sociology*, 47(4), 671–686.

Scoats, R. (2017). Inclusive masculinity and Facebook photographs among early emerging adults at a British university. *Journal of Adolescent Research*, 32(3), 323–345.

Threadgold, S. (2011). Should I pitch my tent in the middle ground? On 'middling tendency', Beck and inequality in youth sociology. *Journal of Youth Studies*, 14(4), 381–393.

UN Women (2017). *Facts and figures: Leadership and political participation* [online]. www.unwomen.org/en/what-we-do/leadership-and-political-participation/facts-and-figures

Vickerstaff, S. (2003). 'Apprenticeship in the Golden Age': Were Youth Transitions Really Smooth and Unproblematic Back Then? *Work, Employment and Society*, 17(2), 269–287.

Walker, C., & Roberts, S. (Eds.). (2017). *Masculinity, Labour, and Neoliberalism: Working-Class Men in International Perspective*. Springer.

Wilott, S., & Griffin, C. (1996). Men, masculinity and the challenge of long term unemployment, in M. Mac an Ghaill (Ed.), *Understanding Masculinities*. Buckingham: Oxford University Press, pp. 77–94.

Woodman, D. (2009). The mysterious case of the pervasive choice biography: Ulrich Beck, structure/agency, and the middling state of theory in the sociology of youth. *Journal of Youth Studies*, 12(3), 243–256.

Woodman, D. (2010). Class, individualisation and tracing processes of inequality in a changing world: A reply to Steven Roberts. *Journal of Youth Studies*, 13(6), 737–746.

Woodman, D. (2012). Life out of synch: How new patterns of further education and the rise of precarious employment are reshaping young people's relationships. *Sociology*, 46(6), 1074–1090.

Woodman, D. (2013). Researching 'ordinary' young people in a changing world: The sociology of generations and the 'missing middle' in youth research. *Sociological Research Online*, 18(1), 7.

Woodman, D., & Wyn, J. (2015). Class, gender and generation matter: Using the concept of social generation to study inequality and social change. *Journal of Youth Studies*, 18(10), 1402–1410.

Wyn, J. (2004). *Youth Transitions to Work and Further Education in Australia*, paper presented to the American Educational Research Association Annual conference, San Diego, April 2004.

Wyn, J., & White, R. (1997). The concept of youth. *Rethinking Youth*, 8–26.

Wyn, J., & Woodman, D. (2006). Generation, youth and social change in Australia. *Journal of Youth Studies*, 9(5), 495–514.

2 Dominant representations of working-class masculinity

The so-called 'crisis of masculinity' and the academic response

Introduction

The processes of social and economic change, especially deindustrialisation and changes in education, are seen to have particularly profound effects on young men, underscoring one part of a recurring obsession in the popular press and the public imagination across western contexts: the 'crisis of masculinity'. This crisis is often argued to be underpinned by, but also result in, boys' and men's lower academic achievement relative to girls and women, higher rates of completed suicide, and lower rates of treatment-seeking for physical and psychological ailments.

The first section of this chapter critically discusses this proclaimed crisis. Despite being an issue that many academics have tackled, its enduring prevalence in the political and public imagination makes it an important backdrop to study. The second half of the chapter turns to the academic treatment of this notion of 'crisis' and the ways that working-class masculinity tends to be observed and presented in sociological research. Despite sterling efforts in academic research to deconstruct and reveal the ways the working-class cultures and working-class selves are stigmatised, this sits in tension with how research and scholarship often positions (especially white) working-class men. While many sociologists appreciate the degree to which many working-class young men are disenfranchised, and indeed equally negatively affected by the expectations of masculinity, the approach to understanding and eradicating the worst excesses of orthodox masculinity leaves little room for anything other than a broad pathologising of this very group. As such, where older research has been critiqued for lionising certain behaviours (as is often argued to be the case in pioneering work of Paul Willis in *Learning to Labour*), many other accounts paint a picture of the young working-class man as a repository of sexism, homophobia and resistance to authority, often with little to no assignment of similar levels of 'guilt' to middle-class young men. The analysis of masculinity's intersection with class, then, ignores that many of these 'masculine ills' (Ingram, 2018) are not features of working-class masculinity alone.

The so-called 'crisis of masculinity': a prominent, problematic, durable discourse

The durability of this theme means that academic texts on masculinity are often obligated to problematise the notion of crisis, while still recognising this rhetoric as an important contextual backdrop to empirical findings (see for example Beynon, 2002; McDowell, 2003; Ward, 2015; Stahl, 2015). It is unavoidable, then, yet essential, that I follow suit. Initially, two points are worth making in brief, both of which will be returned to in greater detail in Chapter 3. First, despite much research suggesting that maleness must be decoupled from masculinity (e.g. Messner, 1993; Sedgewick, 1985; Beynon, 2002; MacInnes, 1998), and an emphasis that masculinity is what men *do* rather than what they *are* (West & Zimmerman, 1987; Morgan, 1992), the popular discourse of the crisis of masculinity is *almost always* used in a way that implies it is actually, and only, a crisis for men. Second, despite masculinity being better understood as the plural *masculinities* (Connell, 1987, 1995), the crisis is often documented in popular thought as being about men as a unitary category.

A recent high-profile iteration of the crisis of masculinity logic exemplifies this quite nicely. In May 2013, as part of a lecture series for the think-tank *Demos*, then Labour shadow public health minister Diane Abbott gave a speech entitled 'Britain's crisis of masculinity'. Abbott raised concerns about how rapid economic and social change had affected male identity and suggested that this 'crisis' had created a number of largely 'unspoken problems'. Given the discursive resonance of the issue of crisis over the last 100 years or so (Beynon, 2002; Roberts, 2014), the idea that any of it remains unspoken seems rather ironic; nonetheless, Abbott's contention was that this contemporary crisis included some widely accepted 'inescapable truths'. These included: fewer men than ever being able to connect the fabric of their lives to traditional archetypes of masculinity; more people being employed behind tills than in mining coal or other heavy industries, which were in decline; and many men feeling uncomfortable about the kinds of jobs on offer to them – particularly service jobs. Abbott rounded off these concerns by arguing that there exists a lack of respect for women's autonomy, and a normalisation of homophobia among men.

This apparent redundancy of male roles was also picked up by Geoff Dench in his writings, including his verbal response to Abbott's speech. Contemplating the 'worthlessness' felt by men, Dench echoed some of Abbott's concerns, claiming that *many* young men seem under-motivated at school, and are likely to remain workless and feel 'unwanted', in part due to the 'success' of feminism in making more women financially independent. Here, Dench taps into not just the alleged crisis faced by men in the sphere of work, but also the presumed crisis facing boys in the classroom that has followed girls' surpassing of boys' attainment and participation beginning in the mid-1990s (Arnot, 1996; Roberts, 2014). All of these claims necessitate critical appraisal, as does the rhetoric of crisis itself.

The cyclical nature of crisis talk: crisis as constitutive of masculinity

The decline of manufacturing and heavy industry, the increasing participation of women in the workforce, and the relative underachievement of boys in school are, indeed, realities of life today. But does this really constitute or underpin a 'crisis of masculinity'? Certainly, crisis does seem to be widely accepted as fact, and is routinely reproduced in popular texts. This can be seen in the prolific publication of books in the late 1990s and the early 2000s (Beynon, 2002), such as Waller Newell's (2003) *The Code of Man*, and, more famously, Susan Faludi's (1999) *Stiffed*, whose subtitle decried the 'betrayal of modern man'. This trend continues today, exemplified by authors like Steve Biddulph (2010) and Guy Garcia (2008) – who both assert the need for boys and men to reconnect with 'traditional manliness' – and Jack Myers (2016), who is slightly more flexible in proposing that crisis can be overcome by redefining what it is to be a man. The proposed need to return to and reinvigorate particular forms of manliness is also found in various popular websites. These include style and activity guides on how to 'revive the lost art of manliness', such as www.artofmanliness.com, or, in more extreme ways, the hyper-misogynistic blog site 'Return of Kings' lamenting efforts 'to marginalize masculine men with a leftist agenda that promotes censorship, feminism, and sterility'.

It is worth noting that, far from being a novel concern, the 'masculinity-in-crisis' theme is well rehearsed, and has a long history. Both historians and literary scholars have identified historical periods, both predating and following the women's movement and the development of the industrial order, where masculinity can be considered in crisis (Beynon, 2002). As an example, we can point to the discourse around a 'crisis' in masculinity that emerged in the 1890s. Stimulated by anxieties surrounding the losses of key battles across the empire, the rise of the United States as an economic power, and Germany's imperial ambitions, this period emphasised concerns about the economic, political, social, psychological, and even physical deterioration of English men (Kestner, 2010). Regarding the latter, this period saw schools begin to focus not just on the cultivation of boys' minds, but also on the development of their athleticism. This concern resulted in a moral panic over the supposed 'softening' of boys, and manifested in the British cultural obsession with competitive team sports that we now consider the norm. Masculinity has also regularly been subject to 'crisis talk' as a result of changes to the nature and availability of work over the last 100 years. The 1930s Great Depression damaged many men's efforts to be a breadwinner, while the development of Fordism and the associated simplification and standardisation of work practices had, by the 1950s, already started to undermine levels of skill and autonomy in the workplace. The de-industrialisation of the late 1970s and 1980s, with its peaks in unemployment and the start of an ongoing reduction of industrial- and manufacturing-based workplaces, also raised concerns for men and masculinity. In combination with the effects of some small victories for second-wave feminism in respect of women's equality, this transition to a more 'feminised' service-based economy saw more women entering paid work – albeit often part-time work. Again, this brought with it concerns about the role of men in society. During this period serious academic attention began to be given towards researching men as gendered beings, giving rise to the emergence of critical masculinities studies.

The more recent debates about the crisis of masculinity through the 1990s and 2000s appear to have taken the 1980s as a starting point and often emphasised similar concerns. But in addition, the mid-1990s witnessed a profound change in the level of political and research attention given to boys' academic performance in the UK (Arnot et al., 1996) and internationally (see e.g. Martino, 1999, in respect of Australia). Since that point, extensive research attention has been paid to masculinity and the school setting in the UK and beyond (e.g. Mac an Ghaill, 1994; Gilbert & Gilbert, 1998; Griffin, 2000; O'Donnell & Sharpe, 2000; Keddie, 2007; Haywood & Mac an Ghaill, 2013; Singleton, 2008). This body of work has done much to destabilise and deconstruct the simplistic 'boys are losing out to girls' rhetoric, revealing that this worry has been underpinned by a 'discourse of crisis and loss' (Griffin, 2000). Concerns about boys' achievement then seem anchored to mourning the erosion of male dominance (Petersen, 1998) in educational achievement, and disregarding the strides made by girls (McDowell, 2000). Such concerns also ignore the ways power can be and is enacted by boys in classrooms, even in apparent times of crisis (e.g. Ringrose & Renold, 2010; Keddie, 2007).

The more contemporary concerns about masculinity and the economy, as proffered above by Abbott and Dench, *might* apply to a minority of men, but these concerns are presented as if they are more widely representative. Even though it is a great concern that many young people are unemployed, Dench's comments about a lack of motivation and the links he makes to worklessness seem to run contrary to evidence. Academic research in this area suggests that the vast majority of all unemployed people want paid work (Shildrick et al., 2012), and much recent work in the sociology of education outlines the reality of young people's positive aspirations (St Clair & Benjamin, 2011; Archer et al., 2014). Dench's remarks also serve to downplay the complex interplay of class, race and gender in educational achievement. For example, in 2011, only 26% of white British boys eligible for free school meals (FSM) obtained the benchmark GSCE level of five 'good' passes, compared with 32% of FSM-eligible girls. In other words, the majority of both boys and girls in this cohort did not achieve the benchmark, yet girls seem to be left out of this discussion. Many sociologists have pointed to the fact that gender has a smaller impact than social class or race, but this often remains overlooked (Roberts, 2012b; Ashley, 2009), and as Ward (2014: 53) states, any 'crisis of school to successful adult futures may not really be linked to a "crisis" of masculinity at all, but more social class inequality'.

Not only does popularly accepted talk of a crisis in masculinity incorrectly promote an idea of a unified group of men all somehow out of sync with contemporary realities, it also ignores the likelihood that, rather than being new, crisis is something that is experienced in different ways by different generations (Beynon, 2002). Beynon (2002: 90) quotes Mangan (1997: 4) in a way that perfectly captures the historical contingency of various crises in masculinity: 'Masculinity is never stable; its terms are constantly being redefined and renegotiated ... Certain themes and tropes inevitably re-appear with regularity but each era experiences itself in different ways'. In this sense, as Allan (2017) observes, masculinity might even be thought of as a mechanism that always has and must produce in men a sense of shame, fear, and dread of inadequacies – in short, masculinity is reliant on the idea of crisis by its very definition. Ultimately, however, while crisis might be constitutive of masculinity in as much as it is inherently unstable, changeable and always unattainable, I concur with Whitehead (2002: 47), who delicately queries 'how is it possible that men are in "crisis" given the continued, worldwide, material inequalities that favour males and men?' Despite raising this question over 15 years ago, it remains highly pertinent. The crisis of masculinity discourse, as applied to actual people, might be durable, and this durability speaks volumes for the significant and unequal regard with which men's entitlement is held, but it is also a discourse that is fundamentally absurd.

Not exactly a 'crisis': sociology's reflections on changes, challenges and continuities to masculinity in new times

The crisis of masculinity rhetoric endures in political, popular and media representations in ways that feel very cyclical. While not quite a consensus, sociologists have for the most part been quick to problematise discourses of masculinity in crisis, and have done so frequently (e.g. Connell, 1995; Hearn, 1998; Griffin, 2000; Martino & Meyenn, 2001; McDowell, 2003; Roberts, 2014; Stahl, 2015; Ward, 2015). Even those who do not wholly dismiss crisis talk insist that it should be carefully qualified; as O'Donnell and Sharpe (2000: 15) note, radical transformation of the British economy and, consequently, the class structure 'to an extent [...] justifies references to a crisis ... [but] experiences of this generalised crisis can be very different' according to social background. So, where young men are increasingly defined as a problem category (Hearn, 1998), what should be made clear is that,

> it is young men from low income backgrounds who are most often associated with this 'crisis' anxiety and with public fears of disorder, disrespect and delinquency around their performances of masculinity.
> (Ward et al., 2015: para 3)

Sociologists, then, tend towards a more critical understanding of 'crisis', giving significant attention to the impacts of economic and social change upon men and masculinity. As Hearn (1999) reminds us, the presence of change for men should not be confused with any general assertion of a so-called 'crisis in masculinity', but the nature of changes, whom exactly they impact and how, are questions that require close sociological scrutiny (see also Whitehead, 2002).

As noted above, the very real changes underpinning the presumed 'crisis' stem largely from structural changes in industrialised economies, which, since the 1970s, have evolved from being reliant on manufacturing and heavy industry, to becoming dominated by service sector employment. Such de-industrialised economies, it was argued, needed a highly skilled, flexible workforce to best serve the requirements of technology and service-based employment (OECD, 1996). Alongside equal rights legislation, increased educational access and the subsequent academic success of young women, such changes have been argued to destabilise earlier notions of working-class masculinity. The changes in work, of course, were most fundamentally changes to working-class work. Working-class masculinities, until these changes, had long been 'embedded in the productive manual skills, experience and relations of all male shop floor life' (Mac an Ghaill, 1996: 67), and augmented by the value ascribed by working-class men to tasks that required effort, strength and physical skill (Willis, 1977; Corrigan, 1979; Marks, 2003; McDowell, 2003; Simpson et al., 2016; Nixon, 2017).

As Nixon (2017: 57) explains, 'working-class masculinity is a form of masculinity that valorises certain types of "embodied" hard and heavy manual labour'. This valorisation is built upon the understanding that risky and physically demanding work offers compensations for one's seemingly inferior position in the social hierarchy, such that working-class men can develop a sense of dignity and pride because they are brave and hard-working compared to those who cannot do such labour, such as women, or men who embody more 'rational' and cerebral, middle-class masculinities (McDowell, 2003; see also Willis, 1977; Bradley, 1989; Lamont, 2000). Given it was long perceived that such work required no or few qualifications, a corresponding rejection of the mental work required for schooling was seen as necessary for many working-class young men; education was associated with compliance, femininity and middle classness and, thus, having no social value (Sennett & Cobb, 1972; Willis, 1977; Corrigan, 1979; Frosh et al., 2002; Lingard et al., 2009). A rejection of the feminine also underscored the gendered division of spheres, where men held to the idea that paid work as a form of breadwinning was a man's role, whereas women were responsible for the private sphere of homemaking and childrearing (Delamont, 2001; Nayak, 2003a, 2003b). Masculinity, then, was highly contingent upon heterosexuality and heteronormativity (see Chapter 3 for more detail).

The enduring effect of studies of working-class 'lads'

Paul Willis's (1977) seminal ethnography, *Learning to Labour*, which documents the transition from school to work of a group of working-class 'lads', continues to illustrate the *ne plus ultra* of adherence to such working-class masculine ideals among young men. The 'lads' in Willis's study – in contrast to their more studious, compliant peers – were the archetypal adherents to the type of masculinity outlined above, in that they rejected the value of school, resisted authority and valued macho sentiment and typically male, manually focused workplaces. The lads also centred their time on 'having a laff', often at the expense of others through sexist and/or racist behaviours, and held 'traditional' views about women, denigrating them as objects of gratification or imagining them as adornments and/or comforters of the domestic sphere (see also Connell, 2001; Pascoe, 2007). Compliance at school, indeed anything that could be connoted feminine or subordinate, was the very antithesis of their existence.

Importantly, they also evidenced a 'partial penetration' of the myths of meritocracy, seemingly aware that greater compliance at school would not alter their future employment prospects, and that work of any kind anyway had little intrinsic value. This penetration was only partial, though, because ultimately their 'cross-valorisation of manual labour with the social superiority of masculinity' (Willis, 1977: 148) served to facilitate their entry into work at the bottom of the labour market and thus reproduce the very basis of capitalist relations. The denigration they suffered as workers was in some sense, as noted above, compensated by working jobs through which they might demonstrate worth through tasks considered 'manly' and – just as they had done at school – by displaying resistance to authority as a 'self-worth protection strategy' (Ingram, 2017: 73).

Despite these incredibly valuable insights, for me the most enduring aspect of *Learning to Labour* (and others, e.g. Corrigan, 1979; Robins & Cohen, 1978) has been the caricaturing of working-class masculinity for decades to follow. While these authors did much to highlight the political, economic and social marginalisation and exclusion of the boys they studied, they went to little effort to balance these accounts with the views of other young men with alternative experiences.

These other groups are identified through the words of troubled and troublesome 'lads' – such as Willis's boys' reference to the educationally-committed and conformist 'ear'oles' – but their own actual perspectives remain comparatively muted. As a result, the moniker 'lads' and the associated qualities of being 'anti-school, anti-feminine and homophobic' (Ingram, 2017: 75) came to be representative of working-class masculinity, while definitions of 'laddishness' retained the same sentiments as those portrayed by Willis for decades (see e.g. Francis & Skelton, 2005: 496). Even for forms of masculinity not associated with laddishness or 'macho' behaviours, the othering of women was and continues to be seen as an important feature for developing solidaristic relations between men (O'Donnell & Sharpe, 2000). As too does the continued 'repudiation of the spectre of failed masculinity' (Pascoe, 2007: 5; Marks, 2003; Mac an Ghaill, 1994) through taunting and marginalising boys who deviate from the 'appropriate' gender script by being studious or evidencing a lack of sexual interest in and objectification of girls and women.

Being so concerned with understanding counter school cultures and the experiences of the most disaffected young people, the key texts of the late 1970s created a slightly simplified and bifurcated picture of working-class experience. This clearly defined 'them and us' was the world as understood by the lads in these studies, but failing to fully explore a fuller range of experiences and outcomes led to the creation of an influential false binary. Upon these foundations emerged the current dominant explanation of working-class masculinity and its relationship with, for example, school disengagement. Despite the efforts of some researchers in the 1980s to consider the experiences of 'ordinary kids' (Brown, 1987) and the fluid and contextually contingent nature of subjectivities (Jenkins, 1983), the duality remains ingrained such that the fixed caricature of working-class boys as 'lads' – with all their negative attributes – are given particular explanatory power in considerations of working-class male educational 'failure' (Roberts, 2012b). Even when moving to a four-part typology of 'macho lads', 'academic achievers', 'new enterprisers', and 'real Englishmen', Mac an Ghaill's (1994) influential text allows only for total disengagement by those considered lads, and (albeit differentiated) forms of successful outcomes for the rest. On this basis, 'a lack of attention given to heterogeneity within working-class masculinity result[s] in a representation of the working-class lad as a monolithic character' (Ingram, 2017: 72), and ultimately, the label 'lads' 'shuts down the possibilities of nuanced, conflicted and complex identities' (ibid.).

Changing circumstances, changing working-class masculinity?

Working-class masculinity then, however inadvertently, is often presented as being rather static or fixed, especially in education-focused research (see Chapter 4 for more detail). The origins, mechanics and embeddedness of 'fixing mechanisms' (Connell, 2001) in such respects are worthy and necessary foci for masculinities researchers, but they alone are not sufficient. Attention to only how masculinity is fixed ensures in some ways that working-class boys are made 'to bear the weight of white racism and male sexism' (Reay, 2002: 222; also Haywood, 2008; Ingram, 2017), and renders only a very simplified picture. A richer view might be unearthed if we follow Diane Reay's (2002) lead in digressing from then perceived (academic) popular wisdom in 'Shaun's Story'. Reay's sensitive, considered, single case study account detailed the need to understand working-class masculinity as 'far more complex, nuanced and fragile than any of the stereotypical representations in dominant discourses' (Reay, 2002: 221).

Rather than simply reproducing discourses that seem more in keeping with the articulation of working-class masculinity up until the 1970s, Reay's words invite us to take seriously how contemporary complexities are managed and negotiated by young men. This pivotal sentiment has been echoed in a number of important studies in the 2000s that considered nuances in the construction of working-class masculine identity in relation to schooling (e.g.

O'Donnell and Sharpe, 2000; Ingram, 2009, 2011; Stahl, 2015) and the wider transition to adulthood (e.g. Nayak, 2003b, 2006; McDowell, 2000, 2003, 2015; Ward, 2014, 2015). For the most part, such studies note that 'today's working-class male social identities are increasingly fragmented and complex [with] uncertainty surrounding sense making practices' (Stahl, 2015: 31).

Making efforts to better grasp the challenges of constructing masculine identities in 'new times', characterised by the greater than ever need for educational credentials in a precarious labour market, researchers have often heeded Connell's (1989) call to document the implications and contradictions negotiated in 'multiple spaces of gender production' (Ward, 2015: 2; see also Ward et al., 2017). Here, for example, Ingram (2009, 2017) has paid attention to the challenges faced by academically successful working-class schoolboys as they manage the contradictions of their educational trajectory and its incompatibility with their class background (cf. Stahl, 2013). Ingram presents the local context as being crucial in developing any credible analysis of the boys' negotiation of their identity. This focus is part of an important trend in other recent analyses concerned with understanding the relationship between masculinity, class and place (e.g. Hopkins & Noble, 2009; Jimenez & Walkerdine, 2011; Hardgrove et al., 2015; Stahl et al., 2017; Ward et al., 2017).

Particularly instructive here for the context of this book is the work of Nayak (2003a, 2003b, 2006), McDowell (especially 2000, 2002, 2003; McDowell et al., 2014) and Ward (2014, 2015), all of whom take as their starting point the ramifications of de-industrialisation in the UK, upon men's youth transitions in locales imbued with a particular heritage of manual labour – Newcastle (Nayak), the South Wales valleys (Ward), and, working with a point of comparison, the contrasting cities of Sheffield and Cambridge (McDowell). Despite the different locales, the three writers' work coheres in respect of how the studied area's substantial industrial legacy creates incongruence for young men, with the fundamental concern being how men are 'adapting to insecure times and an expanding post-industrial economy in which the rich reservoir of labouring jobs has all but evaporated' (Nayak, 2003b: 146). Each of these authors' findings is now discussed in some detail to present a picture of what I think is the predominant sociological account of working-class masculinity in an era of de-industrialised economies.

Anoop Nayak's research on young masculinities in the North-East of England

Nayak makes explicit and regular reference to the 'prominent masculine legacy of manual labour [that] ran through their familial biographies' (Nayak, 2003b: 150) as a way of making sense of how young men in Newcastle negotiated their subjectivity and their 'complex, fractured and "insecure transitions" mediating across school-work, local-global, boyhood-manhood'. The relationship between occupation and identity is seen for Nayak as being central, with the 'local lads' of his study aspiring to join the labour aristocracy of mining, shipbuilding, steel works, and other heavy engineering their fathers' generation had transitioned into, but which had recently disappeared.

An accompanying understanding of non-manual work as being 'soft and babyish' (Nayak, 2003b: 152) was widespread. Echoing the sentiments of their own fathers, as well as Willis's lads' 'penetration', that learning would not equate to greater earning given the limited types of jobs available, Nayak's young men denounced the contemporary obsession with human capital theory, rejecting the rhetoric of then Prime Minister Tony Blair (among others) that '[i]n today's world, there is no such thing as too clever. The more you know, the further you'll go'. These findings then are in keeping with Taylor and Jamieson's (1997: 162) assertion that the diminution of traditionally masculine work results in 'the sudden and total evacuation of men from the symbolic terrain of work'.

This legacy then acted as a 'fixing mechanism' (Connell, 2001) of sorts, one which meant, as Nayak (2003b: 153) conveys so poetically, that these men were reminiscent of 'flies in amber [who] had become petrified in the hardened solution of an older period from which their values descended, making metamorphosis ever more difficult to achieve'. Paradoxes and seeming contradictions punctuated the men's narratives, though, because while many of them turned to 'fiddly careers' or minor criminality in response to these new economic realities, many also undertook 'part time work in the service sector' (Nayak, 2006: 819), including 'sport shops, petrol stations, record stores and cafes' (Nayak, 2006: 819). This seems to be at odds with Nayak's (2006: 817) prognosis and initial concerns that certain white working-class males may be out of step with the new economy.

However, the seeming recalcitrance for metamorphosis *might* be better understood as being emblematic of a future ideal of masculinity for these lads. In their extended present there was clear evidence of malleability because many of them entered the kinds of service work we are led to presume they detest and are incompatible with. The malleability, though, was articulated as being necessary for financing 'the rituals of drinking, football and working-class exhibitionism' (Nayak, 2003b: 154), which Nayak (2006: 818) deemed essential to the processes by which masculinity is 'preserved, recuperated and ultimately refashioned'.

Those who remained unemployed and/or have histories of family unemployment – those disparaged as 'Charvers' by other young people in Nayak's study – went about 'recuperating the material and symbolic value of labour through theft, risk and the culture of the street' (Nayak, 2006: 827). An additional layer – albeit *perceived* by others rather than articulated by men in this position themselves – was that such young men resorted to the body to demonstrate a 'hard' masculinity through a pronounced walk, 'an unapologetic posture of survival that was "ruff", tough and street-wise' (Nayak, 2006: 826). Working-class masculinity's key tenets, for Nayak, prove durable in the context of social and economic change, but with re-fashioning methods used to adhere to and exhibit those older traditional characteristics, such as hardness, resistance, machismo, and claims of social superiority.

Linda McDowell's comparative research on masculinity and youth transitions in contrasting British towns and cities

McDowell's (2000, 2003; McDowell et al., 2014) longitudinal research on young men and their school-to-work transitions in the contrasting cities of Sheffield and Cambridge, and later in her comparison of Luton and Swindon (McDowell et al., 2014), also brings similar issues to the fore, but identifies considerably more nuance. The legacy of an industrial heritage, and/or the legacy of manual work of any kind, was that for several young men in McDowell's study various forms of 'manly work' were desired. Measuring their future aspirations for work whilst at school, only one of the young men hinted at the service sector, though this was tightly constrained to a 'sports-shop', while most others aspired to semi- or unskilled manual work or apprenticeships in painting and decorating, mechanics, engineering, or building work; joining the army; or being a professional footballer or radio broadcaster. A few considered college courses desirable. While this sentiment towards continued education was only a minority view, in complete contrast with Nayak's lads, the recognition of the importance of qualifications in the new economy was a prominent view among McDowell's participants.

Beyond the school gates, the narratives of McDowell's young men were characterised by serious efforts to obtain paid work, with many being overtly attracted to typically masculine jobs. For most, though, there were at least some dalliances with service work in various guises, such as fast food service jobs. The negotiation of such work is another prominent nuance in McDowell's findings; remaining deferent to customers even when being subjected to rudeness was a constant theme. Here, McDowell (2003: 176) interprets that the young men recognised some customer behaviour 'challenges masculine attitudes and pride', but for the most part[1] let go of their right to 'stick up for yourself' and retained an ingratiating manner so as not to get sacked. This is positioned as being an acceptance of indignities 'in exchange for a feeling of pride in working hard' (McDowell, 2003: 177), pointing to a reliance on some traditional markers of masculinity (the relationship between paid work and men's identity) at the expense of others (being deferent and docile instead of 'hard'). This type of work, though, holds low symbolic value and is perceived by many commentators to be 'without redeeming value' (McDowell, 2003: 227; Bauman, 1998; Nixon, 2009).

McDowell also highlighted another significant and complex negotiation of identity in relation to two subject positions, 'domestic respectability' and 'hard laddishness', both of which the young men were able to manoeuvre despite their seemingly contradictory natures. For example, in terms of male (hetero)sexuality, they simultaneously subscribed to predatory discourses, emphasising and exaggerating sexual prowess and both denigrating and celebrating women who have casual sex, as well as an idealised discourse of romantic love, commitment and enduring relationships that emphasise the importance and scope of 'family values'. McDowell notes how this seeming incompatibility can ensure respect is gained from both peers and the wider community by ensuring that 'particular aspects of masculine identity are most evident in different arenas and locations' (McDowell, 2003: 213; reminiscent of what Ward calls 'chameleon masculinity' – see below).

Despite this significant nuance being a hallmark of McDowell's research and reflections, the bottom line, she contends, is that there exists

> [a] continued dominance of a version of traditional sexist masculinity, in both the laddish behaviours exhibited in leisure arenas and in the domestic attitudes that affect workplace participation and attitudes towards young women and family life. New versions of masculinity more in tune with the dominant attributes of the service economy and with young women's changing social position and a more general recognition of the arguments of feminism have yet to find any expression ...
>
> (McDowell, 2003: 226)

This continuance of traditional masculinity, McDowell (2016: 54) concludes, ensures that for working-class young men service sector employment is seen as 'women's work, and so beneath their dignity'. Simultaneously, employers read working-class masculinity as being incompatible with service sector roles, so even those young men who are prepared to explore such work are often disqualified in the recruitment process because of their 'appearance (piercing, tattoos or inappropriate clothes)', 'attitudes', 'bodily demeanour, dress and language' (ibid.). Additionally, McDowell is reticent to consider that economic restructuring can challenge long-standing masculine attitudes, and instead echoes Nayak's (2006: 815) view that 'new youth transitions do not automatically result in "new men"', insisting such change can preserve traditional gendered relationships in working-class communities (see also Kenway & Kraack, 2004, in the Australian context), and that waged work remains the central element in the development of acceptable and respected masculinity (McDowell, 2003: 226, 236). In many ways I find this conclusion somewhat surprising, and think at least some of this assessment ought to be reconsidered.

Michael Ward's study of youth transitions and masculinity in South Wales

The third analysis of young men's transitions within changing economic landscapes that I examine is the more recent work of Michael Ward (2014, 2015). Somewhat surprisingly, given the significant contouring of local employment change as the study's backdrop, little attention is given to young men's engagement with or rejection of service jobs. Nonetheless, in combining longitudinal design with a focus on several existing subcultural groupings of young men – usefully labelled as 'analytic sets' – Ward provides greater nuance to his study of the end of young men's educational careers than made visible by Nayak's. Following these young men through the end of secondary school and beyond, Ward captures different, multiplex and often contradictory performances of masculinity, as well as the continued influence of older local traditions which ultimately limit the performance of masculine identity.

The old local traditions Ward identifies insist that 'distance from anything seen as "feminine" was essential for a strong masculinity' (Ward, 2014: 54), and that, even in the face of a de-industrialising economy, there is necessity to deploy '"masculine" affirming practices of playing sports, engaging in physical and aggressive behaviours and certain ideas of male embodiment' (Ward, 2014: 55). Another overwhelming legacy has been the cultural valorisation of the breadwinner model of the family, where men are encouraged, indeed demanded to be primary workers and providers of finance for their family. Here, Ward provides a strong sense of how working-class masculinity is shaped by place, as well as how 'masculine identities shape and influence the specific character of places' (Ward, 2015: 34).

Simultaneously, however, Ward's research evidences how contemporary young men in that locality engage in 'a degree of chameleonising [...], where individuals can adjust and alter performances with different audiences' (Ward, 2015: 150). This chameleonising, which has been relatively widely acknowledged for some time (see e.g. Jenkins, 1983; Fisher, 2009; Atkinson, 2011; Matthews, 2016), is a form of code shifting that enables boys and young men to segue from being predominantly a typical lad – in terms of engaging in contact sports, choosing risky leisure practices, intimidating non-conforming boys or rejecting mental labour – to exhibiting a great deal of trust and intimacy with friends, acts that might have previously been considered feminine. Additionally, and conversely, chameleonising enabled those more studious young men in Ward's sample, who usually distanced themselves from 'laddishness', to deviate from this and to occasionally embrace some forms of machismo, such as the objectification of women.

In cases where young men performed alternative versions of masculinity, through, for example, attachment to and presentation of 'emo' subculture, 'older legacies of masculinity still endure and weave in and out of their narratives' (Ward, 2015: 152). Such 'emos' portrayed themselves as heroic and resilient while describing instances of being bullied, and suggested that aspects of their subculture – such as skateboarding and American football – were simultaneously more extreme and more mature than mainstream activities such as playing football (soccer) or drinking in pubs. Like almost all the participants in Ward's study, these men subscribed to homophobia and relatively heterosexist worldviews. Despite instances of code shifting, then, Ward is clear that the re-traditionalising of masculine ideals and gender relationships was prominent (see also Segal, 1993).

A relatively singular account of masculinity across variations in place and space

McDowell, Nayak and Ward each contain their discussions in some respects by paying sustained attention to how locality, heritage and identity intersect and interact. Yet, while the specifics of place are central to their respective analyses, the overlaps in their findings speak to relative homogeneity: de-traditionalised, de-industrialised economies, rather than freeing men from traditional gender scripts, lead to relatively little change in the way working-class masculinity is performed and socially reproduced. The changing economic landscape has ensured that 'synchronicity between subjective and objective structures is broken' (Adkins, 2003: 21), which in theory (according to Beck, 1992; see also Giddens, 1991; Bauman, 1998) creates circumstances or possibilities for reflexive practices that lead to an ability to question norms around, for example, performances of gender. Instead, the conclusions of McDowell, Nayak and Ward are that the incongruence between current circumstances and socially imprinted masculine traditions leads to a re-traditionalisation of gender norms, a reassertion of masculinity and a reinforcement of gender stereotypes as 'particular localities [are] inflected not only by actually-existing regimes of work but also by nostalgic evocations of such regimes, even in the aftermath of their disappearance' (Taylor & Jamieson, 1997: 150).

While not a fatal flaw, some of these assessments are undermined when considering that, despite the significance of work in traditional industrial economies forming a huge part of the backdrop, men's attitudes towards so-called 'feminised' service work are not discussed in great depth. It is striking in the accounts by Ward and Nayak that, despite one of the central arguments being that the low-level service economy is at odds with such young men's masculine identity, their respondents' engagements in various types of work is almost entirely overlooked and not critically considered. McDowell is much clearer on the contrasts between young working-class men's negative discursive positioning of such work and their lived reality of often having no choice but to take this work. Here still, though, the rich nuances in the narratives do not quite square with the overall argument of the incompatibility between service work and working-class masculinity.

Nonetheless, these are important studies of young men's transitions and, beyond their self-noted focus on the local, they speak to a much wider recognition of how employment change has ensured that the 'reproduction of working-class masculinity has been ruptured' (Kenway & Kraack, 2004: 107; see also Dolby et al., 2004; Marks, 2003; Jimenez & Walkerdine, 2011). Working-class men are, generally speaking, no longer observed as learning to labour – given the decline of labouring work – and instead are grappling and *struggling* with the need to 'learn to serve' in the new economy (McDowell, 2003).

The literature indicates that 'becoming a man is a matter of constructing oneself in and being constructed by the available ways of being male in a particular society' (Gilbert & Gilbert, 1998: 46), but that, often, the currently *available ways* are seen to be at odds with the perceptions of *locally sanctioned appropriate ways* of being a man that many men have internalised through an intergenerational transmission of knowledge (Jimenez & Walkerdine, 2011) and the inheritance of localised industrial psyches. Despite, as above, sociologists being keen to play down talk of a 'crisis' in masculinity, it is such circumstances where 'crisis' (always in inverted commas) is perhaps more sympathetically considered appropriate terminology. This seems to capture the struggle of reconciling a traditionally valorised masculine identity with the onset and continuation of four decades (since de-industrialisation kicked in) of social change outlined in some literatures.

This struggle is clearly observed in research that considers unemployed young men's attitudes towards service sector employment (e.g. Nixon, 2009; Lindsay & McQuaid, 2004; Furlong & Cartmel, 2004; McDowell et al., 2014; Jimenez & Walkerdine, 2011). The female-dominated work environs and the perceived feminine characteristics required to do front-line service work are held as particularly challenging for unemployed men from working-class backgrounds. Nixon's (2006, 2009) research found an utter rejection among unemployed men of almost anything other than male-dominated manual occupations, and service sectors were generally only considered if there was the possibility of a masculine occupational niche such as security and driving jobs, or 'backshop' environments in retail (see also Nixon, 2017). This rejection was premised largely on an inability to 'put a smiley face on' when confronted by demeaning or angry customers, but also the low pay which would not provide a perceived working man's wage. While not as focused on the incongruence of manliness and service work, similar findings were found by Lindsay and McQuaid (2004) and Furlong and Cartmel (2004), who document unemployed men's concerns about pay, required skills and a lack of full-time work in low-level service sector jobs. Jimenez and Walkerdine (2011) report an even clearer psychological cost for young men contemplating front-line service roles as an exit route from unemployment, documenting the presence of stigma and ridicule from fathers, peers and the wider community in areas where manual work had until recently predominated.

This instructs that, yes, unemployed men seem to often very strongly reject service sector work. However, the experiences of men *who are in* front-line service work remain comparatively absent (Nickson & Korczynski, 2009: 298). For over 20 years, research has identified stigma around men working in 'feminised' jobs (Williams, 1995), and concerns about how this status may underscore practices of reconstituting job roles to assert masculinity or disassociate from 'women's work' (e.g. Milkman, 1997; Cross & Bagilhole, 2002; Simpson, 2005; Huppatz, 2012; McDonald, 2012). However, this body of research, especially recently, has tended to focus on professions nothing like the front-line service work that has taken the place of the mines and heavy industry it situates as its backdrop. Huppatz's (2012) account of Australian men in feminised occupations, for example, considers social work, exotic dancing, nursing and hairdressing, while another influential piece of UK-based research by Simpson (2005) examines nurses, airline cabin crew, librarians and primary school teachers. Clearly, these are not necessarily the roles that low-skilled, low-qualified men might enter after the disappearance of manufacturing and heavy industry. As such, they constitute something of a false comparison in any attempt to determine how masculinity is being affected by and affecting mass economic transformation.

Despite increasing attention and importance given to the *particularities* of place, orthodox thinking – and research – seemingly depicts working-class masculinity not just in very specific locales with a long history of industrial work, but seemingly across the board. This image is characterised by 'efforts to preserve tradition, uncertainty, survivalist mentalities, unrealistic expectations, and new searches for "respectability" and "authenticity"' (Stahl, 2015: 29). Yet, the foundation for this apparently universal truth emerges from studies of some marginalised men in particular places. Any progress made elsewhere, complicated or limited as that may or may not be, is overlooked. This gives us only a *partial* reading of contemporary working-class masculinity.

Conclusion

While academics have repeatedly challenged the popular and simplified notion of the 'crisis of masculinity', it perseveres in popular representations in Britain and beyond. In part this is because, unquestionably, there has been significant social and economic change, meaning today's young men are growing up in a world that is very different to that of their fathers and grandfathers. This is especially the case for working-class young men, who are faced with the reality that traditional masculine identities built through a process of 'learning to labour' are no longer the social resource they once were; indeed, these are increasingly thought to be 'redundant' because of a new imperative to learn to serve (McDowell, 2000, 2003). Yet, and despite long-standing recognition that the demand for 'masculine physicality' is falling (Lovell, 2000), the dominant picture of working-class masculinity that pervades academic literature and popular media has, until recently, continued to correspond with traditional representations: adherence to male breadwinner ideals, homophobia and misogyny, alongside suspicions of anything connoting femininity (Roberts, 2013; Ingram, 2018). The resilience of this mode of masculinity, as presented in much research, is quite staggering. I would argue, however, this presentation is problematic, limited and limiting.

Given that masculinities have been recognised as plural for several decades (see Chapter 3), and that the construction of masculine identity is a contested and contradictory process, the rigid, unitary version of working-class masculinity painted in the literature seems too simplified. While I don't doubt the validity of representations of working-class men's voices in work by Nayak, Nixon, Ward, McDowell and others, how far they extend is of crucial importance for sociological theorising. How far does the dominant version of traditional sexist masculinity extend beyond, or indeed *within*, the locales studied by such writers? How far does it extend into the life course beyond a year or two? That is, are these *partial* insights into contemporary working-class men's lives? We cannot know the answer to these questions for those specific men; however, we can note that in all those locales, many young working-class, relatively low-qualified young men do work in front-line service work (Roberts, 2011).

This tells us that these landmark studies have done the great job of explaining why and how their participants, those on the periphery of working lives, retain an adherence to older models of masculinity through a focus on 'fixing mechanisms' (Connell, 2001). While these are important voices, they represent a minority of young men, yet they have gained hegemonic status in the literature. This serves to collectively pathologise working-class young men, however inadvertent that might be, as sexist, traditionalist throwbacks who are incapable of being anything other than the kinds of men that their fathers were and, perhaps, 'needed' to be. This pathology is illustrated by Nayak's (2006: 814) statement that the contemporary world is characterised by 'new masculine subject positions struggling to adjust to a shifting gender order'. It is further extended through, for example, Ward's and Nayak's analyses of drinking rituals and the sexualisation of women in ways that seem to position them as attributes of working-class masculinity, when in fact these are just as likely to occur in middle-class settings, but are less researched. Ward's (2015) attribution of 'studious' boys' attendance at a strip club to their locale's working-class traditions is a very particular example of this.

In such analyses, then, the dominant narrative paints young working-class men as unchanging and unchangeable, and simultaneously, and somewhat more kindly, removes any blame by painting them as constrained by the tradition of embedded masculine heritage. In these cases, while some attention has been given to the complexities of the person – something that Connell (2005) suggests sociologists often overlook – the very bottom line is that this complexity is distilled into a dominant and largely negative set of traits.

I concur with Nayak's (2006: 817) statement that 'processes of gender cannot be set apart from economic restructuring, but instead are embedded within the restructuring process itself'. However, Nayak's research, like that of many others explored above, discusses the economy as fundamentally changed and restructured, while depicting the construction and performance of working-class masculinity as immutable. The processes of gender in this formulation then appear embedded in existing, older economic structures rather than in economic *re*-structuring. The possibility for any change in the development and construction of gender identities is reduced to practically zero as, it seems, people 'cannot fail to make themselves in particular ways' (Skeggs, 1997: 162), or, as McNay (1999) contends, that any attenuation of conventional masculinity or femininity in recent decades is likely to have done so in a piecemeal, discontinuous fashion through individual action and negotiation.

Thus we ought not presuppose that a reformulation of working-class masculinity is impossible, and should consider this an empirical question: Does economic re-structuring engender any *productive possibilities* for contemporary working-class masculinities or do they remain impossible? How might these come to bear on the wider aspects of the transition to adulthood? As I go on to demonstrate, we can gain newer and more holistic insights if, following McDowell's (2003) suggestion, we follow relatively lowly educated working-class young men for prolonged periods through their twenties, and if we avoid focusing solely on the most dispossessed when we refer to 'the working class' (Byrne, 2005; MacDonald, 2011).

Compared to previous generations, working-class, low-to-moderately educated young men in particular are faced with very different transition routes to contemporary labour markets, and indeed to adulthood. A decline in urban manufacturing employment and many heavy industries means that their employment opportunities are limited and the possibilities of gaining and retaining relatively well-paid work have declined in recent decades. These things are something of a truism. However, whether traditional working-class masculinity will have a lasting legacy, or whether the very nature of masculinity is subject to change alongside the labour market (Marks, 2003: 91), is not a given.

Before discussing the detail of changes and continuities in masculinities in the data analysis chapters, the following chapter first outlines the theoretical frameworks used in analysing these data.

Note

1 One young man in McDowell's study does indeed report getting sacked for fighting with a boy at work who had bad-mouthed the participant's mother.

References

Adkins, L. (2003). Reflexivity: Freedom or habit of gender. *Theory, Culture and Society*, 20(6), 21–42.

Allan, J.A. (2017). Masculinity as cruel optimism. *NORMA* [online], 1–16.

Archer, L., DeWitt, J., & Wong, B. (2014). Spheres of influence: What shapes young people's aspirations at age 12/13 and what are the implications for education policy? *Journal of Education Policy*, 29(1), 58–85.

Arnot, M., David, M., & Weiner, G. (1996). *Educational Reforms and Gender Equality in Schools*. Manchester: Equal Opportunities Commission.

Ashley, M. (2009). Time to confront Willis's lads with a ballet class? A case study of educational orthodoxy and white working-class boys. *British Journal of Sociology of Education*, 30(2), 179–191.

Ashton, D., & Field, D. (1976). *Young workers: From school to work*. London: Hutchinson.

Bauman, Z. (1998). *Work, Consumerism and the New Poor*. Buckingham: Open University Press.

Beck, U. (1992). From industrial society to the risk society: Questions of survival, social structure and ecological enlightenment. *Theory, Culture & Society*, 9(1), 97–123.

Beck, U. (2002). *Individualization: Institutionalized individualism and its social and political consequences.* Sage: London.

Beck, U., Giddens, A., & Lash, S. (1994). *Reflexive Modernisation: Politics, Tradition and Aesthetics in the Modern Social Order.* Cambridge: Polity.

Beck-Gernsheim, E. (1998). On the Way to a Post-familial Family from a Community of Need to Elective Affinities. *Theory, Culture and Society*, 15(3–4), 56–57.

Bennett, A., & Kahn-Harris, K. (2007). *After subculture: Critical studies in contemporary youth culture.* Basingstoke: Palgrave.

Berry, C. (2015). The final nail in the coffin: Crisis, manufacturing decline, and why it matters, in J. Green, C. Hay, & P. Taylor-Gooby (Eds.), *The British Growth Crisis*. Basingstoke: Palgrave.

Beynon, J. (2002). *Masculinities and culture.* McGraw-Hill Education (UK).

Biddulph, S. (2010). *The New Manhood: The handbook for a new kind of man.* Sydney: Finch.

Bradley, H. (1989). *Men's work, women's work: A sociological history of the sexual division of labour in employment.* Minneapolis, MI: University of Minnesota Press.

Brown, P. (1987). *Schooling ordinary kids; inequality, unemployment and the new vocationalism.* London: Tavistock.

Byrne, D. (2005). Class, culture and identity: A reflection on absences against presences. *Sociology*, 39(5), 807–816.

Chisholm, L., & du Bois-Reymond, M.D. (1993). Youth transitions, gender and social change. *Sociology*, 27(2), 259–279.

Cockburn, C. (1983). *Brothers.* London: Pluto.

Connell, R.W. (1987). *Gender and power.* London: John Wiley & Sons.

Connell, R.W. (1989). Cool guys, swots and wimps: The interplay of masculinity and education. *Oxford Review of Education*, 15(3), 291–203.

Connell, R.W. (1995). *Masculinities.* Cambridge: Polity Press.

Connell, R.W. (2001). Introduction and overview. *Feminism & Psychology*, 11(1), 5–9.

Connell, R.W. (2005). *Masculinities* (2nd edn). Berkeley, CA: University of California Press.

Corrigan, P. (1979). *Schooling the Smash Street Kids.* London: Macmillan.

Cross, S., & Bagilhole, B. (2002). Girls' jobs for the boys? Men, masculinity and non-traditional occupations. *Gender, Work & Organization*, 9(2), 204–226.

Delamont, S. (2001). *Changing women, unchanged men?: Sociological perspectives on gender in a post-industrial society.* Buckingham: Open University.

Dench, G. (2011). Rethinking the Sociology of the Family. *Sociology Review*, July. www.men-for-tomorrow.org/wordpress/wp-content/uploads/2011/10/ARTICLE-SOC-REVIEW-2011-071.pdf.

Dolby, N., Dimitriadis, G., & Willis, P.E. (2004). *Learning to labor in new times.* London: Psychology Press.

Du Bois-Reymond, M. (1998). 'I don't want to commit myself yet': Young people's life concepts. *Journal of Youth Studies*, 1(1), 63–79.

Faludi, S. (1999). *Stiffed: The Betrayal of the American Man.* New York: William Morrow and Company.

Fisher, M.J. (2009). 'Being a Chameleon': Labour processes of male nurses performing bodywork. *Journal of Advanced Nursing*, 65(12), 2668–2677.

France, A. (2007). *Understanding youth in late modernity.* London: McGraw-Hill Education (UK).
France A., & Roberts, S. (2017). *Youth and social class.* Basingstoke: Palgrave.
Francis, B., & Skelton, C. (2005). *Reassessing gender and achievement: Questioning contemporary key debates.* London: Routledge.
Frosh, S., Phoenix, A., & Pattman, R. (2002). *Young masculinities: Understanding boys in contemporary society.* Palgrave Macmillan.
Furlong, A., & Cartmel, F. (1997). Risk and uncertainty in the youth transition. *Young,* 5(1), 3–20.
Furlong, A., & Cartmel, F. (2004). *Vulnerable young men in fragile labour markets: Employment, unemployment and the search for long-term security.* York: Joseph Rowntree Foundation.
Furlong, A., & Cartmel, F. (2007). *Young people and social change.* London: McGraw-Hill Education (UK).
Furlong, A., Cartmel, F., Biggart, A., Sweeting, H., & West, P. (2003). *Youth transitions: Patterns of vulnerability and processes of social inclusion.* Edinburgh: Scottish Executive Social Research.
Garcia, G. (2008). *The decline of men: How the American male is tuning out, giving up, and flipping off his future.* New York: Harper Collins.
Giddens, A. (1991). *Modernity and Self-identity: Self and Society in the Late Modern Age.* Cambridge: Polity.
Gilbert, R., & Gilbert, P. (1998). *Masculinity goes to school.* New York: Routledge.
Goodwin, J., & O'Connor, H. (2005). Exploring complex transitions: Looking back at the 'Golden Age' of from school to work. *Sociology,* 39(2), 201–220.
Goodwin, J., & O'Connor, H. (2015). *Norbert Elias's Lost Research: Revisiting the Young Worker Project. Rethinking Classical Sociology.* Farnham: Ashgate.
Griffin, C. (2000). Discourses of crisis and loss: Analysing the 'boys' underachievement' debate. *Journal of Youth Studies,* 3(2), 167–188.
Hardgrove, A., Rootham, E., & McDowell, L. (2015). Possible selves in a precarious labour market: Youth, imagined futures, and transitions to work in the UK. *Geoforum,* 60, 163–171.
Haywood, C. (2008). Genders and sexualities: Exploring the conceptual limits of contemporary educational research. *International Studies in Sociology of Education,* 18(1), 1–14.
Haywood, C., & Mac an Ghaill, M. (2013). *Education and masculinities: Social, cultural and global transformations.* London: Routledge.
Hearn, J. (1998). Troubled masculinities in social policy discourses: Young men, in J. Popay, J. Hearn, & J. Edwards (Eds.), *Men, Gender Divisions and Welfare.* London: Routledge, pp. 37–62.
Hearn, J. (1999). A Crisis in Masculinity, or New Agendas for Men?, in S. Walby (Ed.), *New Agendas for Women.* London: Palgrave Macmillan, pp. 148–168.
Hopkins, P., & Noble, G. (2009). Masculinities in Place: Situated Identities, Relations and Intersectionality. *Social and Cultural Geography,* 10, 811–819.
Huppatz, K. (2012). *Gender capital at work: Intersections of femininity, masculinity, class and occupation.* Springer.
ILO (International Labour Organization) (2015). *World Report on Child Labour 2015.* Geneva: ILO.
Ingram, N. (2009). Working-class boys, educational success and the misrecognition of working-class culture. *British Journal of Sociology of Education,* 30(4), 421–434.

Ingram, N. (2011). Within school and beyond the gate: The complexities of being educationally successful and working class. *Sociology*, 45(2), 287–302.

Ingram, N. (2017). 'I'm not just one type of person': Aspirational working-class Belfast boys and complex embodied performances of educationally successful masculinities, in G. Stahl, J. Nelson, & D. Wallace (Eds.), *Masculinity and aspiration in an era of neoliberal education*. London: Routledge, pp. 71–88.

Ingram, N. (2018). *Working-Class Boys and Educational Success: Teenage Identities, Masculinity and Urban Schooling*. Basingstoke: Palgrave Macmillan.

Jenkins, R. (1983). *Lads, citizens, and ordinary kids: Working-class youth life-styles in Belfast*. London: Routledge.

Jimenez, L., & Walkerdine, V. (2011). A psychosocial approach to shame, embarrassment and melancholia amongst unemployed young men and their fathers. *Gender and Education*, 23(2), 185–199.

Keddie, A. (2007). Games of subversion and sabotage: Issues of power, masculinity, class, rurality and schooling. *British Journal of Sociology of Education*, 28(2), 181–194.

Kenway, J., & Kraack, A. (2004). Reordering work and destabilizing masculinity. *Learning to Labor in New Times*, 95–109.

Kestner, J. (2010). *Masculinities in British adventure fiction, 1880–1915*. Farnham, Surrey: Ashgate Publishing.

Kimmel, M. (2006). *Manhood in America* (2nd edn). New York: Oxford University Press.

Lamont, M. (2000). *The dignity of working men: Morality and the boundaries of race, class, and immigration*. Harvard University Press.

Lindsay, C., & McQuaid, R.W. (2004). Avoiding the 'McJobs' unemployed job seekers and attitudes to service work. *Work, Employment and Society*, 18(2), 297–319.

Lingard, B., Martino, W., & Mills, M. (2009). *Boys and Schooling, Beyond Structural Reform*. Basingstoke: Palgrave Macmillan.

Lovell, T. (2000). Thinking feminism with and against Bourdieu. *Feminist Theory*, 1(1), 11–32.

Mac an Ghaill, M. (1994). *The Making of Men: Masculinities, Sexualities and Schooling*. Buckingham: Open University Press.

Mac an Ghaill, M. (1996). *Understanding masculinities: Social relations and cultural arenas*. McGraw-Hill Education (UK).

MacDonald, R. (2011). Youth transitions, unemployment and underemployment: Plus ça change, plus c'est la même chose? *Journal of Sociology*, 47(4), 427–444.

MacInnes, J. (1998). *End of masculinity: The confusion of sexual genesis and sexual difference in modern society*. McGraw-Hill Education (UK).

Mangan, M. (1997). *Shakespeare's first action heroes: Critical masculinities in culture both popular and unpopular*. Unpublished.

Marks, A. (2003). Welcome to the new ambivalence: Reflections on the historical and current cultural antagonism between the working class male and higher education. *British Journal of Sociology of Education*, 24(1), 83–93.

Martino, W. (1999). 'Cool boys', 'party animals', 'squids' and 'poofters': Interrogating the dynamics and politics of adolescent masculinities in school. *British Journal of Sociology of Education*, 20(2), 239–263.

Martino, W., & Meyenn, B. (2001). *What about the boys?: Issues of masculinity in schools*. London: McGraw-Hill Education.

Matthews, C.R. (2016). Exploring the pastiche hegemony of men. *Palgrave Communications*, 2, 16022.

McDonald, J. (2012). Conforming to and resisting dominant gender norms: How male and female nursing students do and undo gender. *Gender, Work & Organization*, 20(5), 561–579.

McDowell, L. (2000). The trouble with men? Young people, gender transformations and the crisis of masculinity. *International Journal of Urban and Regional Research*, 24(1), 201–209.

McDowell, L. (2002). Transitions to work: Masculine identities, youth inequality and labour market change. *Gender, Place and Culture: A Journal of Feminist Geography*, 9(1), 39–59.

McDowell, L. (2003). *Redundant masculinities?: Employment change and white working class youth*. London: John Wiley.

McDowell, L. (2016). Youth, identity, class and gender, in A. Furlong (Ed.), *Handbook of Youth and Young Adulthood*. London: Routledge.

McDowell, L., Rootham, E., & Hardgrove, A. (2014). Precarious work, protest masculinity and communal regulation: South Asian young men in Luton, UK. *Work, Employment and Society*, 28(6), 847–864.

McNay, L. (1999). Gender, habitus and the field: Pierre Bourdieu and the limits of reflexivity. *Theory, Culture & Society*, 16(1), 95–117.

Messner, M. (1993). 'Changing men' and feminist politics in the United States. *Theory and Society*, 22(5), 723–737.

Miles, S. (2000). *Youth lifestyles in a changing world*. McGraw-Hill Education (UK).

Milkman, R. (1997). *Farewell to the Factory. Auto Workers in the Late Twentieth Century*. Berkeley: University of California Press.

Morgan, D. (1992). *Discovering Men*. London: Routledge.

Myers, J. (2016). *The Future of Men*. Oakland, CA: Inkshares.

Nayak, A. (2003a). Last of the 'Real Geordies'? White masculinities and the subcultural response to deindustrialisation. *Environment and Planning D: Society and Space*, 21(1), 7–25.

Nayak, A. (2003b). 'Boyz to Men': Masculinities, schooling and labour transitions in de-industrial times. *Educational Review*, 55(2), 147–159.

Nayak, A. (2006). Displaced masculinities: Chavs, youth and class in the post-industrial city. *Sociology*, 40(5), 813–831.

Newell, W. (2003). *The Code of Man*. New York: Harper Collins.

Nickson, D., & Korczynski, M. (2009). Aesthetic labour, emotional labour and masculinity. *Gender, Work & Organization*, 16(3), 291–299.

Nixon, D. (2006). 'I just like working with my hands': Employment aspirations and the meaning of work for low-skilled unemployed men in Britain's service economy. *Journal of Education and Work*, 19(2), 201–217.

Nixon, D. (2009). 'I Can't Put a Smiley Face On': Working-class Masculinity, Emotional Labour and Service Work in the 'New Economy'. *Gender, Work & Organization*, 16(3), 300–322.

Nixon, D. (2017). Yearning to Labour? Working-class Men in Post-industrial Britain, in C. Walker, & S. Roberts (Eds.), *Masculinity, Labour, and Neoliberalism: Working-class Men in Perspective*. Springer.

O'Donnell, M., & Sharpe, S. (2000). *Uncertain masculinities: Youth, ethnicity, and class in contemporary Britain*. London: Psychology Press.

Organisation for Economic Co-operation and Development (OECD) (1996). *The Knowledge-based Economy, OCDE/GD(96)102*. Paris: OECD Publishing. www.oecd.org/sti/sci-tech/1913021.pdf.

Organisation for Economic Co-operation and Development (OECD) (2015). *In It Together: Why Less Inequality Benefits All*. Paris: OECD Publishing.

Pascoe, C.J. (2007). *Dude, you're a fag: Masculinity and sexuality in high school*. CA: University of California Press.

Pease, B. (2002). *Men and gender relations*. Tertiary Press.

Petersen, A. (1998). *Unmasking the masculine: Men and identity in a sceptical age*. London: Sage.

Reay, D. (2002). Shaun's story: Troubling discourses of white working-class masculinities. *Gender and Education*, 14(3), 221–234.

Reay, D. (2004). 'Mostly roughs and toughs': Social class, race and representation in inner city schooling. *Sociology*, 38(5), 1005–1023.

Ringrose, J., & Renold, E. (2010). Normative cruelties and gender deviants: The performative effects of bully discourses for girls and boys in school. *British Educational Research Journal*, 36(4), 573–596.

Roberts, K. (2003). Change and continuity in youth transitions in Eastern Europe: Lessons for Western sociology. *Sociological Review*, 51(4), 484–505.

Roberts, K. (2009). Opportunity structures then and now. *Journal of Education and Work*, 22(5), 355–368.

Roberts, S. (2010). Misrepresenting 'choice biographies'?: A reply to Woodman. *Journal of Youth Studies*, 13(1), 137–149.

Roberts, S. (2011). Beyond 'NEET' and 'tidy' pathways: Considering the 'missing middle' of youth transition studies. *Journal of Youth Studies*, 14(1), 21–39.

Roberts, S. (2012a). One step forward, one step Beck: A contribution to the ongoing conceptual debate in youth studies. *Journal of Youth Studies*, 15(3), 389–401.

Roberts, S. (2012b). 'I just got on with it': The educational experiences of ordinary, yet overlooked, boys. *British Journal of Sociology of Education*, 33(2), 203–221.

Roberts, S. (2013). Boys will be boys … won't they? Change and continuities in contemporary young working-class masculinities. *Sociology*, 47(4), 671–686.

Roberts, S. (2014). *Debating Modern Masculinities: Change, Continuity, Crisis?* Basingstoke: Palgrave.

Robins, D., & Cohen, P. (1978). *Knuckle-Sandwich: Growing Up in the Working-Class City*. Harmondsworth: Penguin.

Sedgwick, E.K. (1985). Gender asymmetry and erotic triangles, in *Between Men: English Literature and Male Homosocial Desire*. Columbia University Press, pp. 21–27.

Segal, L. (1993). Changing men: Masculinities in context. *Theory and Society*, 22(5), 625–641.

Sennett, R., & Cobb, J. (1972). *The hidden injuries of class*. New York: Vintage.

Shildrick, T., MacDonald, R., Webster, C., & Garthwaite, K. (2012). *Poverty and Insecurity: Life in Low-pay, No-pay Britain*. Bristol: Policy Press.

Simpson, R. (2005). Men in non-traditional occupations: Career entry, career orientation and experience of role strain. *Gender, Work & Organization*, 12(4), 363–380.

Simpson, R., Hughes, J., & Slutskaya, N. (2016). *Gender, Class and Occupation: Working Class Men Doing Dirty Work*. London: Springer.

Singleton, A. (2008). Boys in crisis? Australian adolescent males beyond the rhetoric. *The Journal of Men's Studies*, 15(3), 361–373.

Skeggs, B. (1997). *Formations of class and gender*. London: Sage.

Stahl, G. (2013). Habitus disjunctures, reflexivity and white working-class boys' conceptions of status in learner and social identities. *Sociological Research Online*, 18(3), 2.

Stahl, G. (2015). *Identity, Neoliberalism and Aspiration: Educating white working-class boys*. Routledge.

Stahl, G., Nelson, J., & Wallace, D. (Eds.) (2017). *Masculinity and Aspiration in an Era of Neoliberal Education: International Perspectives*. London: Routledge

St Clair, R., & Benjamin, A. (2011). Performing desires: The dilemma of aspirations and educational attainment. *British Educational Research Journal*, 37(3), 501–517.

Taylor, I., & Jamieson, R. (1997). 'Proper little mesters' – Nostalgia and protest masculinity in de-industrialised Sheffield, in S. Westwood & S. Williams (Eds.), *Imagining Cities: Scripts, Signs, Memory*. London: Routledge, pp. 152–178.

Vickerstaff, S. (2003). 'Apprenticeship in the Golden Age': Were Youth Transitions Really Smooth and Unproblematic Back Then? *Work, Employment and Society*, 17(2), 269–287.

Ward, M.R. (2014). 'I'm a Geek I am': Academic achievement and the performance of a studious working-class masculinity. *Gender and Education*, 26(7), 709–725.

Ward, M. (2015). *From labouring to learning: Working-class masculinities, education and de-industrialization*. Springer.

Ward, M., Featherstone, B., Robb, M., & Ruxton, S. (2015). Beyond male role models? *Discover Society*, 24, September 1 [online]. https://discoversociety.org/2015/09/01/beyond-male-role-models-gender-identity-in-young-men/.

Ward, M., Tarrant, A., Terry, G., Featherstone, B., Robb, M., & Ruxton, S. (2017). Doing gender locally: The importance of 'place' in understanding marginalised masculinities and young men's transitions to 'safe' and successful futures. *The Sociological Review*, 65(4), 797–815.

West, C., & Zimmerman, D.H. (1987). Doing gender. *Gender & Society*, 1(2), 125–151.

Whitehead, S. (2002). *Men and Masculinities*. Cambridge: Polity.

Williams, C.L. (1995). *Still a Man's World: Men Who Do Women's Work*. Berkeley, CA: University of California Press.

Willis, P. (1977). *Learning to labor: How working class kids get working class jobs*. New York: Columbia University Press.

Wilott, S., & Griffin, C. (1996). Men, masculinity and the challenge of long term unemployment, in M. Mac an Ghaill (Ed.), *Understanding Masculinities*. Buckingham: Oxford University Press, pp. 77–94.

Wyn, J., & Dwyer, P. (1999). New directions in research on youth in transition. *Journal of Youth Studies*, 2(1), 5–21.

Wyn, J., & White, R. (1996). *Rethinking youth*. London: Sage

Wyn, J., & Woodman, D. (2006). Generation, youth and social change in Australia. *Journal of Youth Studies*, 9(5), 495–514.

3 Making sense of men
Outlining a framework for the study of contemporary masculinities

Introduction

There is a rich tradition of thinking and writing around the concept of masculinity and 'maleness'. The historical and cultural variation in the ways that masculinity was performed and the attendant concerns that followed are well documented by historians and literary scholars (e.g. Hoch, 1979; Tosh, 2005; Kestner, 2010; see Chapter 2). However, it was the emergence of critical men's studies in the late 1970s that led to a research focus on men as *gendered* beings (Kimmel et al., 2005). This approach, inspired by feminist thinking, took up the challenge of questioning the presumed naturalness of gender that had dominated academic thought for centuries. Tackling head on Parsons's functionalist account of gender role specialisation as a means to maintain family equilibrium (Parsons & Bales, 1953) and critiquing sex role theory's (e.g. Brannon, 1976) lack of attention to both ideology and power as well as its seeming emphasis on a simple masculine/feminine binary, this new approach made masculinity visible, examined its negative components and contested its apparent unity. As a result, critical men's studies highlighted the existence of a *plurality* of masculinities, the diversity of existence and the ways men are stratified within this plurality – what Connell (1995) calls the politics of masculinity.

The critical study of men and masculinities has since developed considerable theoretical apparatus. This chapter outlines the major theoretical frameworks utilised in analysing the data in subsequent chapters. As with many scholars studying men and masculinities, I start from the ontological and epistemological perspectives of social constructionism. In the analysis chapters, I draw mainly on the theories of two writers steeped in these traditions, namely Raewyn Connell and Eric Anderson, and further supplement their ideas by incorporating concepts from Pierre Bourdieu's 'structural constructivist' repertoire (Bourdieu & Wacquant, 1992: 11). In combining and critically engaging with the ideas and concepts, I proceed with a 'research tools' approach (akin to those advocated by Bourdieu and Foucault (who favoured the term 'toolbox')). This approach emphasises *using* these frameworks as resources for contemplating and interpreting the data, rather than 'testing' theories. Accordingly, I also make less systematic, but productive use of other theoretical resources – such as 'social generations' – to explain the findings.

The chapter starts with a brief consideration of the differences and overlaps between post-structuralism and social constructionism. I then critically engage with Connell's work – especially her most well known idea, Hegemonic Masculinity Theory – illustrating the need to consider Anderson's Inclusive Masculinity Theory in making sense of social change. I also illustrate how this can be further augmented by reference to the 'social generations' paradigm. Connell and Anderson are very much associated with critical study of men and masculinities, and their works mark important contributions in the field. However, to build a more complete picture of how and why young working-class men engage with and perform masculinities in the ways they do, and the consequences of this, I turn to Bourdieusian theory, especially the concept of habitus, to ensure better explanatory power. In the last part of the chapter focusing on the intellectual apparatus used, I critically engage with a small but recently growing body of work that variously incorporates Bourdieu, or advances quasi-Bourdieusian concepts, into studies of masculinity, ultimately suggesting that a more distilled, 'purer' version of Bourdieu's theorising can better serve the study of change and continuity in the lives working-class young men.

Social constructionism vs post-structuralism: a genuinely entrenched binary?

The approach I take is what Beasley (2012) calls the 'weak structuralism' of many social constructionists in the field of critical studies of men and masculinities (CSMM). Here, social structures do not simply determine subjects, and emphasis is instead placed on the dialectical relationship between structure and agency (Connell, 1987; Giddens, 1984). This approach 'eschew[s] monolithic accounts of structure from above and has room for contesting multiple modes of power, thus providing a more plural, less one-way and therefore less straightforwardly deterministic account of gender' (Beasley, 2012: 754). Despite being a strong statement, this acknowledgement does not stem from or support an absolute rejection of post-structuralist thought. Perhaps much to the chagrin of those who maintain that CSMM's social constructivist orientations remain incompatible with post-structuralist and/or postmodern thinking[1] (see e.g. Beasley, 2012; Whitehead, 2002), I share McCormack's (2012) reservations about just how far apart these two research paradigms actually sit. Consider this quote from Williams (2005: 3–4), for example:

> One aspect of post-structuralism is its power to resist and work against settled truths and oppositions. It can help in struggles against

discrimination on the basis of sex or gender, against inclusions and exclusions on the basis of race, background, class or wealth.

The post-structuralist aim then, advances Williams, is 'disruption' of 'truths' and binaries, to reveal how they act as systems of oppression and to more generally erode the constraints of seemingly fixed identity categories. Being set against the idea of any universalising 'truth', Williams (2005: 1) explains that post-structuralism differs to how 'the structuralist scientist hopes to arrive at some secure understanding' through 'noting a repeated pattern of signs'. However, I remain unconvinced that destabilising accepted knowledge is the sole preserve of post-structuralism, with the substantive content of the above quote also speaking directly to the ambitions of social constructionists.

Similarly, the post-structuralist understanding that '[g]ender does not happen once and for all when we are born, but is a sequence of repeated acts that harden into the appearance of something that's been there all along' (Salih, 2007: 54), seems quite aligned with West and Zimmerman's (1987: 125) classic articulation of 'gender as a routine accomplishment embedded in everyday interaction', such that it is constructed as naturally occurring. Beasley's (2012: 759) contention that 'postmodern interest in "undoing" gender [...] require[s] a reconfiguring of [gender categories] such that these identities are rendered permanently open and contestable' seems to be sensible and logical, too, for social constructionists who reject a simplistic agency/structure binary.

Ultimately, while the premise of post-structuralist thought is often theoretically and philosophically insightful – particularly in regards to its emphasis on the significance of discourses; identity categories as inherently unstable; and power as decentred and possessing productive, rather than simply oppressive, capacities – the practical application of these insights does not seem always or necessarily different from social constructionist accounts.[2] Several researchers have demonstrated how to combine ideas from post-structuralism with aspects of social constructionist thought (see e.g. Aboim, 2010; Pease, 2002; Hearn, 2012; Gahman, 2017). So, in adopting what Pease (2002) calls 'weak post-modernism', for example, we can proceed from a broadly social constructionist starting point, taking note of the multiple differences between men, while not losing sight of power structures (also Aboim, 2010; Hearn, 2012). This means we do not have to accept that men can inhabit only 'a limited set of material positions' (Aboim, 2010: 34; also Haywood & Mac an Ghaill, 2003), but similarly that we need not deny that categories are both 'reductionist and necessary, not only for reasons of intelligibility but also for the pursuit of justice' (Aboim, 2010: 35). The latter is crucial as the post-structuralist idea that 'culturally intelligible subjects' are produced by, rather than the producers/causes of, discourses that conceal their own invention (Foucault, 1977) leaves no room for accountability of either structures or agents, or the way they interact, thus limiting the scope for progressive change.

Connell's theory of hegemonic masculinity

Raewyn Connell's (1987, 2005) theorising has enduringly shaped studies of men, gender, social hierarchy and the field of masculinities more generally. This began with her fierce critique in the 1980s of the then prevailing 'sex role'/'sex-differences' paradigms, and the developments she proposed in their place, namely Hegemonic Masculinity Theory (HMT). To explain Connell's theorising, it is pertinent to briefly outline the development and content of the ideas she was critiquing.

Connell's critique of sex role theory as a launchpad for HMT

For several decades from the 1950s, 'role theory' had been something of a bellwether for progressive thought, emphasising the social rather than biological basis for gender differences. While Parsons and Bales's (1953) notion of men and women respectively performing 'complementary', 'instrumental' and 'expressive' functions was relatively quickly cast as conservative, literature on *sex role* theorising emerged around the 1970s, becoming 'the dominant way of understanding the nature of masculinity (and femininity) for the best part of three decades' (Edley, 2017: 38). Central to sex role theory was the idea that men learn how to be men, which at the time formed a sharp shift away from the biological and psychoanalytic paradigms, both of which argued in various ways that gender was related to some form of inner essence.

One of the most influential social learning ideas relating to the male sex role of this time was Brannon's (1976) four-pronged proposition of socially mandated gender norms for boys: 'No Sissy Stuff' – prohibiting femininity; 'Be a Big Wheel' – endorsing masculinity as measured by success and the admiration of others; 'Be a Sturdy Oak' – requiring stoicism over emotions, and strength over weakness; and 'Give 'em Hell' – valorising risk taking, aggression and agency through resistance.[3] In sex role theory, this process of masculinisation 'requires an ongoing regime of positive and negative reinforcements' (Edley, 2017: 41). These understandings opened up for scrutiny that one is not born but becomes a woman – as per Simone de Beauvoir (1949) – and that one also is not born but becomes a man. Being able to challenge the inevitability and immutability of the categories of man and woman was seen as a significant basis for potential reform of gender inequalities premised on gender difference.

Connell's (1987) critique of sex role theory was fairly fierce (Donaldson, 1993). Echoing an earlier articulation by Edwards (1983) of sex role theory's inadequacies in respect of women, Connell lamented it for failing to theorise structural relations of dominance and power between femininities and masculinities, and for failing to explain the continued global dominance of men over women. Connell also proposed that, as part of an unhelpful, blinkered approach when it comes to issues of power, sex role theory represents any deviation from one's expected sex role (as it applies to the sexed body) as a kind of 'failure' in socialisation. The prospect of such 'failures' then underscores a rather messy understanding of sex role as being both normative, in that it prescribes what men *ought* to be, but also apparently descriptive of what men are commonly *thought to be*. However, what is normative and what is common are very different things, and distinguishing them is a central component in recognising that 'normative' might be 'a definition of what the holders of social power wish to have accepted' (Connell, 1987). Relatedly, and again following Edwards (1983), Connell (1987) illustrated that this focus on the normative necessitated a simplified binary model of gender – commonly thought of as man/woman or masculine/feminine – and that this model assumes that all men and women (besides the allegedly deviant failures) can be neatly captured as one group on either side of the binary – a 'drastic' simplification of the complexities of gender.

An additional layer to Connell's critique was that sex role theory was not much of a social theory at all (Connell, 1987). It lacked an account of change, with Connell labelling it fundamentally static, arguing that sex role theory had 'no way of grasping change as a dialectic arising within gender relations themselves' (Carrigan et al., 1985: 578). The stage was set for Connell to move beyond substantial critique and to offer a more thorough theory of masculinity, paying greater attention to social institutions, social structure and, rather than a binary, gender plurality.

Multiple masculinities: Connell's theorising of masculinity, hierarchy and power

Targeting the prominent shortcomings of sex role theory, Connell's (1987) pioneering work revealed the importance of conceptualising masculinity not as singular monolithic construct, but as relational and plural – *masculinities*. Using this logic, attention could be paid to the 'different ways of enacting manhood, different ways of being a man' (Connell, 2000: 10), and, crucially, to how relations of power and hierarchy were produced, maintained, and contested between different masculinities. This focus was not designed to undermine attention to women's unequal status, as Connell (1995: 77) suggested that understanding the politics of and within masculinity was crucial for understanding wider gender inequalities in the 'gender order'.

Within this pluralised model of power relations, gender is constituted out of the interaction – i.e., the dialectical relationship – between structure and agents, rather than being wholly determined by social structures or individual voluntarism. There are resonances here with Giddens's (1984) model of 'structuration'; Bourdieu's (1990) effort to overcome duality in his theory of practice; and Messerschmidt's (2016) advocation of masculinities as structured action.[4] Central to Connell's theorising is the concept of 'hegemonic masculinity' (Carrigan et al., 1985; Connell, 1987, 1995, 2000), which is favourably viewed as 'the single most influential, recognized and utilized contribution to masculinity research' (Christensen & Jensen, 2014: 60), and has substantially influenced theoretical and empirical work on men, gender and social hierarchy, as well as practical efforts towards justice and equality, such as anti-violence activism (Jewkes et al., 2015).

The foundation of Connell's idea was her incorporation of Gramsci's (1971) well known concept of hegemony into gender theorising. Previously, the idea had been used to illustrate how ruling classes maintained control and authority consensually rather than coercively. However, Connell utilised this notion to explain how hegemonic masculinity operates as a configuration of gender practice that ideologically legitimates 'through discursive cultural influence and discursive persuasion' (Messerschmidt, 2016: 20) the dominant position of men and the subordination of women, and simultaneously facilitates men's access to institutional and economic privilege.

Connell also emphasised the historical contingency of hegemony, explaining it as the '*currently* accepted' strategy (Connell, 1995: 77, my emphasis) for cultural ascendancy. This is again similar to Gramsci's (1971) proposition that hegemony is a 'shifting set of ideas by means of which dominant groups strive to secure the consent of subordinate groups to their leadership' (Strinati, 1995: 170–171). Connell proposed that a culturally idealised form of masculinity maintains a position of hegemonic dominance, which is always contested, and exists through its perceived contrast, and dominant relation, to femininity.

It is now widely accepted that this is also a plural, with competing hegemonies operating at local, regional and global levels (Connell & Messerschmidt, 2005). While not associated with a particular set of traits per se (Messerschmidt, 2012), hegemonic masculinity is often 'characterised by numerous attributes such as domination, aggressiveness, competitiveness, athletic prowess, stoicism and control' (Cheng, 1999: 298). As the archetype of hegemonic masculinity is historically contingent, however, the specific characteristics that form the culturally ascendant archetype are always those that are 'most honoured or desired in a particular context' (Connell, 1995).

This archetype – discursively constructed and reinforced, and culturally celebrated – serves to subordinate and marginalise other masculinities, and ultimately legitimates unequal gender relations between men and women. For most of the latter 20th century, this archetype has accorded with adherence to male breadwinner ideals, homophobia, misogyny, and suspiciousness of anything connoting femininity (see Plummer, 1999). In many ways the characteristics most often linked to this *archetype* (not process) for most of the last half century do not depart too radically from Brannon's articulation of those things that boys and men must learn to do (see above), though it could be argued that such characteristics are both produced by and constitutive of hegemonic masculinity. Recalling some of these key components of masculinity is a useful step in understanding the complex *process* through which hegemonic masculinity is legitimated. For example, according to Schippers (2007, cited by Messerschmidt, 2016), traditionally masculine characteristics only legitimate men's power over women when they are viewed as both complementary to and hierarchically ranked above qualities associated with femininity. For example, an ability to use interpersonal violence only constitutes masculinity when paired with the 'inferior' quality, associated with femininity, of being unable to use strength and violence. Only with this pairing intact does the masculine form become superordinate (Messerschmidt, 2016: 51–52).

Another crucial feature of hegemonic masculinity is that 'only a minority of men express and perform its pattern' (Whitehead, 2002: 93). Indeed, it is an ideal that most men *cannot* attain (Edley, 2017). Accordingly, another issue integral to the legitimisation of hegemonic masculinity is the subordination and marginalisation – but *not* elimination – of other masculinities formed through the hegemonic process (Connell, 1995). For Donaldson (1993: 644), 'heterosexuality and homophobia are the bedrock of hegemonic masculinity',[5] thus it is probably no surprise that the most commonly cited example of *subordinated masculinities* is gay masculinity. With the key contravention appearing to be the repudiation of heterosexual desire, gay masculinities are denied legitimacy and power through a range of material and discursive practices, irrespective of whether gay masculinities are performed as 'macho', 'effete', or anything in between. There is thus a strong symbolic blurring of male same-sex attraction with femininity (Connell, 1995); and gay masculinities represent the repository of all that has been expelled from hegemonic masculinity (Howson, 2006). Being gay is (presumed by heterosexual men) to negate masculinity (Connell, 1992) and is thus a masculinity that often becomes subjected to acts of violence as disciplinary action.

It is not just heterosexuality that is central to hegemonic masculinity, with white, middle-class, able-bodied men also benefiting most from the hierarchical arrangement. Outside of these are what Connell (1995: 80) labels *marginalised masculinities* – those that emerge from the interplay between gender and other structures such as class and race. The marginalisation of black masculinities reminds us that various forms of oppression are dynamically interdependent (Messner & Sabo, 1990). Similarly, Coston and Kimmel (2012) persuasively argue that marginalised masculinities should include those men marginalised on the basis of disability.

This dominance over subordinated and marginalised masculinities gives rise to an important question about just how hegemony can be achieved if it must be consented to. Connell's answer to this question is twofold. First, some level of 'authorisation' occurs (Howson, 2006: 64), because *some* marginalised or subordinated men can escape (especially economic) powerlessness – perhaps through the media, music or sports. However, such exceptions do not unsettle the gender order or lead to a trickle-down effect that empowers marginalised or subordinated masculinity more broadly. Secondly, sandwiched between hegemonic and subordinated masculinities are *complicit masculinities*. *Most* men fit within this latter form, and while they do not necessarily achieve the normative standards of hegemonic masculinity, they are seen to be 'the central allies of those holding power ... [and] a strong pillar of patriarchal gender order' (Aboim, 2010: 42). While being respectful, non-violent husbands, partners, fathers – and simply colleagues and friends to women – men performing complicit masculinity sanction and validate hegemonic forms.

They may enact some of its attributes (for example, in team sports cultures that demand physical strength and aggression, or that engage in homophobic 'banter' and/or feminising 'sledging'[6]), and certainly benefit from the 'patriarchal dividend' resulting from women's economic oppression (Connell, 1995). Men who follow this pattern of masculinity are not actively advocating for or realising the needs for political change. Howson (2006: 65) notes, then, that this 'strategic unity' between 'the mass of men (and not insignificant number of women)' maintains the current gender order, and is built on their (collective) decisions to compromise housework, childcare, leisure and work routines. Thinking about complicity in this way is a clear example of Gramscian thought, such that the dominated 'accept the ideas, values and leadership of the dominant group not because they are physically or mentally induced to do so, nor because they are ideologically indoctrinated, but because *they have reason of their own*' (Strinati, 1995: 165–166, my emphasis).

What we can derive here is that hegemonic masculinity acts as a regulating force within the gender hierarchy both internally (between masculinities) but also externally (within relations between masculinities and femininities), to provide legitimacy to the contested problem of male dominance (see Demetriou, 2001; Caruso & Roberts, 2017). Evidently, in this formulation 'the capacity to exercise power and to do sex, gender, and sexuality is for the most part a reflection of one's place in sex, gender and sexual structured relations of power' (Messerschmidt, 2016: 50).

Critiques of Hegemonic Masculinity Theory

Connell's theorising has, like all good social theory, been subject to extensive critical engagement, with various scholars highlighting perceived limitations and/or proposed adaptations or reformulations.[7] These include: the vagueness and convenience of catch-all terms like hegemony and complicity (McCormack, 2012); inconsistent use of hegemonic masculinity as both an archetype and a process (see Messerschmidt, 2016); questions over how to delineate various masculinities, given that what is subordinated in one context might be hegemonic in another (Aboim, 2010; see also Donaldson, 1993 on the differing gender practices of various movie stars; also Whitehead, 2002); and that complicity and resistance to hegemonic norms can co-exist or be combined (Wetherell & Edley, 1999). Further, arguing the virtues of postmodernist perspectives, Beasley (2012: 759) posits that Connell's work encourages development of unhelpfully homogenising typologies, leaving 'the political logic of hegemonic positioning to be characterized in terms of a specific homogenized group of actual dominant men, transnational businessmen'. Meanwhile, Hearn (2004, 2010) has made clear that hegemonic masculinity renders absent any discussion of the hegemony – and violence, control, etc. – of 'real' men. The critiques then are wide and varied. In the remainder of this section, however, I want to pay more substantive attention to engagements with Connell's theorising that pertain to the issue of social change.

A salient example is Demetriou (2001), who argues for greater recognition of the reciprocal influence of masculinities; the agency of subordinated groups; and, importantly, the ways hegemony is accomplished through incorporation of non-hegemonic masculinities, rather than solely oppression through discredit or violence. Demetriou (2001) further contends that HMT overlooks any potential for hegemonic masculinity to become reconfigured into a more positive form of masculinity, highlighting the barriers to dismantling gender hierarchies in practice. I return to this latter point below, as it is an issue that many scholars diagnose as a weakness in Connell's theorising.

Most pertinently, Demetriou suggests that hegemonic masculinity might be better understood as a *hegemonic bloc* that remains in a state of 'constant hybridisation'. Using the example of heterosexual men's use of some elements of gay aesthetic, and strongly resonating with earlier work by Messner (1993), Demetriou (2001: 349) says this hegemonic bloc is characterised by efforts 'to articulate, appropriate, and incorporate rather than negate, marginalize, and eliminate different or even apparently oppositional elements'. Change in patterns of masculinities, and especially in the expression of hegemonic patterns, is argued to be better understood as style than substance (Messner, 1993), and likely more associated with fortifying power than challenging systems of inequality.

While Connell and Messerschmidt (2005) remain 'unconvinced that hybrid masculinities are illustrative of a transformation in hegemonic masculinity beyond local subcultural variation' (Bridges & Pascoe, 2014: 247), this idea has retained influence for some scholars who maintain that contemporary changes in masculinity leave power relations unaltered (see de Boise, 2014; O'Neill, 2015; Bridges, 2014). These notions of hybridity are contended by such authors to help *extend* rather than *dismantle* HMT; however, their effect is to further instantiate a more significant problem with the theory. Connell (1995) maintains that we must pay attention to the changing structure of relations, arguing that any theory of masculinity worth having must give an account of this process of change; yet, both in her own writing and that of advocates of masculinity hybridity (e.g. Bridges & Pascoe, 2014), social change cannot be understood as anything other than a top-down reconfiguration and fortification of existing power relations. Hegemonic masculinity, then, becomes a shorthand for male power, with the entire gender order reduced to *only* 'the systematic pursuit of power by heterosexual men' (Whitehead, 2002: 95; Anderson, 2009; Duncanson, 2015). The theory thus predicts relations of power in reductionist ways akin to a strong structuralist approach (see Beasley, 2012), which ensures that the individual is 'absent from both history and theory, having been made invisible within a system of

50 Making sense of men

domination *that changes, and somehow never changes*' (Whitehead, 2002: 96, my emphasis).

Connell offers consideration of the need for the culturally ascendant to maintain their power through a renewal of legitimation and consent. This speaks to the idea that hegemony is 'never complete', but little room exists for the effects of the exercise of resistance, either at the level of individuals or groups. By giving these such short shrift, Connell obviates a key component of hegemony: i.e. the ongoing nature of collective struggles and, crucially, the *prospect for change*. In almost all empirical work that follows Connell's lead, there is a tendency to render hegemony as something that can never be overcome, despite this being at odds with the very character of hegemony as articulated by Gramsci (1973) and others (e.g. Williams, 1973). This is perhaps nowhere better expressed than in the work of Richard Howson (2006, 2008).

Howson (2006: 5) makes clear that, in Connell's model, hegemony can only be usurped by another form of hegemony, which would be equally dominative. Yet, hegemony can be understood to resemble the *lack of total domination* (see also Whitehead 2002). This is clear in Howson's triparite model of hegemony, which offers the theoretic possibility that 'masculinity may be productive of new socio cultural practices, meanings, alliances and feelings' (Moller, 2007: 275).

Howson's point of departure is Weberian social theory, noting that even prior to Gramsci, there is a clear line of thought that expresses that domination is always open to the possibility of change. Moving to the tools offered by Gramsci, Howson (2006: 26–32) outlines three types of hegemony: detached, dominative and aspirational. The first two are characterised as regressive, as both have an exclusionary nature, and emerge from and end with various forms of crisis, which 'ensures that the hegemonic group, in the final analysis, dominates all other groups' (Howson, 2006: 60). The reproduction of existing power relations is a feature of both detached and dominative hegemony, but operates differently in each.

In detached hegemony, possibilities for change are closed down by the distance between the elite rulers and the dominated, and a lack of apparatus for the dominated to engage with the powerful. The dominative mode, which is the cornerstone of Connell's model of hegemony, is premised on a 'restorative function' (Howson, 2006: 61) where traditionally accepted practices of heterosexual marriage, men 'owning' or occupying public space, being breadwinners, and being compelled to expel emotional impulses must be upheld and constantly re-legitimated. Connell's version of hegemony is spoken of as historically contingent, but its flexibility is limited to ensuring that the idealised characteristics of masculinity remain legitimate and desired – achieved, perhaps, through the logic of hybridity.

The third version of hegemony is a progressive form, better understood as premised on a benevolent motivation, in which the dominant social group 'align[s] itself ideologically to the broader community of interests and identities' (Howson, 2006: 60). This leadership can of course become dominative, and this might come about as a result of crisis, yet only this form of hegemony offers the prospect for socio-positive change; it is not simply an alternative form of domination. In this aspirational form, 'hegemony involves moral and intellectual leadership whose task is not to neutralise and close down demands and interests, but rather to link them within an ethico-political collective, underpinned by openness [...]' (Howson, 2006: 31). Achieving this is not easy, and may seem fantastical at a time when a self-confessed 'pussy grabber' occupies the seat of President of the United States. However, this is to miss two vital points: first, the theory needs to be able to theorise the prospects for change and, second, as Howson states, 'usurpation of power from the traditional ruling groups requires profound patience' (ibid.).

In short, Howson's argument renders problematic Connell's reduction of social justice to the elimination of hegemony, insisting that this betrays key productive possibilities of hegemony as originally laid out by Gramsci. Reflecting on this and others (e.g. Demetriou, 2001), Connell and Messerschmidt (2005: 883) concede that it is 'perhaps possible that a more humane, less oppressive, means of being a man might become hegemonic, as part of a process leading toward an abolition of gender hierarchies'. Meanwhile, Messerschmidt (2012) has provided some important clarifications, reminding us that, beyond the hegemonic ideal, which contributes to patriarchal domination, there exist 'dominant', 'dominating' and other forms of non-hegemonic masculinities. Understanding and distinguishing between these forms is critical if we are to identify what Messerschmidt (2012: 73) calls 'equality masculinities'. Nonetheless, moving attention away from the dominant analytical and empirical investigations of the global north towards 'the majority world' reveals, for Connell (2016: 313), 'multiple tiers, where different configurations of masculinity are at work, and come into conflict'. The outcome of such competition is that there remains 'only a little ground for democratic projects of change in masculinity' and, in respect of the global economy, that there remains lacking a 'kinder, more inclusive, or more feminized capitalism' (Connell, 2016: 313).

The constraints of HMT's deterministic outlook

Connell has herself often emphasised the historical contingency of hegemonic masculinity, and noted that it is subject to ongoing contestation. Connell (1987, 1995), too, has insisted that change is not only possible, but can also come about from *within* gender relations, through the productive process of social movements, for example, and not just as a result of cultural forces (see Segal, 1990, 2007). Nonetheless, and despite Connell's assertion that HMT does not predict men's behaviours, her work has influenced particular and pronounced research attention into dominant forms of masculinity. That is, the prospects for socio-positive change, or an alternative type of hegemony as per Howson, have been absent not solely from Connell's theorising but also from much research that has utilised her frameworks. Moller (2007: 265) captures this especially well, lamenting HMT's tendency to inhibit empirical nuance by reducing gendered power 'solely to a logic of domination'. Thus, while Christensen and Jensen (2014: 64) caution against assuming 'that the most normative and legitimate form of masculinity in any society and at any historical point in time is also one that legitimates patriarchy', much masculinities research seems to do just that, suffering from a narrow approach that invites researchers to 'look out there' for 'particularly nefarious instances of masculinist abuses of power' (Moller, 2007: 275).

This is an approach that I think has come to dominate research on working-class young men in particular. Some key studies of young men's transitions provide good examples of how the literature has presented young men, especially working-class young men, as being unable to move beyond what might be termed a 'falsely homogeneous and universalised masculinity' (Segal, 2007: xxxi). My contention, then, is that despite working-class men being barred from an ascendant position in Connell's conceptual hierarchy of masculinity by their marginalised social class, they are also *a priori* characterised as adherents of the model of masculinity set out above, where dominance and toughness, homophobia and heterosexism are all essential to men's gender identity (Kimmel, 2008). There is a great risk of confirmation bias in such circumstances. HMT does offer some flexibility through the concept of protest masculinities, which, depending on the definition adopted, can be understood as:

> being structurally complicit, [but still] challeng[ing] the defining hegemonic principles by expressing behaviours such as deep affection for children, egalitarian attitudes towards the sexes and a sense of personal hygiene and fashion that, traditionally, were attached to subordinate masculinities and femininities.
>
> (Howson, 2006: 65)

Despite this nuance in Connell's repertoire, it is a much under-used or researched aspect of hegemonic masculinity. In part this is because protest masculinities have predominantly been characterised as representing resistance to the demands and abuses of capitalism, perhaps through acts of violence or collective urban unrest by those needing to re-work male superiority in the absence of economic security (e.g. McDowell, 2003; McDowell et al., 2014; Groes-Green, 2009; Ward, 2015). This narrow version of protest masculinity suffers from a problem that appears to be the hallmark of HMT – it allows only for the pursuit of power, and reduces masculinity to a fixed and limited set of motivations or practices. Duncanson (2015: 240) sums this up by suggesting that '[i]t is as if any shift in gender relations is inevitably hegemony at work; and there is little point in asking whether such shifts might be signs of progressive change, and, more importantly, how they could be furthered'. She further contends that 'the risk is that we come to our analysis of gender relations with a framework within which progressive change cannot be conceptualized' (Duncanson, 2015: 240), yet this is more than a risk, and an actuality of the HMT approach. Indeed, as McCormack (2012: 38) contends, HMT 'maintains most utility when investigating the patterns of masculinity within a particular institutional or local context', and, I would add, especially when conceptualising the presence and function of, and relations to, dominance.

The armoury of tools offered by Connell retains a strong heuristic utility for specific elements of the study presented in the later chapters, but its effectiveness as a wholesale theory of gender relations between men and masculinities is compromised by its inability to theorise change, and by a reluctance by some who use it to acknowledge change as anything other than a buttress of male dominance. Such selective accounts are in danger of framing masculinity as a deficit category, and this is amplified when these accounts are positioned as reflecting a widespread norm. In fact, I suggest that much like Connell's critique of sex role theory, much research focusing on problematic masculinities suffers from normativity. This is evident, for example, in a recent paper by Ward et al. (2017: 4, my emphasis), who observe:

> *Some* studies conducted with young men offer a more complex account, highlighting that young men's identities can be more fluid and complex, and that there are possibilities for constructing alternative masculinities that are *not necessarily* marked by negative behaviour.

Here, the possibility for, and observations of change are relegated to being anomalistic, and, equally, that masculinity is generally understood as deficit. Indeed, in sharp contrast to the 'complex accounts', Ward et al. refer to swaths of literature evidencing how 'acceptable forms of working-class masculinities are still often displayed through dominant, toxic or extreme forms of behaviour' (Ward et al., 2017: 4). I am not suggesting that Ward et al. and the many they cite are wrong in the portrayal of these problematic performances, but I question the logic that follows whereby masculinity is seen as unchanged and always negative. As the next section makes clear, there is abundant empirical and theoretical work that better offers a chance to understand the complexities in ways that move beyond equating masculinity with the pursuit of power. This has been mostly led by research adopting the lens of inclusive masculinity.

Theorising change: Anderson's Inclusive Masculinity Theory

While Ward et al. (2017), among others, note that 'some' studies have observed change in masculinity, this is an understatement. Research concerned with men's performances, expressions and understandings of gender has increasingly reported the changing nature of masculinities (Anderson,

54 Making sense of men

2014). Deviating from positions associated with traditional, orthodox or hegemonic forms of masculinity, empirical evidence increasingly suggests that heterosexual (especially young) men appear to be exhibiting social behaviours characterised by a softened version of masculinity (Anderson, 2009; McCormack, 2012), compared to similar research from decades ago (e.g. Pronger, 1990; Messner, 1993). This 'attenuated form' (Roberts, 2013) includes changed attitudes towards same-sex attraction, comprising a move from acceptance to overt support for gay peers and friends, and an expansion of acceptable and even esteemed behaviours relating to physical and emotional contact between straight men, and in leisure activities, consumption and employment (Adams, 2011; Anderson, 2009; Hall & Gough, 2011; McCormack, 2012; Roberts, 2013; Anderson et al., 2016; Maloney et al., 2017).

These more positive developments have been captured primarily[8] through the lens of Eric Anderson's (2009) Inclusive Masculinity Theory (IMT). While it is accurate that 'a closer look at the masculinities of the main power-holding elites in the contemporary world shows the huge task still ahead for the project of gender equality' (Connell, 2016: 312), Anderson and many other proponents of IMT contend that close inspection lower down the social order reveals changing patterns of gender behaviour, particularly among ordinary boys and young men in the West. These changing behaviours have important theoretical implications.

According to Anderson (2011: 731), and as above, a function of hegemonic masculinity is that one archetype of masculinity is esteemed above all others, so that boys and men who most embody this standard are accorded the most respect. Conversely, those who behave in ways that conflict with this valorised masculinity are marginalised, with those at the bottom of the hierarchy often publicly homosexualised as a means of chastisement for failing to adhere to rigid heteromasculine boundaries. Accordingly, in this model homophobia is used as a weapon to stratify men in deference to a hegemonic mode of heteromasculine dominance.

In light of contemporary social changes within North American and Western European cultures, Anderson (2009) theorises that hegemonic, or orthodox, forms of masculinity – characterised by heterosexuality, misogynistic attitudes, disembodied rationality and emotional restraint – are becoming less prominent within particular male cohorts. Anderson (2009) attributes this to the declining rates of homophobia and what he calls 'homohysteria' (the fear of being seen as gay) within most Western cultures over recent years. Given homophobia has been widely held by theorists of masculinity to be so central to men's identities and gender scripts, I now detail this concept and its significance.

Anderson's concept of homohysteria

Anderson's IMT, and especially the concept of homohysteria, is a development that allows us to contextualise and give due explanatory power to homophobia's historical contingency. For instance, Anderson (2009, 2011) highlights how the period from the 1980s to the late 1990s can be seen as an apex of cultural homophobia, with three factors combining to create a culture of heightened homohysteria: 1) a widespread understanding of 'homosexuality' as a static sexual orientation; 2) a zeitgeist of disapproval towards this orientation; and 3) a suspicion and concomitant condemnation of men's femininity as a relational signifier of being gay.

One of the driving forces of the stigmatisation of same-sex attraction during this period was the emergence (and subsequent reporting and misunderstanding) of the AIDS crisis, which facilitated an increase of the proportion of the British public who deemed 'homosexuality' as 'always wrong' from around 50% in 1982 to almost 64% in 1987 (British Social Attitudes Survey, 2016).

Widespread recognition of same-sex attraction, alongside a discriminatory and disparaging political discourse (exemplified by the Thatcher government's introduction of the infamous Section 28 legislation), produced an environment in which anything coded as feminine was seen to be the opposite of appropriate masculinity. This perfect storm of homohysteria ensured that men felt compelled to avoid suspicion of being gay by aligning their behaviours with those befitting a heterosexual identity (Anderson, 2011). Such a compulsion and its consequences led Kimmel (2008) to suggest that fear of being seen as 'not a real man' is fundamental to the formulation of masculinity, with men of this time symbolically defining themselves as '"soldiers" in a war of masculinity over femininity; heterosexuality over homosexuality' (Anderson et al., 2016: 3).

Subsequent decades, however, witnessed slow but steady erosion of this homohysteric culture; something McCormack and Anderson (2014) suggest is fuelled by rapidly improving cultural attitudes toward same-sex relationships. The reversal on public attitudes has been quite profound, with the proportion of British people perceiving 'homosexuality' as 'always wrong' declining from its 1987 peak to just 22% in 2012, and the proportion of those who considered being gay 'not wrong at all' growing from 11% in 1987 to 64% in 2016 (British Social Attitudes Survey, 2016).

Of particular interest here are observed generational effects but also period effects; i.e. while 74% of people born during the 1980s[9] feel same-sex relationships are 'not wrong at all', indicating a sharp generational effect, people born in all cohorts from the 1940s onwards have become more accepting of same-sex relationships since the early 1990s. While some ambivalence remains, in that some consider being gay as 'rarely or sometimes wrong', the direction of the trend is unmistakable, supporting that we are now in an epoch of relatively diminished cultural homophobia as per Anderson's theory. Indeed, the British Social Attitudes Survey (2016: 8) summary chapter on moral issues suggests that 'increased liberalisation of views therefore appears to mainly be a period effect – driven by a society-wide cultural shift'.

The vital thing to note here, and of relevance to my study, is that the concept of hegemonic masculinity cannot sufficiently theorise masculinity in Western cultures, as they are characterised by decreasing or lower (but not entirely diminished) levels of cultural homophobia. Anderson (2009) proposes IMT as a way of better making sense of this current trend. Men who espouse inclusive masculinity are likely to adopt attitudes and gendered behaviour that undermine the values of orthodox masculinity, particularly in relation to women and gay men (Anderson, 2009).

This opening up of behaviours is, as stated, made possible by the declining significance of homophobia in the construction of a masculine self (McCormack, 2012). The outcome is that, where Connell (2005: 77) observed that 'at any given time, one form of masculinity rather than others is culturally exalted', Anderson (2009: 8) contends that 'in cultures of diminished homohysteria, two dominant (but not dominating) forms of masculinity will exist: One conservative and one inclusive'. Co-existing within the inclusive form are multiple masculinities, and gendered behaviours of boys and men that are less differentiated from girls and women (Anderson, 2011: 733). Consequently, inclusive masculinities may be culturally esteemed among particular male peer groups, yet are not 'hegemonic' as they do not attempt to dominate, marginalise or subordinate any of the other masculinities within a given culture (Anderson, 2009; McCormack, 2011).

Empirical and theoretical developments related to IMT

Anderson's writing over the last decade or so is premised on data from over 40 distinct projects, and his ideas have enjoyed prolific uptake and support in empirical research (e.g. Channon & Matthews, 2015; Roberts, 2013; McCormack & Wignall, 2017; Haltom & Worthen, 2014; Drummond et al., 2015; Murray & White, 2015). Based on this research, McCormack and Anderson (2014; also Anderson & McCormack, 2016a) have asserted that significant numbers of young heterosexual men are engaging in homosocial relationships characterised by: 1) social inclusion of gay male peers; 2) embracing of once-feminised artefacts; 3) increased emotional intimacy; 4) increased physical tactility; 5) erosion of the one-time rule of 'homosexuality'; 6) eschewing violence. IMT has also been used as a framework for understanding the experience of bisexual young men (Anderson & McCormack, 2016b), men with non-exclusive sexual orientations (McCormack & Wignall, 2017), and gay men (McCormack et al., 2016).

What becomes clear is that IMT research finds, but also can theorise, something that HMT research does not. Connell holds that the feminisation of other groups of men is central to the achievement of hegemonic status, and many have contended that the policing of homo/heterosexual boundaries is *the* central dynamic of the relations between and performances of masculinity (Kimmel, 2008; Hooper, 2001). So as these old certainties erode is it any wonder that we see such change in masculinities? Some claim these changes are overstated or misinterpreted, as I will now illustrate, but ultimately reject.

Critiques of IMT

Although Connell has not entertained the theory, IMT has been subject to critique along lines established by her ideas. Some striking examples appear in the edited collection of empirical projects using and engaging with IMT, *Debating Modern Masculinities* (Roberts, 2014), with Simpson (2014) arguing that 'inclusive' attitudes represent simply civil indifference. In the same volume, Ingram and Waller (2014: 39, 40) consider IMT too 'optimistic', insisting that Anderson is guilty of presenting a 'postmodern co-existence of multiple male cultures that entail no relationship of power'. They also contend that while changes in masculinity are notable and research worthy, they are better understood as a 'repackaging of forms of domination'. This concern regarding unaltered power relations, as well as the implications for transformed or hybridised forms of masculinity, is taken up further in the wider recent literature (see de Boise, 2014; O'Neill, 2015; Bridges, 2014) in ways that mostly rely on arguments related to hybrid performances of masculinity (as noted above; e.g. Demetriou, 2001). The problem with these critiques is that they presuppose that masculinity is always and only about the pursuit of power.

Emphasising that 'there *must* be a correspondence between institutional power and group practice' (de Boise, 2015: 325, emphasis in original), those critiquing IMT in this fashion cannot and will not fathom any change unless it occurs under the guise of hybridity, such that men alter practices, or have their practices altered, in ways that 'provide the impression of progress while still protecting the interests of historically privileged groups' (de Boise, 2015: 324). Thus, de Boise (2015: 334) argues that IMT offers nothing new to CSMM because change is already captured in the notion of hybridity as articulated by Demetriou (2001), and that attitudinal changes as measured by survey data do very little to disrupt broader inequalities, hidden prejudice, and the continued institutional privilege of some groups of men. However, the softening of hegemonic masculinities, identified across many contexts, is not always inevitably a superficial change, masking the retention of power and the creation of new hierarchies (Duncanson, 2015). That is clearly borne out in Anderson's research and the work of those who have employed IMT; they have not assumed that 'softer' or hybrid masculinities always entail new racial, class-based or sexual oppression, but have let such issues, and the question of institutional power, emerge in their empirical findings.

On those empirical results, though, further criticisms emerge. De Boise (2015), O'Neill (2015) and Negy (2014) all posit that IMT relies on studies of white, educated, middle to upper-middle class, heterosexual male youth, arguing that the relatively privileged position these men occupy permits enactments of a range of gendered behaviours. Further, it is argued that there is currently no account of how butch lesbian, trans and gender-diverse, or bisexual individuals fit into the schema of the respondents' more 'inclusive' practices and attitudes (de Boise, 2015). These critiques, however, are problematic and rely on a narrow, selective reading of the literature.

First, Anderson (2009) holds that decreasing homophobia is a socially uneven process. I would further suggest that presuming working-class men are homophobic, 1) is reliant on older research, 2) situates working-class masculinity as in deficit, and 3) without more evidence could be observed as explicit prejudice. Each of these points is captured in de Boise's (2015: 326) somewhat contentious reminder that 'middle-class men, historically, have not necessarily been considered the most chauvinistic, homophobic, or "physically" powerful'. Secondly, while more studies are needed on varying populations, to suggest an absolute absence of inclusive attitudes beyond middle-class, heterosexual men is misleading because social class position is not understood as a barrier to performing softer, attenuated practices of masculinity in schools or workplaces (Roberts, 2013; McCormack, 2014).

Working-class discourses can act as a 'buffer', but as McCormack (2014: 143) maintains, they are not an entirely prohibitive factor in the development of more inclusive attitudes and behaviours among working-class male youth (see also Roberts et al., 2016). Anderson and Bullingham (2014) use an adapted version of homohysteria to make sense of the ways that lesbian athletes compete in more supportive environs and enjoy almost universal inclusive social settings. Meanwhile, Magrath (2015) argues religiosity, rather than 'race', underpins homophobia, with several black boys in his study stating they would aspire to be best man at the wedding of a gay best friend. These are, clearly, accounts of groups who are not middle-class, white, male university students.

O'Neill (2015) has also critiqued IMT for failing to focus on gendered power relations by de-emphasising key issues of sexual politics, ultimately reflecting and reproducing a postfeminist logic in which gendered inequalities are overlooked. Given the IMT research to date, I agree that this area requires more research and theorising, and the findings chapters in this book offer observations in what should be fruitful areas of future research. That said, O'Neill overstates her claim; the IMT literature is replete with unambiguous statements about changing masculinities not being synonymous with a gender utopia.

Overall, IMT holds exceptional utility as part of a toolbox approach for understanding contemporary masculinities. IMT provides coherency that an uncritical commitment to HMT does not permit, giving conceptual mileage to processes of change, and moving beyond relatively static approaches that only conceptualise power and that stabilise gender identities/masculinities as plural yet largely homogenous and predictable groupings (Beasley, 2012; Aboim, 2010). As Duncanson (2015) notes, the formation of hegemonic masculinity through the subordination – often feminisation – of others, requires that any transitory stage must be one where traditionally disparaged, feminised traits are newly valued and incorporated into 'softer' masculinities. Taken as a form of hybridity that does not assume men's change 'always camouflages the continuation of patriarchy, militarism, and neoliberalism' (Duncanson, 2015: 245), IMT offers a chance to understand contradictions and to push towards relations of equality. This is because inclusive practices and attenuated masculinities – including the incorporation of the feminine – are a necessary, 'more achievable and therefore more likely first step' (Duncanson, 2015: 244) *towards* a socio-positive hegemony.

IMT also offers a strong focus on generational distinctiveness; indeed, that contemporary young people engage in bottom-up processes of social change is one of the core arguments for its proponents. However, as I now explain, IMT can be usefully augmented with a formal extension of generational theorising, which might be aided through reference to youth sociology's recent conceptual developments regarding 'social generations'.

Making the most of Mannheim's legacy: masculinities and the sociology of generations

Accurately understanding the complex contexts of young people's lives requires drawing on a range of theories (Woodman & Wyn, 2015). Therefore, I propose that the sociology of generations can augment IMT to better theorise contemporary social change pertaining to masculinities. I have elsewhere critiqued the homogenising discourses that sometimes emerge from the application of social generations theory in youth sociology, such that young people are collectively characterised as a precarious generation, positioned in contrast to the 'gold-plated' baby boomer generation (France & Roberts, 2015). This means that intra-generational differences among both become overlooked (France & Roberts, 2015), limiting our understanding of nuances in attitudes and experiences.

Mannheim's (1952) theory of generation, however, offers conceptual tools permitting a sophisticated theorisation of social change. Moreover, it can complement IMT in understanding the relationship between generational location and 'certain modes of behaviour feeling and thought' (Mannheim, 1952: 291). Simply put,

> [the] concept of generations focuses on the reality that at particular points in time young people face distinctive conditions that require their active engagement in 'rewriting' the rules for making a life. At such times young people face new demands to 'invent' youth and young adulthood.
> (Woodman & Wyn, 2015: 1404)

This understanding aligns with the reflexive and subject-driven 'bottom-up' approach signalled by McCormack's (2012) argument that it is boys and young men themselves who are redefining masculinity. Similarly, this echoes earlier points made by Wyn and Woodman (2006) that understanding the specific conditions that shape a generation requires an accompanying consideration of young people's subjectivities.

Youth is important because it is in this biographical phase that social circles of generational discourse crystallise (Corsten, 1999). Generations exist as specific collective identities, unlike an arbitrary age group, and they share a picture of 'their' time or a script of 'their' collective development in the course of 'their' historical phase (Corsten, 1999). Traces of this are evident in Figure 1.1 (Chapter 1), where the UK's 65+ generation more collectively see themselves as completely masculine, something almost universally rejected among the youngest generation. This is indicative of a form of 'self-reference' that is also essential in the formation of a generation (Corsten, 1999), such that, rather than simply sharing a background of experience, the members of a collective also have a 'sense' that they share similar assumptions to others of their generation. This is clear in McCormack's (2012; McCormack et al., 2016) work on the changing nature of 'gay discourse', where large numbers of young men – straight, gay or otherwise, both working and middle class – hold that among their generation the word gay has a meaning beyond being a homophobic slur.

A generational framework accounts for the impact of political, social and economic context to understand the complex and differentiated ways in which young people interpret and give meaning to their lives. The intertwining of these dimensions has particular implications for young men's identity constructions at a time when, after decades of restructuring, employment prospects vary massively in terms of content, title and contract tenure from their parents' generation. These structural realities are norms for the contemporary generation of young men, and intersect with wider contributors to diminishing homohysteria as noted by IMT scholars (see above), working in a reciprocal manner to re-fashion the possibilities for masculine identity.

Mannheim (1952) also offers ways to understand heterogeneity within a generation through his concept of 'generational units'. These are different groups within a generation who 'work up the material of their common experiences in different and specific ways' (Mannheim, 1952: 304). I have argued elsewhere (France & Roberts, 2015) that generational units ought not to be aligned with or substituted for social characteristics like class. Avoiding such conceptual slippage is essential in moving away from reductive, class-based characterisations of, for example, working-class boys valorising 'fighting, fucking and football' (Mac an Ghaill, 1994), towards understanding that, even within a similar class location, different articulations of masculinity can emerge. Indeed, Mannheim's intention was to consider intra-generational difference in the production, receipt and transmission of knowledge, and its attendant effects (France & Roberts, 2015). This is useful for conceptualising how various forms of masculinity will co-exist (Anderson, 2011), sometimes hierarchically, but not always in the presence of hegemony (McCormack, 2011).

A final noteworthy point is that the social conditions of a generation's experience is argued to shape people's consciousness throughout the life course, such that having 'grown into it' in youth, they will never grow out of 'it' (Wyn & Woodman, 2006). A real life example here might be that young people will not 'grow out' of their support for equal marriage, or their generally higher pro-gay sentiment compared to older groups. That is to say, modes of inclusive masculinity developed among recent generations of young people might be very durable. This is exemplified by Magrath's (2017) interviews of the same men Anderson based his theory on over a decade ago, finding that they maintained their friendships with each other and their social dispositions on masculinity and gay people.

In sum, a formal conceptualisation of generation augments the IMT approach by providing conceptual tools that allow serious consideration of the conditions of social change and – if used properly – can avoid overly homogenising all men, all young men, or even all young working-class men. However, theories of masculinity can only get us so far in analysing young working-class men's transitions to adulthood. That is, masculinity is only part of the issue being examined in this study of working-class lives. As I now illustrate, Pierre Bourdieu's conceptual toolbox lends itself particularly well to explaining the role of classed processes in young people's negotiation of life domains, and the issues of inequality and difference that ensue (France & Roberts, 2017; see also Atkinson, 2015 on Bourdieu's wider relevance for class analysis), and moreover, has a significant role for theorising masculinities.

Bringing in Bourdieu: a fuller account of the social actor

Pierre Bourdieu's work has enjoyed enormous uptake in recent years, especially as it applies to social class (Savage et al., 2013; Atkinson, 2015; France & Roberts, 2017). His theory of practice is a well-rounded approach to human action that, despite his critics' misgivings (e.g. Adkins & Skeggs, 2004), centres the intersection of various forms of social difference (see Atkinson, 2017: 127–8). Permitting such a focus on the intentions, dispositions, possibilities and 'choices' of action of the individual actor ensures that the young men who are the focus of this study are not reduced solely to their masculinity. Moreover, this approach obviates the post-structuralist argument (e.g. Whitehead, 2002) that social constructionist theories of masculinity, despite rejecting the either/or binary of macro-structural determinism and micro-level agency by voluntarist subjects, make the actor (or 'subject', in post-structuralist parlance) somewhat absent.[10] In this section, I describe some of Bourdieu's main concepts and explain how, despite some academics' misgivings, his ideas can be seen as complementary to the theories set out above.

Bourdieu's ideas initially offered a limited foray into the realm of masculinities, at least explicitly. His most famous work in this area, *Masculine Domination* (Bourdieu, 2001), was chided by Connell and Messerschmidt (2005: 844) as having an essentialist edge that gives 'a new lease of life to functionalism in gender studies'. This critique rests in some ways on the perennial and arguably misconstrued readings of Bourdieu's work as lacking an emphasis on agency and/or being unable to account for change and transformation (Archer, 2000; Goldthorpe, 2007). The criticism of essentialism, especially, appears to be a mistake. Atkinson (2017: 107, emphasis in original), for example, notes Bourdieu's precise articulation of gender as 'linguistic-perceptual *constructions*', i.e. cultural ideas of what men and women should be, that have come about as a result of long-standing struggles over classification, and also that Bourdieu (2001: 3n.3) lamented psychologists for ignoring the 'degree of overlap between the distributions of male and female performances ... in the various domains (from sexual anatomy to intelligence)'. Further, in relation to masculinity specifically, Jo-Anne Dillabough (2004: 494) makes plain:

> [Bourdieu's] view of the performance of masculinity has an anti-essentialist character in that male domination can be traced to historical ideas that are embodied by social actors in the present. It is not simply a straightforward or objective derivative of contemporary social and cultural power formations. Arbitrary enactments of masculine domination are expressed and, therefore, to be read differently through social structures, discourses, relations and bodily representations.

Dillabough also uses Bourdieu's words to make clear just how ripe for analysis masculinity becomes through a Bourdieusian lens: 'as a man or woman [...] we have embodied the historical structures of the masculine order in the form of unconscious schemes of perception and appreciation' (Bourdieu, 2001: 5). This refers to Bourdieu's notion of *habitus*, which, along with the concepts of *field* and *capitals*, forms part of his conceptual triad for understanding the *logic of social practice*. I emphasise 'social practice' because, while mostly used to understand the power dynamics of domination and the legitimacy of one social group over another, Bourdieu's tools offer ways to theorise society beyond forms, tactics and realities of oppression. Indeed, resistance and the struggle for recognition are crucial dimensions to Bourdieusian theorising (Atkinson, 2017).

Bourdieu's conceptual tools

Before outlining Bourdieu's concepts, it is important to state that 'theorists [ought] not "mine" data to capture, for example, evidence for habitus, capital and field', and instead these must be understood as 'theoretical tools to better understand empirical data and think inductively and critically' (Webb et al., 2017: 141). The task of the present research, then, is to use these concepts as appropriate rather than being concerned with 'counting up' the instances they become present.

Habitus is a 'system of durable and transposable dispositions through which we perceive, judge and act in the world ... acquired through lasting exposure to particular social conditions and conditionings via the internalizing of external constraints and possibilities' (Wacquant, 2006: 267). These 'dispositions' are formed in childhood through a relational dialectic with the surrounding ecology of social life (i.e., the family, community, media, early education, etc.; see Bourdieu & Wacquant, 1992).

They are reflections of individuals' lived journeys in classed or collective contexts, premised largely on the shared conditions of work and life. Habitus is a durable lens through which we interpret the world, but happens 'without any deliberate pursuit of coherence ... without any conscious concentration' (Bourdieu, 1984: 170), and provides justification for individuals' perspectives, values, actions and social positions. However, rather than being fixed, habitus is 'endlessly transformed' (Bourdieu, 1984: 466), meaning that it can be seen 'as much as an agent of continuity and tradition as it can be regarded a force of change' (Costa & Murphy, 2015: 4). The latter is important if habitus is to have any utility in analysing changing working-class masculinities. In direct relation to youth and young adulthood, Woodman and Threadgold (2015: 558) posit that the key question is 'what growing up in a changing world might mean for the type of habitus that is formed'; relatedly, it is important to ask what this might mean for changing gender expressions.

The habitus cannot be considered in isolation, for it is always referenceable to the second of Bourdieu's interlocking tripartite model: social fields. Starting from an overarching 'field of power', which denotes the broader social world, Bourdieu theorised the field of power as composed of multiple intertwining fields. These fields are autonomous social arenas, governed by their own laws, in which competitive 'games' are played out for position – or, in Bourdieu's terms, recognition – such that 'agents and groups of agents are thus defined by their relative positions within that space' (Bourdieu, 1985: 724). Examples include the fields of art, education, employment, politics, housing and the family (Silva & Wright, 2009; Atkinson, 2015). These fields, despite their autonomy, are interdependent and influence one another. Habitus furnishes agents with 'feel for the game' that takes place in a specific field, thus it is easier to succeed if one's habitus (i.e. one's dispositions, inclinations) is commensurate with the rules of the field, such that one feels like a 'fish in water' (Bourdieu, 1989: 43, in Wacquant, 1989). Mismatch between habitus and field – most overtly and expansively explored in the sociology of education (e.g. Crozier & Reay, 2011; Lehmann, 2013) – forms the basis of inequalities that are *mis*-recognised as being legitimate because 'underlying processes and generating structures of fields are not consciously acknowledged in terms of the social differentiation they perpetuate' (Grenfell & James, 1998: 23). Bourdieu (1998: 40) suggests, though, that habitus and field have a dialectical relationship, which is underpinned by 'struggle for the transformation or preservation of the field'. This relationship is neatly explained by Ingram (2018), who states that 'habitus develops within a field according to its position, and the field develops in response to the multitude of differently positioned habitus'.

The social world (and its various fields) are negotiated not just through the lens of habitus, but also through access to, deployment of and efforts to accumulate *symbolic* resources, or in Bourdieu's vernacular, *capitals*. Primarily Bourdieu refers to three types of capital in his symbolic economy: economic, cultural and social. Economic capital encompasses material wealth, money and assets. Cultural capital includes certain forms of knowledge, cultural preferences, styles of speech and even manner of comportment.

Importantly, while some capitals are held as legitimate, others are seen to lack value. The classic example here is the difference between different types of knowledge, such that knowledge of 'highbrow' activities, such as classical music, is more highly valued than, for example, knowledge of popular music.

The distinction between the two is arbitrary, but this arbitrariness is, for Bourdieu, disguised such that difference in value is perceived – read, *misrecognised* – as legitimate and objective. Bourdieu (1986: 48) also notes that acquisition of cultural capital can occur through a process of unconscious inculcation, such that 'inequalities associated with cultural capital reflect unequal capacities to acquire capital which themselves reflect prior inequalities in the possession of cultural capital' (Moore, 2008: 109). Such a statement veers towards a highly deterministic understanding of inequality, but the main point here is that what Bourdieu offers is an explanation of social reproduction – indeed, Lovell (2007) suggests Bourdieu is thus better thought of as a pessimist than a determinist.

Social capital is 'the aggregate of the actual or potential resources which are linked to possession of a durable network' (Bourdieu, 1986: 46). Siisiäinen (2000) suggests that in contemporary times social capital might be exemplified by voluntary associations, trade unions, political parties, secret societies or fraternities. These associations can be drawn on for advantage and are 'convertible, in certain conditions, into economic capital [but also] may be institutionalized in the form of a title of nobility' (Bourdieu, 1986: 242). This of course depends on the size of the network of connections that one can effectively mobilise (Bourdieu, 1986: 249; Siisiäinen, 2000), and it is important to note that social capital is produced by the configuration of relationships, rather than merely a common 'quality' of the group. Crucial to note here is that Bourdieu's version of social capital is very different from Putnam's (1993) formulation, as the former remains a resource in social struggles carried out in different social fields, while the latter relates to a notion of generalised trust and reciprocity. The composition of capitals is observed as a vital 'organising principle', such that without analysis of capitals, Bourdieu (1986: 46) argues, it is 'impossible to account for the structure and functioning of the social world'. Capitals are important, in conjunction with habitus, for understanding how people have greater or lesser capacity to act and thus achieve a 'position' in a particular social *field*.

How gender – in this case masculinity – informs capitals and habitus is of crucial importance. I explore this in the forthcoming chapters in relation to young working-class men's transitions to adulthood. Using Bourdieu to understand men's lives and behaviours is not especially new, but what I show now is that a specific reading of gender in Bourdieu is required if his tools are to be useful, which necessitates critical engagement with some of the more recent advances that have sought to build on his ideas.

Critically assessing the use of Bourdieu's concepts in studies of masculinity

Various studies of masculinity have drawn upon feminist scholars' (e.g. Adkins & Skeggs, 2004; Skeggs, 1997; Reay, 2004) re-articulations of Bourdieu's concepts. For example, the notion of 'gender capital' builds upon the idea that to qualify as capital, a practice ought to have value within a social field such that it can be deployed to one's advantage (Skeggs, 2004). Huppatz (2009), for instance, writing on the Australian care sector, teased out the classed nature of how 'gender capital' structures the life trajectories and career pathways of women. More recently, Huppatz's approach has focused on the interrelationship of both male and female forms of gender capital and how this impacts men and women's life chances and opportunities (Huppatz & Goodwin, 2013). As Huppatz and Goodwin (2013: 297) state, 'both femininity and masculinity are resources that are drawn on both consciously and unconsciously with varying success in movements through social space, particularly in the labour market'.

Here, the authors show how masculine and feminine forms of capital differently position particular genders in the labour market and the public and private spheres, and reveal how the same capital has different effects as used by different genders. Tellingly, Huppatz and Goodwin (2013: 304) note that the 'transgression of gender norms and the mobilisation of feminine capital can be so profitable it can sometimes assist men in moving class position', and that 'mobilisation of feminine embodiments may be particularly advantageous for working-class men who need to "halt losses" and find that most low-skilled employment opportunities in Australia are in service work'. These ideas suggest '[f]or both men and women gender is increasingly taking the form of a self-conscious artifice which can be managed, strategically deployed and performed' (Adkins, 2004: 202).

Despite these developments, I align myself with Atkinson's (2017: 119, his emphasis) determination that 'while both masculinity and femininity *appear* to operate as resources, this is in fact nothing more than an illusion'. Men and women – and any identification between those discursive poles – possess stocks of capital that plot them in more or less dominated/dominant positions in social space. In this space there are symbolic struggles over ideas and visions of and for gender, and these refract the ways gendered practices and ideas are perceived, valued and embodied (Atkinson, 2017: 128). These feed into distinguishable variants and expectations both across and within social space, such that those that turn to the body or practical skill for recognition in the absence of economic and cultural capital are split between opposing strategies of physical hardness and glamorous beauty, or – in the field of work – between manual trades and personal/caring services.

Meanwhile, abundant cultural capital ensures a different kind of (still gendered) divide between the pursuit of masculine 'hard sciences' – such as business and political science, which lead to positions of power and influence – and the 'softer' sciences and the arts, which carry lesser symbolic and material rewards (Atkinson, 2017: 129–30). Gender is then a perceptual linguistic category that unites, divides and mobilises people and practices. Therefore, instead of a general gender capital, our understanding is better served if we accept that actors have, as part of/formed by their habitus, a gendered *social surface* (Atkinson, 2017), and that 'particular gender*ed* capitals are mobilised in specific structural contexts' (Atkinson, 2017: 119, emphasis in original).

Ultimately, possession of different stocks of economic, cultural and social capitals equip men and women with differential capacities to deal with and challenge masculine domination.

Several related conceptual developments have come to light in recent years. Morris's (2017) ideas on 'gay capital' and Hakim's (2012) 'erotic capital', for example, each offer interesting insights, but are both conceptually limited. The former falls into the same trap as the notion of subcultural capital developed in youth sociology by Thornton (1995), as it illuminates the function of legitimate behaviour and activity in what might be described as an 'alternative field' (see Threadgold, 2015). Morris shows that gay capital can be converted into various social benefits, yet this does not mean that gay capital can necessarily be presumed a form of cultural capital in the Bourdieusian sense; its translation to 'legitimate' fields is unproven, and many would argue that it has little or neutral value in wider fields and the field of power. As for Hakim (2012), hers is a crude formulation that rests on individualist impulses and the notion of free choice, overlooking that this apparent 'currency' operates as a form of 'double domination' (Atkinson, 2017), such that those who are unattractive are dominated, and even those who are dominant or endowed with ample 'erotic capital' are ultimately recognised only as a result of men's desires.

A second notable development is Coles's (2009: 39) theoretical approach, contending that habitus, capitals and field permit better attention to how 'masculinity as an unconscious strategy forms part of the habitus of men that is both transposable and malleable to given situations to form practical dispositions and actions to everyday situations'. Coles's analysis also includes important acknowledgment of the (contested) role of the male body in relation to the production of 'physical capital' and what Bourdieu referred to as 'bodily hexis', or the embodied outcomes of one's habitus (see also Ingram, 2018). However, Coles's (2009: 38) more nuanced treatment of masculinity seeks to aid our understanding of how 'external sources of influence such as class, age, and ethnicity intersect with the *field of masculinity* to form complex matrices that allow for a variety of masculinities to exist'. While at first appearing commensurate with Bourdieu's notion of field – masculinity does of course seem to have its own rules and on some level be a site of struggles for recognition – the idea of masculinity as a field is ultimately flawed and theoretically incoherent (Robinson & Robertson, 2014). With Coles keen to point out that masculinity can be differentially wielded as a *resource*, this speaks, perhaps inadvertently, to the idea of capitals. Coles (2009: 38) also acknowledges that masculinity informs and is informed by habitus. Masculinity, though, cannot be *all* parts of Bourdieu's interlocking triad. Furthermore, Coles's formulation positions the field of masculinity as largely *structured* by capitals, ethnicity, age and sexuality, but this overlooks Bourdieu's contention that fields are relatively autonomous arenas, and are sites where capitals are deployed, accumulated and struggled over in respect of ensuring legitimacy. The multiple ways in which masculinity can be deployed and manifest as dominant or subordinated across other fields – employment, education, the family, etc. – renders the idea of masculinity as field untenable. Ultimately, gender – and in this case masculinity – 'enters into the "game" of different social fields in ways specific to each field' (Krais, 2006: 128, cited by Robinson & Robertson, 2014).

Aligning Bourdieu with theories of masculinity

The last point I want to address is the apparent tension between HMT and Bourdieusian theory. Despite critique of Connell's ideas, and Connell's critique of Bourdieu (see above), I believe that within a toolbox approach various tools can, when necessary, work together.

There has been a long-standing trend in German-speaking literatures to combine HMT and Bourdieusian conceptualisations to useful effect (Meuser, 2009), a method relatively absent in Anglo literatures on masculinity. Meuser (2009) explains how German-speaking sociologists align these two allegedly competing positions, using the Bourdieusian idea of masculine habitus to consider how individuals become disposed to acting according to the given gender order, and thus viewing masculinity as constructed within the competitive games played among men. Meuser and Scholz (2005) further argue that as Bourdieu's analysis of masculine domination highlights incorporation, it provides a better model than Connell to explain the persistence of established patterns of masculinity. Additionally, I would suggest that Bourdieu offers methods of understanding and theorising change as per Anderson's IMT. Bourdieu thus provides the conceptual bridge for understanding persistence of the socio-negative *and* change towards more socio-positive forms of masculinity, and a broader understanding of the lives of young men.

This can be seen empirically through recent English-language Bourdieu-inflected readings of working-class young masculinities. In the German-speaking tradition, these studies utilise Bourdieu to make sense of the existence of change alongside elements of persistence. For example, Roberts et al. (2016) emphasise the enduring nature of the institutional habitus of a professional football club, but also highlight a stark distancing from older, restricted codes of gender expression among elite-level, young, professional footballers. Here, Bourdieu is used to explain how and why behaviours change as young men traverse their home locality and the 'football locality' – and the limited emotional expression permitted therein. Similarly, Stahl (2013) adopts the frame of institutional habitus to explore how working-class boys' learner identities are (sometimes problematically) restructured by attendance at a high-performing school in a socially marginalised area, pointing to the role of institutions in transforming or producing a divided habitus. Moreover, Stahl (2015: 75) identifies among working-class schoolboys an 'egalitarian habitus', which 'is not about accruing power over others; it instead upholds the inverse of such a practice'. In a refreshing break with the trend towards understanding working-class schoolboys as problematic, Stahl emphasises that, despite being a counter habitus (inasmuch as it was at odds with the school's demands and expectations), the predominantly observed masculine identity was resistant to hegemony as per Connell because it was 'infused with *traditional working-class values of non dominance*' (ibid., my emphasis). Habitus has been used for work on masculinities in non-western contexts, too, such as research in Hong Kong that finds middle-class fathers resistant to being primary caregivers, in sharp contrast to working-class men who embrace the caring role as a means of being valued in the absence of capitals that would permit a more traditional provider role (Liong, 2015; see Chapter 7).

Similarly, McCormack (2014) employs Bourdieu more fully by considering how habitus and capitals interlock to produce classed differences around embracing certain types of tactility. McCormack uses Bourdieu's symbolic economy to explain relatively conservative levels of tactility among working-class teenagers, without presenting working-class culture as deficit or pathological.

He also shows how differences in the production of habitus can explain intergenerational difference in expressions of masculinity. Finally, a coherent Bourdieusian theoretical approach is adopted by Thorpe (2010: 202), who, in her study of young adult snowboarders, notes how 'men's snowboarding identities, behaviours, and interactions (with other men and women) often change as they age and enter new life stages and gain (or lose) access to particular forms of capital (e.g., physical, symbolic, masculine, economic)'. Informed by a gendered reading of the habitus–field complex, Thorpe (2010: 202) illustrates 'how men's movement across, and within, social fields can prompt critical reflection on masculine practices and performances within the snowboarding culture as well as gender norms and values in other social fields'.

What such developments alert us to is that Bourdieu offers scope to understand change and continuity, not simply social reproduction, and, furthermore, permits scope to better understand relationships between social positions in structural hierarchies (Robinson & Robertson, 2014), which seem to be quite absent in, for example, HMT.

Conclusion

This chapter has emphasised how concepts and theories should 'serve as tools, mobilised in specific programmes of research, for making sense of the social world' (Atkinson, 2017: 139). The engagements and conclusions herein have been presented in the spirit of arriving at the best possible position to analyse young working-class men's transitions to adulthood.

According to Hearn (2012), recent progressivist studies on men and masculinities have witnessed HMT become almost hegemonic in itself. Questioning HMT's hegemonic status, however, should not be simply a case of demanding new ideas or concepts for the sake of newness. If, after being critically considered, a theory retains its overarching explanatory function and is supported by data, then it would be fit for purpose. However, for HMT to retain its relevance for my study and more broadly, we must remain *certain* that there operates for men a personal and collective project that emphasises aggression, dominance, heterosexual performance and homophobia as normal, pervasive, and the orientation point men sit in relation to and are influenced by. We may not want to take this as a given, but at the very least, as Segal (2007: xxix) noted over a decade ago, even if we find them 'unconscionably slow', 'the trends to equality [are] in the right direction'. These trends, then, demand more detailed discussion. Alongside recent research findings using IMT, it becomes clear that the process and implications of changes in masculinities are central issues for further empirical investigation, and something that a longitudinal investigation of young working-class men's lives is well placed to contribute.

Having initially defended its social constructionist epistemological foundations and its wholesale relevance for a certain historical period, I have proposed that, for two main reasons, HMT is not sufficient for the present analyses. While Connell's theory has been and remains crucial to understanding both the internal power relations of masculinity, and the potential for a multiplicity of gendered identities and practices, there seems very little room for change in her theorisation, nor room for much more than analysis of abuses of power. This is made most apparent through Howson's writings on the prospects for positive hegemony – a theme absent from Connell's version of hegemony, which, as per her post-structuralist critics, renders her theory static, incapable of theorising change, and at risk of imposing false unity and fixedness on fluid, contradictory realities and practices. Where an understanding of the dynamic between competing hegemonies has been offered (e.g. Demetriou, 2001), while there has been an emphasis upon internal and external distinctions and contestations, the replacement of one negative form of hegemony with another equally negative form, or even hybridised form, is the best that Connell can offer. The ambition here is not to reject that power hierarchies exist, nor to insist that Connell's apparatus is not useful for theorising power, but instead to contribute to the emerging literature in ways that recognise 'the question of power relations between men and women (and between men) is considered an open and empirical question related to different contexts and local settings' (Christensen & Jensen, 2014: 71). This is best served through an approach that emphasises historical specificity, meaning that IMT, especially when complemented with ideas from 'social generations' within youth sociology, can act as an important vehicle for understanding how masculinities are constructed in an era characterised by relatively low levels of cultural homophobia, or homohysteria.

Moreover, HMT, or any theory of masculinity, cannot sufficiently theorise the dynamics of young men's everyday lives. While masculinity is an important component of identity and, as such, a pervasive influence upon young men's experience of and engagements with education, work, living arrangements, friendships and romantic/domestic relations, young men cannot and should not be reduced to masculinity. I have thus insisted that a fuller understanding of how and why, and with what consequences, these young men negotiate these various domains can be delivered through Bourdieu's theory of practice. Habitus, in particular, but also capitals and field are important tools for understanding how, as I will show, contemporary young working-class masculinities are characterised by a co-existence of continuity and change. Furthermore, while there has been some encouraging dissolution of gender constraints, leading to (complex) developments towards gender equality, these tools are used in the following chapters to illustrate how working-class lives, even when men change and respond well to their repositioning, remain relatively difficult. That is, class power relations between dominant and subordinate groups remain a feature of contemporary life in England.

Notes

1 Postmodernist and post-structuralist are terms often used interchangeably. This is not unproblematic (see Beasley, 2012), and my preference would be to use the term post-structuralism. However, for the purposes of the discussion in this section for the chapter, they are used interchangeably as is the case in various writings.
2 One difference which has been highlighted by several social constructionist scholars is the use of an obfuscatory writing style in post-structuralist theorising. See e.g. McCormack, 2012; Anderson, 2014; Magrath, 2017, who all note this to be an elitist and somewhat exclusionary practice.
3 Later developments by other sex role theorists included adding in components of 'required' homophobia and instrumental attitudes to sex (e.g. Levant et al., 1992).
4 There are differences between all these positions. Giddens, for example, has been criticised for overstating individual agency, while Bourdieu is accused often of inescapable determinism. Nonetheless, all are united by efforts to avoid an either/or situation when it comes to structure and agency.
5 See also Kimmel (2000, 2008), who has argued that masculinity is constitutive of homophobia.
6 Sledging is a discursive practice often used in competitive sports which involves using feminising or homophobic slurs to distract or belittle opposing players.
7 Masculinity, more broadly, has been subject to sustained interrogation and positioned as conceptually flawed. Examples include MacInnes (1998) and Petersen (1998, 2003).
8 See also Duncanson (2015) on peacekeeper masculinity, and Elliott (2015) on caring masculinities.
9 The data for the 1990s cohort have not been made available.
10 See also Woodman and Threadgold's (2015) in-conversation piece about youth sociology, which illuminates the value of Bourdieu's theorising of the individual actor, versus, for example, its virtual absence in Beck's theorising.

References

Aboim, S. (2010). *Plural Masculinities: The Remaking of the Self in Private Life.* London: Ashgate.

Adams, A. (2011). 'Josh wears pink cleats': Inclusive masculinity on the soccer field. *Journal of Homosexuality*, 58(5), 579–596.

Adkins, L. (2004). Reflexivity: Freedom or habit of gender? *The Sociological Review*, 52(2_suppl.), 191–210.

Adkins, L., & Skeggs, B. (Eds.). (2004). *Feminism after Bourdieu.* Oxford: Blackwell, pp. 191–210.

Anderson, E. (2009). *Inclusive masculinity: The changing nature of masculinities.* New York: Routledge.

Anderson, E. (2011). Updating the outcome: Gay athletes, straight teams, and coming out in educationally based sport teams. *Gender & Society*, 25(2), 250–268.

Anderson, E. (2014). *21st century jocks: Sporting men and contemporary heterosexuality.* London: Springer.

Anderson, E., & Bullingham, R. (2014). Openly lesbian team sport athletes in an era of decreasing homohysteria. *International Review for the Sociology of Sport*, 50(6), 647–660.

Anderson, E., Magrath, R., & Bullingham, R. (2016). *Out in sport: The experiences of openly gay and lesbian athletes in competitive sport.* London: Routledge.

Anderson, E., & McCormack, M. (2016a). Inclusive Masculinity Theory: Overview, reflection and refinement. *Journal of Gender Studies*, 1–15.

Anderson, E., & McCormack, M. (2016b). *The changing dynamics of bisexual men's lives: Social research perspectives.* New York: Springer.

Archer, M.S. (2000). *Being human: The problem of agency.* Cambridge: Cambridge University Press.

Atkinson, W. (2015). Putting habitus back in its place? Reflections on the homines in extremis debate. *Body & Society*, 21(4), 103–116.

Atkinson, W. (2017). *Beyond Bourdieu.* London: John Wiley & Sons.

Beasley, C. (2012). Problematizing contemporary Men/Masculinities theorizing: The contribution of Raewyn Connell and conceptual-terminological tensions today. *The British Journal of Sociology*, 63(4), 747–765.

Bourdieu, P. (1984). *Distinction: A social critique of the judgement of taste.* Cambridge, MA: Harvard University Press.

Bourdieu, P. (1985). The social space and the genesis of groups. *Information (International Social Science Council)*, 24(2), 195–220.

Bourdieu, P. (1986). The forms of capital, in J. Richardson (Ed.), *Handbook of Theory and Research for the Sociology of Education.* Greenwood Publishing Group, pp. 280–291.

Bourdieu, P. (1990). *The logic of practice.* Redwood, CA: Stanford University Press.

Bourdieu, P. (1998). *The state nobility: Elite schools in the field of power.* Stanford University Press.

Bourdieu, P. (2001). *Masculine domination.* Redwood, CA: Stanford University Press.

Bourdieu, P., & Wacquant, L.J. (1992). *An invitation to reflexive sociology.* Chicago, IL: University of Chicago Press.

Brannon, R. (1976). The male sex role – and what it's done for us lately, in R. Brannon & D. Davids (Eds.), *The forty-nine percent majority.* Reading, MA: Addison-Wesley, pp. 1–40.

Bridges, T. (2014). A very 'gay' straight? Hybrid masculinities, sexual aesthetics, and the changing relationship between masculinity and homophobia. *Gender & Society*, 28(1), 58–82.

Bridges, T., & Pascoe, C.J. (2014). Hybrid masculinities: New directions in the sociology of men and masculinities. *Sociology Compass*, 8(3), 246–258.

British Social Attitudes Survey (2016). www.bsa.natcen.ac.uk.

Carrigan, T., Connell, B., & Lee, J. (1985). Toward a new sociology of masculinity. *Theory and Society*, 14(5), 551–604.

Caruso, A., & Roberts, S. (2017). Exploring constructions of masculinity on a men's body-positivity blog. *Journal of Sociology*, doi:1440783317740981.

Channon, A., & Matthews, C.R. (2015). 'It is what it is': Masculinity, homosexuality, and inclusive discourse in mixed martial arts. *Journal of Homosexuality*, 62(7), 936–956.

Cheng, C. (1999). Marginalized masculinities and hegemonic masculinity: An introduction. *The Journal of Men's Studies*, 7(3), 295–315.

Christensen, A.D., & Jensen, S.Q. (2014). Combining hegemonic masculinity and intersectionality. *NORMA: International Journal for Masculinity Studies*, 9(1), 60–75.

Coles, T. (2009). Negotiating the field of masculinity: The production and reproduction of multiple dominant masculinities. *Men and Masculinities*, 12(1), 30–44.

Connell, R.W. (1987). *Gender and power*. Cambridge: Polity, pp. 279–304.

Connell, R.W. (1992). A Very Straight Gay: Masculinity, Homosexual Experience, and the Dynamics of Gender. *American Sociological Review*, 57, 735–751.

Connell, R.W. (1995). *Masculinities*. Cambridge: Polity Press.

Connell, R.W. (2000). Arms and the man: Using the new research on masculinity to understand violence and promote peace in the contemporary world, in I. Breiness, R. Connell, & I. Eide (Eds.), *Male roles, Masculinities and Violence*. Paris: UNESCO Publishing, pp. 21–33.

Connell, R.W. (2005). *Masculinities* (2nd edn). Oakland, CA: University of California Press.

Connell, R. (2016). Masculinities in global perspective: hegemony, contestation, and changing structures of power. *Theory and Society*, 45(4), 303–318.

Connell, R.W., & Messerschmidt, J.W. (2005). Hegemonic masculinity: Rethinking the concept. *Gender & Society*, 19(6), 829–859.

Corsten, M. (1999). The time of generations. *Time & Society*, 8(2–3), 249–272.

Costa, C., & Murphy, M. (Eds.). (2015). *Bourdieu, habitus and social research: The art of application*. London: Springer.

Coston, B.M., & Kimmel, M. (2012). Seeing privilege where it isn't: Marginalized masculinities and the intersectionality of privilege. *Journal of Social Issues*, 68(1), 97–111.

Crozier, G., & Reay, D. (2011). Capital accumulation: Working-class students learning how to learn in HE. *Teaching in Higher Education*, 16(2), 145–155.

De Beauvoir, S. (1949). *The Second Sex*. Trans. and ed. H.M. Parshley. London: J. Cape.

de Boise, S. (2014). Cheer up emo kid: Rethinking the 'crisis of masculinity' in emo. *Popular Music*, 33(2), 225–242.

de Boise, S. (2015). I'm Not Homophobic, 'I've Got Gay Friends': Evaluating the Validity of Inclusive Masculinity. *Men and Masculinities*, 18(3), 318–339.

Demetriou, D.Z. (2001). Connell's concept of hegemonic masculinity: A critique. *Theory and Society*, 30(3), 337–361.

Dillabough, J.A. (2004). Class, culture and the 'predicaments of masculine domination': Encountering Pierre Bourdieu. *British Journal of Sociology of Education*, 25(4), 489–506.

Donaldson, M. (1993). What is hegemonic masculinity? *Theory and Society*, 22(5), 643–657.
Drummond, M.J., Filiault, S.M., Anderson, E., & Jeffries, D. (2015). Homosocial intimacy among Australian undergraduate men. *Journal of Sociology*, 51(3), 643–656.
Duncanson, C. (2015). Hegemonic masculinity and the possibility of change in gender relations. *Men and Masculinities*, 18(2), 231–248.
Edley, N. (2017). *Men and Masculinity: The Basics*. London: Routledge.
Edwards, A. (1983). Sex Roles: A Problem for Sociology and for Women. *Journal of Sociology*, 19(3).
Elliott, K. (2015). Caring masculinities: Theorizing an emerging concept. *Men and Masculinities*, 19(3), 240–259.
Foucault, M. (1977). *Discipline and power*. New York: Pantheon.
France, A., & Roberts, S. (2015). The problem of social generations: A critique of the new emerging orthodoxy in youth studies. *Journal of Youth Studies*, 18(2), 215–230.
France, A., & Roberts, S. (2017). *Youth and Social Class: Enduring Inequality in the United Kingdom, Australia and New Zealand*. Springer.
Gahman, L. (2017). Crip Theory and Country Boys: Masculinity, Dis/ability, and Place in Rural Southeast Kansas. *Annals of the American Association of Geographers*, 107(3), 700–715.
Giddens, A. (1984). *The constitution of society: Outline of the theory of structuration*. Berkeley, CA: University of California Press.
Goldthorpe, J.H. (2007). 'Cultural Capital': Some Critical Observations. *Sociologica*, 1(2).
Gramsci, A. (1971). *The philosophy of praxis. Selections from the prison notebooks of Antonio Gramsci*.
Gramsci, A. (1973). *Letters from Prison: Selected, Transl. from the Italian, and Introduced by Lynne Lawner*. London: Harper & Row.
Grenfell, M., & James, D. (1998). *Bourdieu and education: Acts of practical theory*. Hove: Psychology Press.
Groes-Green, C. (2009). Hegemonic and subordinated masculinities: Class, violence and sexual performance among young Mozambican men. *Nordic Journal of African Studies*, 18(4), 286–304.
Hakim, C. (2012). Erotic Capital, Sexual Pleasure and Sexual Markets. *Helsinki*, 3(9), 27.
Hall, M., & Gough, B. (2011). Magazine and reader constructions of 'metrosexuality' and masculinity: A membership categorisation analysis. *Journal of Gender Studies*, 20(01), 67–86.
Haltom, T.M., & Worthen, M.G. (2014). Male ballet dancers and their performances of heteromasculinity. *Journal of College Student Development*, 55(8), 757–778.
Haywood, C. & Mac an Ghaill, M. (2003). *Men and masculinities: Theory, research and social practice*. Buckingham: Open University Press.
Hearn, J. (2004). From hegemonic masculinity to the hegemony of men. *Feminist Theory*, 5(1), 49–72.
Hearn, J. (2010). Reflecting on men and social policy: Contemporary critical debates and implications for social policy. *Critical Social Policy*, 30(2), 165–188.
Hearn, J. (2012). A multi-faceted power analysis of men's violence to known women: From hegemonic masculinity to the hegemony of men. *The Sociological Review*, 60(4), 589–610.
Hoch, P. (1979). *White hero, Black beast: Racism, sexism, and the mask of masculinity*. London: Pluto Press.
Hooper, C. (2001). *Manly States: Masculinities. International Relations, and Gender Politics*. New York: Columbia University Press.

Howson, R. (2006). *Challenging hegemonic masculinity*. London: Routledge.
Howson, R. (2008). Hegemonic masculinity in the theory of hegemony: A brief response to Christine Beasley's 'Rethinking Hegemonic Masculinity in a Globalizing World'. *Men and Masculinities*, 11(1), 109–113.
Huppatz, K. (2009). Reworking Bourdieu's 'Capital': Feminine and female capitals in the field of paid caring work. *Sociology*, 43(1), 45–66.
Huppatz, K., & Goodwin, S. (2013). Masculinised jobs, feminised jobs and men's 'gender capital' experiences: Understanding occupational segregation in Australia. *Journal of Sociology*, 49(2–3), 291–308.
Ingram, N. (2018). *Working-Class Boys and Educational Success: Teenage Identities, Masculinity and Urban Schooling*. Basingstoke: Palgrave Macmillan.
Ingram, N., & Waller, R. (2014). Degrees of masculinity: Working and middle-class undergraduate students' constructions of masculine identities, in *Debating Modern Masculinities: Change, Continuity, Crisis?* Palgrave Macmillan UK, pp. 35–51.
Jewkes, R., Morrell, R., Hearn, J., Lundqvist, E., Blackbeard, D., Lindegger, G., ... & Gottzén, L. (2015). Hegemonic masculinity: Combining theory and practice in gender interventions. *Culture, Health & Sexuality*, 17(sup 2), 112–127.
Kestner, J.A. (2010). *Masculinities in British adventure fiction, 1880–1915*. Farnham, Surrey: Ashgate Publishing.
Kimmel, M. (2000). Masculinity as Homophobia: Fear, Shame, and Silence in the Construction of Gender Identity, in M. Adams, W.J. Blumenfeld, R. Castaneda, H. W. Hackman, M.L. Peters, & X. Zuniga (Eds.), *Readings for Diversity and Social Justice*. New York: Routledge.
Kimmel, M. (2008). *Guyland: The Perilous World Where Boys Become Men*. New York: Harper Collins.
Kimmel, M., Hearn, J., & Connell, R. (Eds.). (2005). *Handbook of studies on men and masculinities*. London: Sage.
Krais, B. (2006). Gender, sociological theory and Bourdieu's sociology of practice. *Theory, Culture & Society*, 23(6), 119–134.
Lehmann, W. (2013). In a class of their own: How working-class students experience university, in *Contemporary debates in the sociology of education*. London: Palgrave Macmillan, pp. 93–111.
Levant, R.F., Hirsch, L.S., Celentano, E., & Cozza, T.M. (1992). The male role: An investigation of contemporary norms. *Journal of Mental Health Counseling*, 14, 325–337.
Liong, M. (2015). Like father, like son: negotiation of masculinity in the ethnographic context in Hong Kong. *Gender, Place & Culture*, 22(7), 937–953.
Lovell, T. (Ed.). (2007). *(Mis)recognition, social inequality and social justice: Nancy Fraser and Pierre Bourdieu*. London: Routledge.
Mac an Ghaill, M. (1994). *The Making of Men: Masculinities, Sexualities and Schooling*. Buckingham: Open University Press.
MacInnes, J. (1998). *End of masculinity: The confusion of sexual genesis and sexual difference in modern society*. London: McGraw-Hill Education.
Magrath, R. (2015). The intersection of race, religion and homophobia in British football. *International Review for the Sociology of Sport* [online].
Magrath, R. (2017). 'To Try and Gain an Advantage for My Team': Homophobic and Homosexually Themed Chanting among English Football Fans. *Sociology*, doi:0038038517702600.

Maloney, M., Roberts, S., & Caruso, A. (2017). 'Mmm... I love it, bro!': Performances of masculinity in YouTube gaming. *New Media & Society*, doi:1461444817703368.

Mannheim, K. (1952). *Historicism. Essays on the Sociology of Knowledge*. New York: Harcourt, Brace & World.

McCormack, M. (2011). The declining significance of homohysteria for male students in three sixth forms in the south of England. *British Educational Research Journal*, 37(2), 337–353.

McCormack, M. (2012). The positive experiences of openly gay, lesbian, bisexual and transgendered students in a Christian sixth form college. *Sociological Research Online*, 17(3), 5.

McCormack, M. (2014). The intersection of youth masculinities, decreasing homophobia and class: An ethnography. *The British Journal of Sociology*, 65(1), 130–149.

McCormack, M., & Anderson, E. (2014). The influence of declining homophobia on men's gender in the United States: An argument for the study of homohysteria. *Sex Roles*, 71(3–4), 109–120.

McCormack, M., & Wignall, L. (2017). Enjoyment, exploration and education: Understanding the consumption of pornography among young men with non-exclusive sexual orientations. *Sociology*, 51(5), 975–991.

McCormack, M., Wignall, L., & Morris, M. (2016). Gay guys using gay language: Friendship, shared values and the intent-context-effect matrix. *The British Journal of Sociology*, 67(4), 747–767.

McDowell, L. (2003). *Redundant masculinities?: Employment change and white working class youth*. London: John Wiley.

McDowell, L., Rootham, E., & Hardgrove, A. (2014). Precarious work, protest masculinity and communal regulation: South Asian young men in Luton, UK. *Work, Employment and Society*, 28(6), 847–864.

Messerschmidt, J. (2005). Men, masculinities, and crime, in M.S. Kimmel, J. Hearn, & R.W. Connell (Eds.), *Handbook of studies on men & masculinities*. Thousand Oaks, CA: Sage, pp. 196–212.

Messerschmidt, J. (2012). Engendering gendered knowledge: Assessing the academic appropriation of hegemonic masculinity. *Men and Masculinities*, 15(1), 56–76.

Messerschmidt, J. (2016). *Masculinities in the Making: From the Local to the Global*. New York: Rowman & Littlefield.

Messner, M. (1993). 'Changing men' and feminist politics in the United States. *Theory and Society*, 22(5), 723–737.

Messner, M., & Sabo, D. (1990). Introduction: Toward a critical feminist reappraisal of sport, men, and the gender order. *Sport, Men, and the Gender Order: Critical Feminist Perspectives*, 1–15.

Meuser, M. (2009). Research on masculinities in German-Speaking countries: Developments, discussions and research themes. *Culture, Society and Masculinities*, 1(1), 33.

Meuser, M., & Scholz, S. (2005). Hegemoniale Männlichkeit – Versuch einer Begriffsklärung aus soziologischer Perspektive [Hegemonic masculinity – attempt to clarify the concept from a sociological perspective], in M. Dinges (Ed.), *Männer – Macht – Körper*. Hegemoniale Männlichkeiten vom Mittelalter bis heute, pp. 211–228.

Moller, M. (2007). Exploiting patterns: A critique of hegemonic masculinity. *Journal of Gender Studies*, 16(3), 263–276.

Moore, R. (2008). Capital, in M. Grenfell (Ed.), *Pierre Bourdieu: Key concepts*. Durham: Acumen.

Morris, M. (2017). 'Gay capital' in gay student friendship networks: An intersectional analysis of class, masculinity, and decreased homophobia. *Journal of Social and Personal Relationships*, doi:0265407517705737.

Murray, A., & White, A. (2015). Twelve not so angry men: Inclusive masculinities in Australian contact sports. *International Review for the Sociology of Sport*, doi:1012690215609786.

Negy, C. (2014). Homohysteria: Useful Construct? Or an Unnecessary Splitting of Hairs? *Sex Roles*, 71(3–4), 137–140.

O'Neill, R. (2015). Whither critical masculinity studies? Notes on inclusive masculinity theory, postfeminism, and sexual politics. *Men and Masculinities*, 18(1), 100–120.

Parsons, T., & Bales, R.F. (1953). The dimensions of action-space. *Working Papers in the Theory of Action*, 63–109.

Pease, B. (2002). *Men and gender relations*. Melbourne: Tertiary Press.

Petersen, A. (1998). *Unmasking the masculine: Men and identity in a sceptical age*. London: Sage.

Petersen, A. (2003). Research on men and masculinities: Some implications of recent theory for future work. *Men and Masculinities*, 6(1), 54–69.

Plummer, D. (1999). *One of the boys: Masculinity, homophobia, and modern manhood*. New York: Psychology Press.

Pronger, B. (1990). Gay Jocks: A Phenomenology of Gay Men in Athletics, in M. Messner & D. Sabo (Eds.), *Sport, Men and the Gender Order*. Champaign, IL: Human Kinetics.

Putnam, R. (1993). The prosperous community. *The American Prospect*, 4(13), 35–42.

Reay, D. (2004). 'Mostly roughs and toughs': Social class, race and representation in inner city schooling. *Sociology*, 38(5), 1005–1023.

Roberts, S. (2013). Boys will be boys … won't they? Change and continuities in contemporary young working-class masculinities. *Sociology*, 47(4), 671–686.

Roberts, S. (2014). *Debating Modern Masculinities: Change, Continuity, Crisis?* Basingstoke: Palgrave.

Roberts, S., Anderson, E., & Magrath, R. (2016). Continuity, change and complexity in the performance of masculinity among elite young footballers in England. *British Journal of Sociology* [online], 1–22.

Robinson, M., & Robertson, S. (2014). Challenging the field: Bourdieu and men's health. *Social Theory & Health*, 12(4), 339–360.

Salih, S. (2007). On Judith Butler and Performativity, in K.E. Lovaas & M.M. Jenkins (Eds.), *Sexualities and Communication in Everyday Life: A Reader*. Thousand Oaks, CA: Sage Publications, pp. 55–68.

Savage, M., Devine, F., Cunningham, N., Taylor, M., Li, Y., Hjellbrekke, J., … & Miles, A. (2013). A new model of social class? Findings from the BBC's Great British Class Survey experiment. *Sociology*, 47(2), 219–250.

Schippers, M. (2007). Recovering the feminine other: Masculinity, femininity, and gender hegemony. *Theory and Society*, 36(1), 85–102.

Segal, L. (1990). *Slow motion: Changing men, changing masculinities*. London: Virago.

Segal, L. (2007). *Slow Motion* (second edition). London: Palgrave.

Siisiäinen, M. (2000). *Social Capital, Power and the Third Sector. The Third Sector in Finland: Review to Research of the Finnish Third Sector*. Helsinki: Finnish Federation for Social Welfare and Health, pp. 7–35.

Silva, E.B., & Wright, D. (2009). Displaying desire and distinction in housing. *Cultural Sociology*, 3(1), 31–50.

Simpson, R. (2014). Gender, space and identity: Male cabin crew and service work. *Gender in Management: An International Journal*, 29(5), 291–300.

Skeggs, B. (1997). *Formations of class & gender*. London: Sage.

Skeggs, B. (2004). Context and background: Pierre Bourdieu's analysis of class, gender and sexuality. *The Sociological Review*, 52(2_suppl), 19–33.

Stahl, G. (2013). Habitus disjunctures, reflexivity and white working-class boys' conceptions of status in learner and social identities. *Sociological Research Online*, 18(3), 2.

Stahl, G. (2015). Egalitarian Habitus: Narratives of Reconstruction in Discourses of Aspiration and Change, in *Bourdieu, Habitus and Social Research*. London: Palgrave Macmillan, pp. 21–38.

Strinati, D. (1995). Marxism, political economy and ideology, in D. Strinati, *An Introduction to Theories of Popular Culture*, pp. 127–176.

Thornton, S. (1997 [1995]). *The social logic of subcultural capital*. London: Routledge.

Thorpe, H. (2010). Bourdieu, gender reflexivity, and physical culture: A case of masculinities in the snowboarding field. *Journal of Sport and Social Issues*, 34(2), 176–214.

Threadgold, S. (2015). Cultural capital, DIY careers and transferability: Towards maintaining 'reproduction' when using Bourdieu in youth culture research. *Youth Cultures and Subcultures: Australian Perspectives*, 53–64.

Tosh, J. (2005). *Manliness and masculinities in nineteenth-century Britain: Essays on gender, family, and empire*. Pearson Education.

Wacquant, L. (1989). Towards a reflexive sociology: A workshop with Pierre Bourdieu. *Sociological Theory*, 7, 26–63.

Wacquant, L. (2006). Pierre Bourdieu, in R. Stones (Ed.), *Key Contemporary Thinkers*. London: Macmillan.

Ward, M. (2015). *From labouring to learning: Working-class masculinities, education and de-industrialization*. London: Springer.

Ward, M., Tarrant, A., Terry, G., Featherstone, B., Robb, M., & Ruxton, S. (2017). Doing gender locally: The importance of 'place' in understanding marginalised masculinities and young men's transitions to 'safe' and successful futures. *The Sociological Review*, 65(4), 797–815.

Webb, S., Burke, P.J., Nichols, S., Roberts, S., Stahl, G., Threadgold, S., & Wilkinson, J. (2017). Thinking with and beyond Bourdieu in widening higher education participation. *Studies in Continuing Education*, 39(2), 138–160.

West, C., & Zimmerman, D.H. (1987). Doing gender. *Gender & Society*, 1(2), 125–151.

Wetherell, M., & Edley, N. (1999). Negotiating hegemonic masculinity: Imaginary positions and psycho-discursive practices. *Feminism & Psychology*, 9(3), 335–356.

Whitehead, S. (2002). *Men and Masculinities*. Cambridge: Polity.

Williams, J. (2005). *Understanding Poststructuralism*. Dundee: Acumen.

Williams, R. (1973). Base and superstructure in Marxist cultural theory. *New Left Review*, (82), 3.

Woodman, D., & Threadgold, S. (2015). Critical Youth Studies in an Individualized and Globalized World: Making the Most of Bourdieu and Beck, in P. Kelly (Ed.), *A Critical Youth Studies for the 21st Century*. Amsterdam: Brill.

Woodman, D., & Wyn, J. (2015). Class, gender and generation matter: Using the concept of social generation to study inequality and social change. *Journal of Youth Studies*, 18(10), 1402–1410.

Wyn, J., & Woodman, D. (2006). Generation, youth and social change in Australia. *Journal of Youth Studies*, 9(5), 495–514.

4 The study context and methods

Introduction

Studies of youth transitions often concentrate on the dichotomy of predominantly unemployed 'sinkers' and mainly employed 'swimmers', or what Jones (2002) describes as 'fast and slow-track transitions'. Through this dualistic thinking, scholars 'run the risk of misunderstanding the structural landscape of the life worlds our research participants inhabit' (Hardgrove et al., 2015: 2). The main aim with my research was to develop a detailed analysis of the 'missing middle' (see Roberts, 2011; Roberts & MacDonald, 2013), those 'ordinary' young people (France, 2007: 57) who fall between this dualism, in order to contribute a more holistic understanding of men's experiences of growing up in the contemporary moment. To do so, I conducted a qualitative study of male 18–24 year-old, front-line retail employees who were 'moderately qualified' – i.e. some Level II (GCSE) qualifications,[1] but no experience in or intention to attend university. To transition into my discussion of the data, here I provide a very brief 'tour' of the research process, highlighting the context of the research sites, how I accessed participants and collected data, and underscoring the motivations for each of these.

The research sites

The study was located in the county of Kent, in South-East England, a contrasting setting to much academic work on young men and changing economies conducted in industrial 'powerhouse' regions (e.g. Furlong & Cartmel, 2004; McDowell, 2003; Jimenez & Walkerdine, 2011; see Chapter 2), but also a locale often popularly mischaracterised. Despite being among the least-deprived third of the UK (Roberts, 2011) and being widely designated as 'the garden of England', this masks stark variations in Kent's wealth distribution. Indeed, 52 of the county's 902 Lower Layer Super Output Areas (LSOAs)[2] feature in England's top 10% most deprived neighbourhoods, and 90 fall inside England's 16% most deprived. For many centuries Kent was an industrial county, with working-class populations able to access semi-skilled or unskilled roles in agriculture, tanning, milling, shipbuilding, quarrying, utility plants, coal mining and warehousing. However, between 1995 and 2007 the county witnessed profound growth in retail, hotels, restaurants and wholesale (Roberts, 2011), and these 'traditional' industries – which represented primary employment prospects for working-class men – fell into decline, or disappeared entirely. This is an important point of consideration given the potential longevity of the legacy of industrial psyches upon men transitioning into adulthood and contemporary labour markets.

I recruited my sample from three relatively large urban centres in the county's east: Maidstone, Canterbury and Dover, which have quite different labour markets and economic climates. Canterbury has a large student population, being home to three universities and a large further education college, but also has several fairly deprived areas on the outskirts of the city. Maidstone, at the study's outset, was home to what is believed to be the ward with the highest teen pregnancy rates in Europe. However, Canterbury city centre and Maidstone town centre both have relatively new and revitalised high street districts similar to a number of other towns across the UK, where shopping is a key feature of the locality's employment and tourism offerings. Dover town centre, however, is relatively dilapidated. Like many UK towns, Dover's high street houses many major national retail chains, but is comparatively 'tired-looking' with growing numbers of unused and closed down shop units and more charity shops emerging in the last decade. Some interviewees from this area described it as 'hopeless', 'the arsehole of the world' and 'a fucking dive', and the town was cast as the 'worst place to live in the UK' according to a 2017 online *Facebook* poll conducted by the website 'I Live Here'. Whilst the other two sites did not suffer from the same kind of comments, they were all linked by the research participants' general recognition that 'retail is all there is' in terms of local employment opportunities.

Accessing the sample

The process of recruiting the sample was long-winded. Initially, I sought the assistance of 15 major, nationally recognised retailers, on the understanding they might offer information on the numbers available and their locations, or even access to those who fit the criteria. I also wrote directly to 16 store managers in these organisations. This process resulted in few people fitting the criteria and willing to participate, so 'snowballing' through participants' friends, peers and colleagues was used to increase sample size. Lastly, I decided to approach store managers, supervisors and staff in person during working hours, on two separate occasions in each locality. These methods sourced 51 eligible participants; 24 took part in the full interviews (6 from Maidstone, 11 from Canterbury and 7 from Dover). Given the nature of these methods, it was by chance that all of the men identified as ethnically white, though this was unsurprising given the relative lack of heterogeneity in Kent. All participants self-identified as heterosexual.

80 *The study context and methods*

Each participant was designated a pseudonym to ensure anonymity. The mean age was 21.6 years, with an even split of part-time (PT) and full-time (FT) employees. There was some variation in job titles, with four occupying limited supervisory roles, but the participants were largely employed as front-line sales/stock assistants. Around two-thirds lived with their parents, with the others residing with a partner or as part of a house share. None of the participants lived alone. Mostly their parents' occupations indicated that the men were from working-class backgrounds, though there was a mix of lower and upper working-class profiles (see Table 4.1). The range of qualification profiles was broader than anticipated, with qualifications obtained at compulsory schooling ranging from one GCSE grade C or above to nine. For those who attempted post-compulsory education, GNVQ/BTEC courses[3] at college were the primary direction, with some choosing to take A-levels[4] and very few having finished the course. None had participated in higher education.

Table 4.1 Sample details at first interview

Pseudonym	Age at first interview	FT/PT	Current type of retail	Occupation of highest earner in household	Living arrangements
Mike*	24	FT	Car/leisure	Retail (self)	Private rent share
Billy*	21	FT	Car/leisure	Retail (self)	Private rent share
Simon	18	FT	Mid-price high street fashion	Police officer (mother)	Parents – mortgage
Rob	21	PT	Lower-price high street fashion	Admin for tourism company (partner)	Private rent with partner
Alex	18	PT	Lower-price high street fashion	Construction site manager (father)	Parents – social accommodation
Damian*	23	PT	Outdoor leisure/equipment	Nurse (mother)	Parents – mortgage
Christian*	24	FT	Music/video	Retail (self)	Private rent share
Dave*	24	FT	Sportswear	Escort/driver for disabled (father)	Parents – mortgage
Richard	21	PT	Lower-price high street fashion	Retail (self – grandparents retired)	Grandparents – social accom.
Danny	21	PT	Lower-price high street fashion	Retail (self – mother unemployed)	Mother – social accommodation
Luke	22	FT	Outdoor leisure/equipment	Retail (self)	Private rent share
Tim*	20	PT	Supermarket	Plumber (father)	Parents – mortgage

Pseudonym	Age at first interview	FT/PT	Current type of retail	Occupation of highest earner in household	Living arrangements
Jason*	23	FT	Upper mid-price high street fashion	Retired telephone engineer (father)	Parents – mortgage
Mark	21	PT	Health food	Retail (self)	Private rent with partner
Peter*	21	PT	Supermarket	Customs and excise (father)	Parents – mortgage
Jake	23	FT	High-price designer fashion	Market researcher (mother)	Mother – mortgage
Carl*	19	FT	Mid-level department	Train driver (father)	Parents – mortgage
James	22	FT	Mid-level department	Teacher (mother)	Parents – mortgage
Gavin*	23	FT	Mid-price high street fashion	School maintenance manager (father)	Parents – mortgage
Adam	21	PT	Mid-price high street fashion	'Entrepreneur' (father)	Parents – mortgage
Bobby*	19	FT	Mid-level department	Delivery driver (father)	Parents – social accom.
Pat*	24	PT	Mid-price high street fashion	Retail (self)	Private rent share
Jez*	21	FT	Fashion/sports footwear	Secretary (mother)	Parents – mortgage
Johnny*	24	PT	Supermarket	Factory operative (mother)	Mother – social accommodation

Asterisk denotes was followed over the seven-year research period.

The research process

Qualitative biographical interviews were used to collect primary data concerning participants' lives and transitional experience. These were chosen over semi-structured interviews, as rich and deep narrative storytelling seemed the best way to access past experiences, present circumstances and future aspirations in the realms of education, work, home and leisure. These interviews gave scope for interrogation of other key issues and permitted a deeper questioning of meaning and feeling; examples included asking for more details on education and employment choices, further elucidation of how the participants *felt* about, for instance, working in service roles, and providing speculative accounts of their future selves in family dynamics. While, for some, truth claims are important, here the account in itself is what was of interest, because these accounts shed light on how events were felt or made sense to the relevant individual (Heath et al., 2009: 88).

82 *The study context and methods*

Setting out in 2009, I met most participants once or twice before the research began. While largely to obtain their 'buy-in', discuss the research and logistics, and/or complete the screening questionnaire or consent forms, men who were recruited in this manner were discernibly more 'open' and communicative than those I met on the day of the interview. Furthermore, when I conducted follow-up interviews a year later, 15 of the 16 whom I managed to re-contact were part of the group I had built good rapport with. In 2014, I began efforts to reconnect with this group of 16 again, and succeeded in signing up 14 to a further stage of the research involving *Facebook* ethnography, which included 'lurking', semi-regular engagement through the *Facebook* and *Messenger* applications, and, in 2016, detailed qualitative interviews by *Skype*.

Including *Facebook* in the later round of the process threw up rich possibilities for researching the construction and negotiation of identities, as Robards (2014: np) makes clear: 'significant parts of [participants'] social and cultural lives have been played out on the site', and as such it is a space 'in which the persona is enacted and made visible [and] ... includes a chronicle of mediated, transitional experiences: birthdays, graduations, the beginning (and end) of relationships, first jobs, travel, and so on'.

As well as the visible *Facebook* activity being data in and of itself, it also facilitated more fruitful discussions via *Messenger* service in the moment or discussed again at the final interview. For example, in November 2015, Pat posted photographs of himself with his two young daughters climbing over him, along with a caption saying his wife was away and he had the children to himself. I sent Pat a brief message saying 'pic with the kids looks fun! and quite a handful!', which developed into a conversation about the family's intention for him to become the primary caregiver, and the attendant implications.

This research process produced a rich dataset that permitted analysis across both time and space, and, importantly, contributes a severely under-researched perspective to the current literature around young men's lives in the UK.

Notes

1 GCSEs (General Certificate of Secondary Education) are the UK qualification exam for each subject, undertaken by 16-year-old secondary school students.
2 This is a statistical measure representing small geographical areas of roughly 1,500 residents and 650 households. There are 32,844 such LSOAs in England.
3 GNVQs were General National Vocational Qualifications, while BTECs are from the Business and Technology Education Council.
4 'Advanced-level' qualifications in the UK. These are generally required for university entry, and are achieved through exams in the final two years of secondary education.

References

France, A. (2007). *Understanding youth in late modernity.* London: McGraw-Hill Education (UK).

Furlong, A., & Cartmel, F. (2004). *Vulnerable young men in fragile labour markets: Employment, unemployment and the search for long-term security.* York: Joseph Rowntree Foundation.

Hardgrove, A., Rootham, E., & McDowell, L. (2015). Possible selves in a precarious labour market: Youth, imagined futures, and transitions to work in the UK. *Geoforum,* 60, 163–171.

Heath, S., Brooks, R., Cleaver, E., & Ireland, E. (2009). *Researching young people's lives.* London: Sage.

Jimenez, L., & Walkerdine, V. (2011). A psychosocial approach to shame, embarrassment and melancholia amongst unemployed young men and their fathers. *Gender and Education,* 23(2), 185–199.

Jones, G. (2002). *The youth divide: Diverging paths to adulthood.* York: York Publishing Services for the Joseph Rowntree Foundation.

McDowell, L. (2003). *Redundant masculinities?: Employment change and white working class youth.* London: John Wiley.

Robards, B. (2014). Mediating experiences of 'growing up' on Facebook's Timeline: Privacy, ephemerality and the reflexive project of self, in *Mediated Youth Cultures.* London: Palgrave Macmillan UK, pp. 26–41.

Roberts, S. (2011). Beyond 'NEET' and 'tidy' pathways: Considering the 'missing middle' of youth transition studies. *Journal of Youth Studies,* 14(1), 21–39.

Roberts, S., & MacDonald, R. (2013). Introduction for Special Section of Sociological Research Online: The Marginalised Mainstream: Making Sense of the 'Missing Middle' of Youth Studies. *Sociological Research Online,* 18(1), 21.

5 Looking back and looking forward at age 18–24

Educational histories and aspirations

Introduction

Using interviews from the initial data collection period in 2009, this chapter analyses the educational experiences of the 24 working-class young men who made up the original sample of the study. I explore the young men's reflections on their educational trajectory and how class and masculinity inflected this experience. This entails an analysis of their journeys through and engagement with compulsory and, in most cases, post-compulsory education, and also their aspirations for and understandings of higher education (HE). Analysing the young men's experiences in this manner reveals the impact of social and cultural processes upon their orientation to formalised learning and its attendant consequences on their 'horizons for action' (Hodkinson et al., 2013). The young men's narratives problematise the polarised manner in which boys' educational effort and attainment is often described. Their experiences also provide a challenge to both the dominant theories of (masculine) resistance which attempt to explain working-class educational failure, and the 'trouble with boys discourse' that pervades contemporary media and political representations (see McDowell, 2003: 60–75; Roberts, 2012).

A key message from this chapter is that theories of masculinity are not especially well suited to understanding the totality of boys' educational engagement. While such theories have been helpful explanatory tools in understanding educational disengagement, and high levels of engagement through processes of intellectual muscularity (Frosh et al., 2002), and the classed nature of both, middle-ground orientations in respect of education have to date remained relatively overlooked and inadequately conceptualised. This does not render theories of masculinity unuseful, but does raise questions about a tendency towards understanding masculinity as deficit. Similarly, what emerges from this chapter is that Bourdieu's conceptual apparatus allows for an understanding of engagement as a spectrum; that is, Bourdieu offers an *explanatory, rather than predictive*, framework for understanding the various subtleties of working-class educational (dis)engagement.

Underachieving and disengaged boys?

Debate surrounding educational performance has implied that underachievement is a concern applicable predominantly to males. Correspondingly, most policy initiatives and media attention in recent years has been, and continues to be, strongly directed towards the underachievement of boys. McDowell (2003: 71), among others (e.g. Roberts, 2012), has noted that year after year the UK summertime is awash with news media headlines about how girls continue to leave boys lagging behind in academic attainment. For example, a House of Commons briefing for a debate on boys' educational performance held on 4 September 2016, led with the summary 'Girls generally outperform boys throughout primary, secondary and higher education', and also pointed to over 20 media commentaries on the issue from the previous 12 months (and there were many more).[1]

Such rhetoric and broad generalisations can manifest a distorted sense of reality where all boys are positioned as failures vis-à-vis the success enjoyed by all girls. This is problematic, and unfounded. Walkerdine et al. (2001), for instance, argue that women from working-class families are commonly faced with situations such as early exit or underperformance at school, early motherhood and low-paid, insecure jobs in contrast to the relative uniformity of the educational performance and general lives of their middle-class contemporaries. Of further significance is that the tendency to associate boys with underachievement and girls with high achievement results in the high-achieving boy being cast as countering gender norms, whereas the underperforming girl is often overlooked altogether (e.g. Jones & Myhill, 2004; Ingram, 2009).

When assessed for underperformance, boys do outnumber girls, yet less starkly than often represented. Recent Department for Education (2016) data on General Certificate of Secondary Education (GCSE)[2] results show that the proportion of boys not achieving five GCSEs at grade C or above (including English and Maths) is 51%, and 41% for girls, figures that have remained relatively similar for at least a decade (e.g. Cassen & Kingdon, 2007). While this is a significant gender gap, and one worth investigation, any calls that underperformance is solely a 'boy' issue are patently inaccurate. On first reading, these figures also mask complexities such as the intersection of gender with ethnicity and class (Reay, 2009). Pupils from socioeconomically disadvantaged backgrounds – often measured through the proxy of entitlement to free school meals (FSM) – irrespective of gender do worse than more advantaged students. Some ethnic groups, though, have worse chances of success, even among the disadvantaged, with white British FSM boys being the lowest performing group overall, with 76% not hitting the five GCSEs at grade C standard. This is only half a percent ahead of black Caribbean boys. In the case of both ethnic groups it should be noted that FSM girls, while doing better than boys in the corresponding category, still fall well below the national average, such that what appears to be a question of gender is, in fact, more a question of class and ethnicity, and the intersection of all three. Ashley (2009: 181) neatly summarises the disproportionate fascination with the actions of boys when stating that 'gender often has a smaller effect size than race or social class, yet it is boys to whom the media often turn first for good stories'.

In discussions of gender and class, then, such variables should not be analysed independently. For many years, the intersection of these two social characteristics has been an important feature of sociological attempts to explain male educational disengagement. Paul Willis's (1977) classic study of working-class schoolboys demonstrates how *working-class* masculinity positions such young men as being counter-school and resistant to 'legitimate' authority. Representations of macho male behaviour have also been utilised to theorise the basis for boys' rejection of educational values by the likes of Mac an Ghaill (1994) and McDowell (2003). The relative strengths of these studies are well documented, yet the weaknesses of such approaches are overlooked. The dominance of 'lads' discourses which have been provided by such research have led to two significant and interrelated problems. The first, as noted by Ashley (2009), is that the disproportionate academic attention given to 'laddishness' can lionise or celebrate a mythical and anti-hero status (see also Chapter 2; Quinn et al., 2006). Relatedly, the second problem is that even when the anti-hero is discussed in reference to its 'other' – the working-class boy who performs well educationally, or 'ear'ole' in Willis's parlance – boys' educational outcomes and experiences are measured and depicted dichotomously. This neglects significant variation in attainment and experiences between boys, and has consequences for wider research. For example, even where trying to problematise the dualistic concepts of 'troublesome boys' and 'compliant girls', Jones and Myhill (2004) utilise a dichotomous framework that identifies simply high-performing/low-performing girls and high-performing/low-performing boys. My interviewees' responses provide an example of experiential variety and illustrate the need to move beyond dualistic understandings.

School days: just an 'in-betweener'

Despite similar working-class backgrounds, the recollection of their school days by the respondents in the present study appeared to have little in common with those described by Willis (1977). Overall, these young men did not consider themselves to be either disruptive lads or swot-like ear'oles. Instead, they regularly implied that they occupied a role of the 'in-betweener', often using remarkably similar language to describe this position

CHRISTIAN: I was sort of an average, sort of, get on with it. I weren't the best student but I weren't the worst … I was always there, never truant or anything. I was like every kid, I didn't wanna go, but I did.

JAKE: I don't wanna be stereotypical, but you have obviously got your sensible, if I can I use the word, geek ... And then you got your real trouble makers, and then you got your group in the middle, and I guess that's the group that I hanged around with.
DANNY: I wasn't a bad kid. I was like an 'in-betweener'. I used to be the kid sitting at the back just trying to stay out of it ...
DAMIAN: I was kind of always in the middle – you look on the classic teen movies, you got the geeks, the jocks and the guys that are in-between.

This self-identification with an in-the-middle status between 'laddish' versus 'swotty' behaviour highlights that these archetypes are polar extremes on a continuum rather than discrete and separate categories. This raises questions about how we theorise identities through the lens of masculinities. An incongruence between the students' habitus and the field of education, and insufficient cultural capitals, resulted in these young men being uncomfortable among the highly engaged 'swotty' group. However, they were not automatically highly disengaged or laddish; this requires deeper consideration.

Despite most participants using variations of this 'in-betweener' metaphor, being situated in this space meant different things to different young men and translated into various behaviours. Most of the young men talked about enjoying the social aspects of school, hanging around with friends and so forth, and this often involved 'messing around' (Tim), 'mucking about' (Peter) and, like Willis's boys, 'having a laugh' (Bobby, Pat, Dave). How the respondents went about having a laugh and enjoying non-educational moments could be deemed a 'laddish' form of resistance (Willis, 1977); however, acts of disruption during the school day varied dramatically across the sample. The following exchange with Peter and the comments by Danny, for instance, serve to highlight the extremes:

PETER: Tried not to [misbehave], but there was always some days where you thought 'I probably shouldn't have done that'.
SR: What's the worst thing you did at school?
PETER: Playing football with another student (in classroom during a break), bouncing it off our head and all that and I smashed a light and it came down and hit the other lad's head and we got pretty done for that.

*****

DANNY: [responding to the same question]: Few harsh comments or something. We made a lot of teachers cry.
SR: Were you part of that?
DANNY: Sometimes. I started to bunk off in my last year as well, which was a bit silly to be honest. It was, I'd say it was [to hang out with] friends to be honest ... They [were] influencing me into a different world ... experimentation shall we say, which was, like, smoking weed.

Between the two poles of playing truant or 'bunking off' to smoke cannabis and accidentally breaking the lights with a football, the majority of the young men reminisced about how they were only occasionally 'mouthy' or 'cheeky', rather than recounting incidents where they had significantly misbehaved and/or demonstrated relentless and outright resistance:

TIM: I was the class joker, you'd never believe it. I didn't really misbehave, it was just the inability to stop talking, then obviously that gets you into trouble and your mouth goes off on one, then you obviously get in trouble.

JAKE: I was never naughty but I was more cheeky ... If I got told off I would switch on, but if I could push my boundaries I would.

DAMIAN: I wouldn't say I was disruptive but I wasn't well behaved, I was kind of like the cheeky chappy, making a laugh but doing my work at the same time, kind of *knowing when to draw the line*, I wouldn't push teachers too far [my emphasis].

Beyond this apparently middle-ground (mis)behaviour, Jake's and Damian's comments highlight a commonplace issue. Many of the participants did, indeed, recall times when they had 'pushed the boundaries', yet they still responded to the direction to re-engage with their work. Such 'mucking about' did not form the staple part of their school experience. It is certainly something that many of the respondents enjoyed recollecting, but their school days were mostly made up of 'getting on with it', perhaps punctuated by occasional and recuperative attempts at having a laugh. This mundanity of everyday life is a feature that is often overlooked in research. Even where responses reflected a typically resistant masculine disaffection with school, they were still very tempered in comparison to the counter-school culture expressed so vividly by the 'lads' in Willis's study, as well as in more recent studies of working-class boys' disengagement (Mac an Ghaill, 1994; Connolly, 2004; Sergeant, 2009). These comments from participants who looked back at their school days with the least affection illustrate this more mundane ambivalence:

TIM: I was anti-school because I didn't wanna go to school, but I wanted to get the grades ... obviously, you don't wanna go to school.

GAVIN: I used to hate school really. I didn't like anything academic. I only went to school to play for the rugby team or cricket team; that was the only reason I wanted to go to school ... I was too lazy, or I just did enough I never did like extra, so I did what I could and then relaxed.

BOBBY: It wasn't learning so much it was just sort of the get up and go part of it to go to school ... Going out in the fields playing football, rugby, I used to do all sports, I loved doing that. But just sitting down in English just didn't interest me at all ... I was quite a good person to be honest with you. Just didn't knuckle down enough, I wouldn't go out and start fights or nothing.

Masculinity here is especially redolent; the emphasis on sports speaks to Connell's (1996: 206) idea that 'masculinising practices are concentrated at certain sites', and reminds us that boys actively construct masculinities. However, this theme of not starting fights mentioned by Bobby is particularly interesting. Physical violence, fighting and bullying formed substantial parts of the pursuit of 'mad laughs' for the boys in MacDonald and Marsh's (2005: 53) research, and for the 'hard lads' identified by McDowell (2003: 117). Examples of this attitude and the value of such actions were also noted earlier by Willis (1977: 36), who stated that 'violence, with its connotations of masculinity, spread throughout the group' he studied. For the young men in my study, bullying and intimidation were recognised, and often freely discussed, but rarely as an activity that they personally took part in. Distancing oneself from an act that is largely socially abhorrent to adults may have been easier through a retrospective lens. However, whereas Willis's ethnography captured the essence and meaning of bullying at its moment of action, respondents in MacDonald and Marsh's (2005: 53) study looked back with the benefit of several years' hindsight and, sometimes still identifying themselves as bullies, also acknowledged the function of their behaviour.

With this in mind, we have no reason to doubt that the recollections of physicality by the respondents in the current study were as conveyed. Their recollections were cut in two particular ways. First, the young men largely framed acts of bullying and intimidation as something that they were aware of but that were performed by others and not frequently visible:

JASON: Some of my friends you may have considered bullies because they picked on less popular kids or made unpopular kids less popular in some ways, but I was never bothered about status, you know. I just got on with what I wanted to do really.
PAT: Some kids were picked on, but it didn't seem very regular. I remember some bigger kids had reputations for being a bit nasty ... or that thought they were dead hard. Like one time an older kid cornered me and made me do up my blazer and then laughed at me for having them done up! That's what we are talking about. Nothing so bad and nothing regular.
LUKE: I'm not saying I got beaten up in the corridors ... [but] the sort of people I was hanging around with, it wouldn't have been good to be seen to be trying too hard. 'Cos that's how you fit in, by just being the same. Like most people don't do that [bullying].

In the last quote, Luke also identifies the prospect of potentially being bullied for trying too hard academically, but he quickly suggested this was also about maintaining a degree of popularity. This change of direction belies that one might feel bullied if, through engaging in academic work, one is excluded, while at the same time downplaying Luke's original statement that implied at least some level of intimidation.

The second set of accounts about intimidation moved beyond a general awareness to overt experiences. Only two participants spoke of being bullied by other peers, but a few more talked about the overly masculine dominance of some male teachers. On the latter, for example:

BILLY: Does it count if [it's] teachers as well? If I think how some teachers treated some of us, like Mr [teacher's name], like thought he was some kind of army sergeant, you know. One time I saw him lose it with a boy and he grabbed him by the neck and lifted [him] off his feet for being cheeky – actually for being silent. That's bullying, right.

ADAM: They probably think they've a right to react back at anyone that gives them a hard time, but I'm not sure it's ok … sometimes, people might be asked to leave [the class] if they spoke out of turn or whatever, but some teachers would have digs at kids as a form of punishment … Kind of make them feel stupid, definitely treat them like shit and get other kids to laugh at them.For Dave, being bullied himself was something that related to his size and also something that could be rationalised and, for him, turned out to be unproblematic and productive in some ways:

DAVE: I was a wimp and I was picked on sometimes, and so was dead quiet … for the first year or two [of secondary school]. I was only little though. A few of the bigger lads bullied another lad and then bullied him into blaming and bullying me for it! But then the following year we all became friends and it just stopped. It's strange.

Given the significance afforded to physicality in the literature on masculinity and school disengagement or underperformance among boys (e.g. Willis, 1977; Mac an Ghaill, 1994), and how physicality is theorised as being central to the operation of hegemony and/or the pursuit of status in such settings (Connell, 1995), the positioning of oneself as separate from much of the antisocial behaviour that occurred, is somewhat surprising. Indeed, laddish behaviour such as bullying, starting fights or causing trouble for teachers, has been noted as being a form of social validation (Stahl, 2015; Jackson, 2003). The interviewees' remarks above might be skewed by rose-tinted retrospective lens, and wanting to conceal previous misdemeanours. The interview setting presents an opportunity for the young men to talk up their hardness or masculine status below the level of bullying behaviours, but any such material was notable only by its absence. Whatever the facts, however, the construction of this past reality and what it now means to the respondents both remain equally interesting if they shed light on how the event was felt and/or made sense of by the individual (Heath et al., 2009). Throughout the sample, the revelations challenge the idea that fighting and physicality 'become permanent possibilities for the alleviation of boredom' (Willis, 1977: 34). If 'violence and the judgement of violence is the most basic axis of … ascendance over conformists' (ibid.), then what we see here is that it is a form of resistance that certainly does not apply or appeal to all schoolboys. It may even be 'one way to make the mundane suddenly *matter*' (ibid., emphasis in original), but it is clearly not the only strategy. For these self-professed 'in-betweeners', at least, it was the extreme and largely non-preferred method of circumventing the mundane.

A better way of understanding this is to think about the correspondences with Stahl's (2015: 75) findings in London, where he emphasises that while working-class boys do hold a counter habitus (in as much as it is at odds with the school's demands and expectations), their masculine identities are resistant to hegemony as per Connell because their habitus is 'infused with *traditional working-class values of non dominance*'. This may seem controversial given it diverges from much work that has emphasised the dominative attitudes of working-class masculinity, but what was most striking in this study is that the clearest translation of habitus to field was the relative avoidance of conflict with peers and teachers. Conflict between working-class habitus and the demands of the education system *might* result in counter-culture behaviours but resistance is not the only course of action. This is not to deny that working-class young people have agency in the education setting, but as a 'generative principle of regulated improvisations' (Bourdieu, 1977: 78), we must also entertain the idea that the working-class habitus has internalised non-dominance, respect and *relative* compliance, rather than dominance, resistance and the pursuit of power. While 'schools have considerable capacity to make and remake gender' (Connell, 1996: 229), circumscribing analyses only to the pursuit of power runs the risk of caricaturing working-class boys' experiences of school in ways that actually understate the powerlessness that coincides with just 'getting on with it' in an antipathetic system.

Such behaviours are best understood in conjunction with the academic attitudes that my participants revealed. The quotations above provide one or two caveats of a broader set of sentiments permeating the responses: wanting the grades, doing at least some work, 'switching on' when it was necessary, doing just enough, and so forth. These sentiments reveal a degree of compliance, but to label these young men conformists in a bipolar model of attainment and experience would be inaccurate and misleading. There is much more to these young men's educational experience than being a 'fish out of water' and having a habitus at odds with the demands of the field, thus resulting in counter-culture-style resistance. In some ways, alongside Luke's comments about not 'trying too hard', the dominant informal culture among students revealed here seemed to have both produced and restricted a degree of (non-)conformity. Following Lareau's (2003) explication of parenting cultures, working-class youth are taught by their parents to obey authority and this might perhaps be why, as schoolboys, the young men in this study appeared to conform when required, though this requires further research. They simultaneously lacked the necessary cultural resources, and their habitus is sufficiently out of kilter with the demands of the education system such that their academic achievements are circumscribed. Understood in this way, working-class boys' position at the mid-point range of experience and engagement becomes easily explicable. It is at once a *safe space* of sorts, in that it permits some boundary pushing, but it ultimately still results in a degree of conformity. Furthermore, it is also a *limiting space* in that it denies them the status that might be afforded by teachers to an academically successful boy, or by peers who invest in the idea that status is achieved through counter-cultural or hegemonic activity.

The participants' school histories in total illustrate that the working-class representations of machismo portrayed by Willis are just one part of a wider canvas of experience. Indeed, this is reminiscent of Jenkins's (1983) critique of cultural reproduction through the contrasting experience of 'lads' and 'ordinary kids'. Illustrating the fluidity of social boundaries, Jenkins highlights how ideal type taxonomies overlook the complexity of real lives because young men can be 'lads' at some points and 'ordinary' at others (see also Ingram, 2018). The weakness of such taxonomies is further illustrated by considering how Mac an Ghaill's (1994) categories of 'macho lads', 'academic achievers' and 'new enterprisers' also neglect any middle-ground potential. Whilst Mac an Ghaill's 'macho lads' have a clear correspondence with Willis's 'lads', the latter two categories are claimed to 'incorporate more adequately both the changing occupational and educational realities ... and the different aspirations of students' (O'Donnell & Sharpe, 2000: 46). 'Academic achievers' is a category that, in many ways, is self-explanatory. In the 'new enterprisers', however, Mac an Ghaill (1994: 63) depicts working-class males who have identified an opportunity for upward social mobility through the new vocationalised curriculum. The moderate level of qualifications, the somewhat moderate misbehaviour, the lack of such obvious instrumentalism (see below) and the lack of upward mobility during their time in the labour market (see Chapter 6), suggest that such categories do not account for the young men in the present research.

'Ordinariness' and alienated instrumentalism

Regarding the problems of Willis's polarised model, Brown (1987: 31) contends that a *majority* of young people, boys and girls, are ordinary kids who 'neither simply accept nor reject school, but comply with it'. As implied above, this notion best fits my participants' accounts. Similar to O'Donnell and Sharpe's (2000) study, boredom and/or wanting to move on did not manifest as the contempt for school conveyed in other research. The young men did not see their school days as articulated by Willis's working-class dualism of 40 years ago, or even in the manner described by some young men more recently in studies of white, working-class masculinity (McDowell, 2003; Nayak, 2006; Ward, 2015). Instead they appear to be articulating a middling position, trading off relative behavioural conformity with a relative lack of academic conformity in terms of 'not trying too hard'. This resonates with the 'alienated instrumentalism' exhibited by Brown's (1987, 1990) 'ordinary' kids. However, whereas Brown acknowledged that 'modest levels of academic achievement appeared to provide access to the sorts of jobs pupils wanted', my participants remained largely unsure about what forms of employment they ultimately hoped to attain, or at least had not foreseen front-line service sector work (the occupation they were all in at first interview) as their destination of choice. None of them, for example, made their GCSE choices on the basis of an aspired career path, as these responses indicate:

CARL: No, I just took them 'cos I enjoyed the subjects themselves, I had been doing them up until GCSEs and then from like 13 lessons you then took your top 3 and then your basic maths, English and sciences.
JAMES: I took economics partly 'cos I liked the teacher, um, [laughs] ... He liked my brother and my brother thought he was good, so ... I thought yeah why not. And to be honest I didn't know what else to do.
DANNY: A lot of my teachers to be honest. Some teachers wouldn't take me for certain subjects just because I wasn't necessarily good enough. I wanted to do geography but the teacher said no, which was 'orrible.

Brown also suggests that, faced with a reality of limited opportunities for attaining desired employment, ordinary kids justify relative compliance in pursuing qualifications as means of getting 'any job' (Brown, 1987: 67). This understanding is problematised by the lack of weight attributed to qualifications by the Kentish young men in relation to obtaining retail work. Jez, for example, was the exception in seeing GCSEs as providing a competitive advantage in retail to date. The element of the instrumentalist attitude more clearly linking the experiences of the ordinary kids of the 1980s with those of today was that working to attain any form of qualification was a moral and social obligation. In fact, it was something participants saw as 'normal':

PETER: My teachers obviously, like, always said I could do better, but *I wanted to push myself, a bit*, as much as I could.
PAT: You don't really wanna be [at] the bottom do you? You have to go to school and do something, that's just how it is. Sometimes you made an effort, *'cos you don't wanna be a complete fucking bum.*
LUKE: Some subjects I was pretty good, like the sciences, um, and maths and I never had to particularly try with those at GCSE, and *I liked being good* at that sort of thing.

This suggests that levels of attainment are not the ultimate goal. This is emphasised by Dave, who despite finishing compulsory education with just one of his nine GCSE passes at grade C or above, insisted that he 'pretty much liked school' and 'enjoyed all the subjects' he was taught.

As per Brown, to have left school completely empty-handed would have been perceived as failure. Therefore, for ordinary kids, then and now, responses such as 'just getting on with it' (Dave), and 'doing it 'cos that's what you're there to do' (Peter) underpin conformist, yet instrumental, attitudes towards school 'and [make] the everyday actions of school life possible' (Brown, 1987: 96). Importantly, however, this instrumentalism is not tied to 'certain historical conditions in which the reward structure of the school and the labour market correspond sufficiently to allow pupils to predict the likely outcome of efforts in school' as much as Brown (1987: 123) suggested in the 1980s. The structure of employment has changed, and the relationship between qualifications and obtaining entry-level retail work, for example, was deemed spurious by the respondents here. Their relatively conformist efforts at school are therefore built on something different: none of the participants put in such effort to achieve a job in retail, but encountered and engaged with a *normalised discourse of compliance* as it was simply the done thing. This is reflected in comments like 'school's school, it's alright, so-so' (Tim) and 'you just didn't like what you didn't like about it' (Luke).

The lack of academic 'success' – in that these young men have moderate qualifications profiles – speaks to a typical Bourdieusian reading. Indeed, without being able to deploy the necessary cultural, social and economic capitals, and with a working-class habitus out of kilter with the demands of the education field, achieving less than students with a more middle-class habitus is unsurprising. However, the fact that these young men did not fall into the kinds of spectacular non-conformity and outright rejection of school described by Willis begs explanation. The young men seem to have engaged in a degree of boundary work such that they adopted a position that was relationally 'respectable'. This resonates with Skeggs's (1997) study of working-class women, which drew distinctions between 'rough' and 'respectable' identity practices. On one hand, an entirely disengaged attitude aligned with boisterousness or even bullying would signal a rough, or undesired identity. Alternatively excessive commitment to education is precluded because, seemingly, it would betray their working-class habitus. As success is out of reach given the mismatch of habitus and field, a middle-ground position of partial compliance is perhaps the logical consequence. There is no tension in the habitus, such that it becomes *divided*, as in the case of some academically successful working-class boys (Ingram, 2018; Friedman, 2016). There is no such misalignment that makes school unbearable, even if it is often unpalatable.

On the issue of locality

MacDonald and Marsh (2005) have argued that the role of local context is crucial in understanding differential levels of educational disengagement. In their study in the North-East of England, for example, a change from an historical abundance of traditional working-class jobs to a relative paucity of employment prospects is highlighted as a key reason for a comparatively higher level of anti-school sentiment versus that which was found by O'Donnell and Sharpe (2000) in their study in four London schools. Indeed, for MacDonald and Marsh (2005: 65), where the rich tradition of working-class job prospects in the locality which they studied had once served to ensure a 'begrudging acceptance of the instrumental value of schooling', the kinds of jobs now available, such as 'serving in cake shops or stacking supermarket shelves', did not require educational engagement. As noted in Chapter 2, this is a theme taken up by others who have studied former industrial heartlands (McDowell, 2003; Nayak, 2006; Ward, 2015). The problem with this explanation is that it is precisely these kinds of jobs that the young men of the present study, and many other young men with low-to-moderate qualification profiles (Roberts, 2011), are engaged in. Many of my participants suggested that 'retail is all there is'. This is not to say that their reaction to and experience of such employment opportunities were always the same (see Chapter 6). Despite the fact that de-industrialisation was more acute in the North-East than the South-East of England, the point here is that the types of contemporary local employment opportunities in both localities were largely understood in the same way, yet educational disengagement was not as sharp among the Kent sample.

The general sense that participants offered was that alienated instrumentalism is not as stable a frame of reference as Brown indicates. The young men's accounts of their school days clearly imply a varied reality of experience. This follows Jenkins's (1983) reasoning that one can be either a lad or ordinary at different times. Similarly, MacDonald and Marsh (2005: 56) indicate that '[s]ometimes the same individuals recounted narratives of school that contained both instrumental engagement and complete disaffection'. As has been shown here, a further form of school experience is plausible – one where limited engagement and limited disaffection occur and provide the basis for an ordinary, but fluid, school experience.

Post-16 'choices'

This section addresses how Brown's 'alienated instrumentalism' operates after compulsory education. Until the relatively recent Raising of the Participation Age legislation, young people in the British school system were technically allowed to leave school after completing their GCSE secondary school qualifications at age 16. However, the vast majority, even before the education age was raised to 18 in 2014, stayed on either at school to undertake A-levels[3] or to engage in various other post-compulsory courses. Thus I am interested in the thinking that underpins the choice to stay on in education rather than enter the labour market at the earliest possible chance.

In terms of educational outcomes, it is insufficient to categorise the respondents as having typically received 'good' (five or more A–C grades) or 'bad' (fewer than five grades A–C) GCSEs. The young men's clutch of qualifications presented them with differing options to consider. For example, Pat, who achieved four A–C grades, was not given the option of staying on at school to undertake A-levels, but this qualification haul was enough to ensure he could access a local further education (FE) college[4] to take A-levels. Similarly, Dave was adamant that despite having only one A–C grade GCSE, his enrolment in computing at college was contingent upon having demonstrated at least some effort in his GCSEs, declaring that "cos in ICT [information communications technology] I got quite a good grade at GCSE level … I got an interview straight away'. Bobby, having been told he could not remain at school for sixth form, enrolled at college to re-sit his GCSE maths and English because 'when you're going for a job … if you haven't got above Cs in those, it's not good really. They [employers] sort of look at people like that'.

Such qualifications, then, formed part of the respondents' 'horizons for action' (Hodkinson, 1998) as they finished their compulsory education. These horizons are partly determined by the availability of external opportunities and partly by internal subjective perceptions of what seems possible and, importantly, 'what might be appropriate' (Hodkinson, 1998: 304). Utilising this concept enables the young men's decisions to be better understood by allowing us to see that, rather than being a totally technical, rational, calculated decision, their post-16 options were pursued as part of 'the socially constructed and historically derived common base of knowledge, values and norms for action that people grow into and come to take as a natural way of life' (Hodkinson, 1998: 304).

So, what choices did these young men make? All but two immediately enrolled in post-compulsory education, and one of the two who did not still enrolled on a college course within 15 months of leaving school. This engagement with post-compulsory education varied significantly across qualification level, subject matter and completion rate. It was no great surprise that of those who undertook A-levels, all except one were from a clearly non-manual background (see e.g. Reay et al., 2001; Reay and Ball, 1998; Furlong and Cartmel, 2007). The horizon for action open to these young men, similar to their established middle-class peers, is likely to have led them towards an academic route, and ensured that more vocational pathways were not just unattractive, but actually perceived as not an option. Concomitantly, the young men who pursued vocationally driven courses were largely from overtly manual backgrounds and this often seemed to be as important an influence on their choices as their qualification levels. Tim, for instance, whose father is a plumber, achieved nine A–C GSCE grades yet left school to pursue a vocational course. Similarly, Jez, who described his parents as 'workers, working-class but not necessarily poor', obtained all A–C passes in his GCSEs but signed up to an FE college course in Business Studies, before dropping out within a week and committing to retail work. Here he explains how his options unfolded and how he made sense of them:

JEZ: Basically, when I turned 16 my mum said I got the option of college and not paying rent, or going out and earning money. So I decided to just earn money. Just 'cos I didn't have much money when I was younger, so I always wanted my own money and to be able to do my own things.

Beyond understanding how horizons for action can influence the more specific choice of educational programme, understanding the decision to participate in any form of post-compulsory education was also important. Despite exhibiting largely alienated-instrumentalist attitudes to school – attitudes that could justifiably lead them to first consider available options in the labour market – further education was deemed the appropriate next step for most of the sample. We might, therefore, expect that the decision to continue in education was a more technically rational one, leaning more towards an instrumental orientation, with a consequence being that the alienated element of such a frame of reference would diminish. Indeed, this is what MacDonald and Marsh (2005: 56) outline with some of their sample, suggesting that '[some] informants described a process of instrumental accommodation in the latter years of compulsory education ... [or] were currently attending Further Education college after earlier dismal experiences'. For my participants, however, 'dismal' experiences and/or episodes of disengagement had not occurred. The reality, once again, was that their decisions about, experiences of, and efforts towards post-compulsory education reflected something of a middle-ground approach rather than an overt instrumentalist one.

The decisions were 'pragmatically rational' (Hodkinson, 1998: 304), i.e. partly rational and partly intuitive in respect of the opportunities which confronted them. Consequently, almost all of the sample noted that they wanted to 'get something behind me' (Christian), or 'get something under my belt' (Bobby), whilst at the same time often acknowledging that 'it meant I wouldn't have to do anything else for a couple of years' (Luke), or that 'it seemed easy, instead of me bumming around' (Danny). In deciding to stay on in post-16 education, the respondents were following the majority trend, which saw around 80% of 16–18 year olds participating in this manner during the 2000s (DCSF, 2008). Despite that opting to participate in post-16 education was seen as a normal step in their transition to adulthood, such decisions were often based on an understanding that, at this stage in their life, they should have been ready to rationally choose a course that would help achieve a desired job. Although never articulated in such a manner, it could be argued that many participants chose subjects reflecting a sense of appropriate (working-class) masculine achievement (see O'Donnell & Sharpe, 2000). Connecting the choice of subject with an aspired job in this manner, however, was rather mixed across the sample. The comments below indicate how these respondents felt they were making a 'rational' decision:

CHRISTIAN: [discussing BTEC in ICT][5] I liked working with computers, and I sort of thought with every sort of job that you get nowadays you tend to have that involved.

ALEX: [BTEC in Public Services] was relevant to what I wanted to do ... I wanted to join the army. It was the most directly, like, relevant course ... Not so much necessary, but it's like, when I went for the interview for it, it gave me an insight into the services.

MIKE: Um, just because I did mechanics all my life [with his dad] so it was either come out and work in a shop, which is quite ironic, [laughs] or go and do college, like get a proper career. I didn't really think about it I was just like, yeah let's do it.

It might have been expected that a relationship would have been more apparent between qualification type and having a relatively fixed career strategy among those undertaking vocational courses. However, such comments occurred across the qualification and subject range. The young men who did not configure a relationship between their post-16 choices and their potential careers also varied in their level of educational engagement:

TIM: [talking about his BTEC in Sports Science] I was gonna stay on [at school] but school was a bit rubbish, so I left, and my mum said 'oh yeah you know, you like sports so why don't you go do sports science' so I did. And then it went from there, parental instinct.

PETER: [discussing his A-levels] I thought I'd try and see where it leads me, and I just done it ... I thought about starting work, but I thought I was a bit too young to, like, get into it.

DANNY: [on deciding he would undertake a BTEC in Business] [I thought] I might as well do it. Like, see if I can go anywhere with it ... I was influenced by my friends, 'cos some of my friends were doing business [studies at college].

JAMES: [considering his A-level choices] I chose subjects I thought I enjoyed the most. In the end I hated economics, 'cos I was probably too lazy to make an effort ... I was never that certain about what I wanted to do.

This relatively even split in terms of understanding or planning how their choice of course might correlate with an aspired occupational outcome produced a rather consistent experience of post-compulsory education. Whilst much of the moderate misbehaviour the young men described in their compulsory school days had declined, this was not necessarily a result of increased effort. The general theme throughout the post-compulsory years was that a degree of alienated instrumentalism was still very much at play. For instance, Gavin, echoing others, suggested that he 'worked a bit harder but was still lazy'. This attitude can be summed up by Danny, who commented that:

DANNY: I'd bunk off here and there. But college was like, we'd all meet up, go in the morning and sometimes we wouldn't come back after lunch 'cos we'd be in the pub, but that's what everyone does.

Alienation might best describe their frame of reference towards the labour market at this particular moment in their lives. For example, as Luke indicates above, being involved in education simply aided avoiding the labour market for another two years. These comments belie the idea that being given the 'choice' of post-compulsory education might result in increased effort and/or instrumentalism. Somewhat contradictorily, alienation persists at this level even though the young men chose to stay on in education. This is strongly reflected by the fact that about half the sample dropped out of their programme of study. In fact, some were involved in multiple enrolments and subsequent drop-outs. Tim, for example, obtained nine A–C grades and then proceeded to leave school and take up a two-year college course in sports science, before dropping out after about 15 months and taking up a college course in music technology, which he then quit within eight months.

In post-compulsory education, these young men mostly continued to 'get on with it', being neither particularly resistant nor conforming to the extent that they exerted additional effort to achieve as much as possible. Having personally opted for this form of study, alienated instrumentalism seems a contradictory frame of reference with respect to my respondents. Nonetheless, it is apparent in the participants' accounts of their choices and experiences at this level. This kind of ambivalent attachment to post-compulsory education throws up interesting contradictions from a Bourdieusian perspective. On the one hand, Bourdieu's concept of *illusio*, which refers to 'the tendency of participants to engage in the game and believe in its significance, that is, believe in that the benefits promised by the field are desirable' (Heidegren & Lundberg, 2010: 12), struggles to capture what is occurring here, given the young men in my study did not presume a relationship between qualifications gained and labour market outcomes. At the same time, however, Heidegren and Lundberg (2010: 12) remind us that 'the norms and benefits of the game force themselves on the participants and seem almost to be dictated by a power beyond the field' and that the *illusio* is 'never questioned'. This lends itself to a determinism of sorts, such that young people appear beholden to what Hage (2012), inferring from Bourdieu, calls 'social gravity' (see Threadgold, 2017 for discussion). As Threadgold (2017: 8) explicates, when young people 'invest themselves in a certain field it creates momentum in and trajectory', and this problematises a simplified notion of choice. Alongside the idea that the working-class habitus emphasises that at least some effort at school produces a sense of moral and social worth, we can make sense of what seems to be an antithetical attachment to an education system from which these young men are unlikely to fully benefit.

Rose's (1999) Foucauldian concept of 'governance through freedom' provides another way to consider the young men's commitment to post-compulsory education as a part of their horizon for actions. This refers to a form of governance that is achieved by shaping people's conduct and the ways in which they construct themselves in an active fashion. Without direct state intervention or force, individuals act upon themselves through the exercise of ostensible freedom and personal choice. More specifically, 'governance through freedom' is about shaping individuals' aspirations and needs, and forging alignments between the aspirations and calculations of ruling and 'independent authorities' – or 'political aims' – and the 'personal aspirations' of free citizens (Rose, 1999: 49). Rose (1999) argues that, in liberal societies, individuals are required to take responsibility and to regulate themselves in a manner that confirms them as autonomous agents – however, their actions need to remain in line with what is defined as possible. This notion of what is possible echoes Bourdieu's concept of *doxa*, which denotes taken-for-granted 'truths' (see Roberts & Evans, 2013). Understood in this way, the decision to stay on is influenced by – and simultaneously supports and reinforces – a normalised discourse of post-compulsory participation. As seen from the comments above, the young men were sometimes unsure why they decided to stay on, but still framed this decision as one they made freely. It is an option, however, which reflects a degree of conformity – their continued participation, or at least their decision to start post-compulsory studies, speaks to Rose's governance through freedom, and the momentum created by *illusio*. Indeed, devoting at least some time to staying on in post-compulsory education appears to have been a central part of the *doxic*, common-sense, accepted norm.

Critical moments in post-16 education engagement and drop out

Despite exhibiting some degree of alienated instrumentalism, and without being particularly non-conformist, about half the sample ultimately abandoned post-compulsory study. This disengagement may reflect an increased sense of alienation towards education. Indeed, some of the sample experienced a form of alienation similar to the young people described by Willis and Brown, which *eventually* led them to reject education and enter the labour market. This often resulted from a mismatch between their expectations and the reality of further education. For example, Simon suggested that he 'felt like a five year old again, completely talked down to' and consequently left his sixth form course after just three days to concentrate on a full-time retail job. Similarly Tim, discussing his BTEC in music technology, explained that:

TIM: [I]t doesn't lead in to anything. It just gives you a better understanding of music and when you are listening to music ... it didn't really give you any clear options [about] how you could get your foot in the door.

Decisions to drop out or remain engaged were, however, often hugely complex and sometimes made in relation to what Thomson et al. (2002) describe as 'critical moments'. Thomson et al. (2002: 339) suggest that this is 'a formal rhetorical device in the unfolding of a story, the pivot, or "complication", on which a narrative structure turns'. Such moments may manifest as a result of agential choice or as a form of fate, something which is out of the control of the individual. The idea resonates with Giddens's (1991: 113) discussion of 'fateful moments' in the reflexive construction of the self. However, Giddens positions these moments as instances of empowerment, where people learn lessons which ultimately 'reshape the reflexive project of identity through the lifestyle consequences which ensue' (ibid.: 143). Contrastingly, of importance for Thomson et al. (2002: 342), and indeed for my work here, is that 'the response of young people to the events, rather than the categories of events themselves, [...] may be most revealing of social inequality'. Such critical moments clearly need to be understood in their particular context, and with due regard given to the various resources available to the young people at the time of the incident. The following very different examples illustrate the impact of such moments on educational dis/engagement.

Mike

At 16, during his last year of compulsory schooling, Mike was accepted into a further education course to study motor mechanics, the occupation his father had been employed in for his whole working life. Enrolment in this programme was not subject to any GCSE requirement. Consequently, Mike felt that continuing with the same effort no longer had much value:

MIKE: I worked hard through most of school ... then it was just like, got to the end and I was like 'I can't be bothered'. I do regret it, big time. 'Cos it'd look so much better on my CV if I actually had some good GCSEs.

Mike's regret stemmed from a critical moment that resulted in an inability to 'get my life sorted until about three years ago'. The critical moment in question was witnessing his best friend be killed by a train. This incident occurred half way through the first year of the mechanics course, and Mike was understandably given time off to grieve and recover. He remained off college for nearly four months, and despite being offered encouragement to return and catch up with the rest of the class, he never got back into his stride:

MIKE: At that point I was just like fuck it, and ended up not going. My dad would drop me off at college and then I'd go to the bus station and go straight home. I did that every day for about a year.In Mike's mind, this tragic event was of incredible significance to the direction of his life:

MIKE: I probably would have stuck at it [if not for the death], 'cos most of my life I did stick at things … And then it came to a point where I'd just had enough.

Mike's tragic loss clearly impacted his educational engagement. It is worth noting that Mike's entire biographical narrative is atypically chaotic relative to the rest of the sample. Teenage fatherhood, losing various jobs due to problems with aggression towards superiors, problematic and usually bilateral violent relationships, moving back and forth between his father's home in Kent and his mother's in Derbyshire, and even a bout of homelessness all punctuated his life story after education. Indeed, each one of these subsequent events was, in hindsight, seen by Mike as connected in some way to this fateful 'critical moment'. Though he is now married with three children and seemingly very settled as a primary caregiver, at the time of this incident, Mike had limited cultural and material resources to draw upon. He and his father lived in a council house on an estate near Canterbury. As a result of increasing problems with Parkinson's disease, his father was employed as a part-time handyman after being a mechanic most of his life. Money was tight, and given the father's occupational history and own cultural capital Mike might have been expected or encouraged to get a job in these circumstances. However, Mike's father persisted in driving him to college, daily. This is indicative of his support for Mike's continuing pursuit of a qualification. Nonetheless, Mike's disengagement ultimately ensured that he did not finish the qualification and that the route into his desired job was closed off.

Rob

Rob's critical moment was not as dramatic as Mike's, yet similarly affected his educational engagement. Rob was studying sports fitness at college with a view to being a personal trainer. He dropped out before the end of his course, however, because of 'financial reasons and the distance I was travelling every day'. Viewed in isolation, this could be seen purely as an issue of social/economic disadvantage. However, in Rob's mind, particularly adverse weather conditions during the period were a crucial factor in his disengagement. Just two months before dropping out, severe snow had caused significant train disruption for several weeks. The only other potential means of getting to college would have been by road, but Rob did not hold a driving licence at the time and indicated a taxi would have been far too expensive (he did not mention, for example, the option of taking the bus). As a result of the absence, Rob felt he had missed too much work, and falling behind began to take its toll. He became de-motivated and unsure about the benefits of staying on when considering the cost of getting to college and being behind the rest of the class:

Looking back and looking forward at age 18–24 103

ROB: I mean I lost a really good career potentially. But we had so much snow, I was behind and it was costing me a fortune – 10 pounds a day, just to get there. I could not do it, no joke. So much money.

Rob's parents earned just above the threshold that would have entitled him to claim Educational Maintenance Allowance (EMA), so he relied on his parents for some financial support. The limited economic capital available to Rob's family meant he needed to generate and use his own money to socialise, and buy items of personal interest. This all impacted his decision to drop out:

ROB: It makes you feel like your mum and dad should have enough money to help you out, but we struggled. Obviously once I left that I just had to find a job, 'cos I was just getting a backlog of debt 'cos I was just living off my own [money], and it was costing me a fortune …

The reason Rob deemed this to be a critical turning point in his biography is that, for him, dropping out completely closed off pursuing the career he had wanted. When asked about potentially returning to college to retake the course, economic resources again were highly influential:

ROB: If I wanted to go back into my personal trainer course it would cost me about 5 grand. Because I'm over 18, so I have to pay for it now … 'cos it's a 2 and [a] half year course there is a lot to learn.

Limited cultural knowledge was also apparent when he talked about potential financing avenues for such courses:

SR: Can you get any help from the government to pay for that or do they …?
ROB: I don't really know, I've not really majorly looked into it, I just looked into it and found out how much it was and that sort of shocked me.

Of significance here, too, was Rob's understanding that he had 'blown his one chance' and that as a result he would not and indeed *should not* be entitled to try again. This was made very apparent in the following exchange:

SR: So, do you think it's unfair that you can't get the same sort of funding as a 17 year old for further education?
ROB: If they are in my situation where they have done it before, then no they shouldn't get it again … they've had that opportunity to do it and excel in whatever they were doing, so I don't think they should get the opportunity to, like, get help from the government … Why should anyone get extra help? It's my fault that I dropped out.
SR: So if you're in the position you are in now and you have never done that before do you think the government should pay for someone who is 21, 22?

104 *Looking back and looking forward at age 18–24*

ROB: Yeah, 'cos everybody should have an equal chance. Everybody's human. If somebody wants to better themselves, no matter how old they are, they should be given that chance.
SR: What about … in the situation you're in now, you tried that course, didn't work out 'cos of the travel, what if you fancied bettering yourself in another fashion?
ROB: Um, well I suppose it's that one chance kind of thing. I have had a chance to do something that I was really interested in, got good grades in, and then just threw it all away. And I regret it now, big time.

This perspective is in line with observations that posit that setbacks or negative outcomes are often perceived as individual shortcomings or failures (Furlong & Cartmel, 2007). This happens because the discourses of individual effort and self-betterment, notions of a meritocratic society in which self-responsible individuals are able to achieve their life aspirations, permeate the media and politics. That economic and cultural resources are still central to an understanding of differential life chances and experiences becomes often overlooked and even obscured (Atkinson et al., 2013).

Danny

Finally, there is Danny, who identified two critical moments: one positive and one negative. His father – 'a manic depressive [who] couldn't ever work' – died when Danny was just 12, and Danny had since lived with his mother and two siblings on a council estate. Household income was a combination of welfare benefits and a small amount of rent that each of the children paid when they later obtained work. The September after finishing school with two A–C grades at GCSE, Danny started a BTEC course in Business Studies at a local FE college. He explained how the course had not been particularly attractive in terms of forging a career, suggesting that he 'would hate to be stuck in an office all day. [But] the course was just like, it was open to me, I could do it'. The idea that he could do this course stems from the fact that horizons for action are also influenced by objectively possible opportunities:

DANNY: I put my application in, for a few things actually, like being a mechanic, and I didn't get that 'cos I don't know anything about cars, I didn't know fuck all [laughs]. Like, I don't have a clue.

Despite the business course not being his first choice, being accepted on to the programme made it a *possibility*. Nonetheless, Danny dropped out after six months because he 'thought it would be easy' and had not realised how much writing, computing and maths was involved – all three being things he disliked at school. After dropping out, Danny said he 'dicked around' before a critical moment changed the direction he was heading in:

DANNY: I left, and I did nothing for a while, I started hanging out drinking on the streets. It was a bad time ... I got in trouble a few times with the law. I had a court case for something I did but I pleaded guilty ... I haven't been in trouble for a long time; my criminal record is spent ... It was just a bad time around that time, but just misbehaviour, drunk and disorderly and stuff like that.
SR: How did you get out of this ... [type of behaviour]?
DANNY: My court case is what stopped me, and when I had a big arse fine that I couldn't pay for and my mum had to pay it ... and I felt so bad. It's not like we got a lot of money in my household, kinda fucked things up so I thought 'you know what, I'm gonna stop it' and didn't do anything after that.

The financial pressure that Danny's court fine placed on his mother, and his ensuing sense of guilt, acted as a catalyst for him to 'sort himself out and try and get a job'. To enhance his employability, Danny went to his local Connexions service for advice and they put him on a training programme called 'E2E' (entry to employment). However, instead of spending three months being prepared for work, Danny was surprised to find himself being ushered back towards education:

DANNY: I didn't do the whole 3 months because, um, well this was based at the college, and from my art experience, they helped me get into the college, not getting like a work placement, they put me onto college and said 'go for the interview take all your old stuff [art portfolio from GCSE] and put a form in and just go there *now*'.

Danny was delighted to be accepted into a BTEC programme in Art and Design, which was a one-year course with the option of going on to a second year at a higher level, subject to satisfactory achievement. Being in receipt of £30 EMA on a weekly basis during Danny's period of study helped pay for some moderate socialising and he felt he was back on track, trying to take the course seriously, though still 'bunking off occasionally' and not entirely enjoying the course's written components. While this critical moment inadvertently ensured that Danny could re-engage with education, another such moment ensured that the re-engagement was short lived.

Halfway through his BTEC programme, Danny inherited £12,500 following the death of his paternal grandfather. This was a moment that led to him 'relaxing quite a lot' and ultimately choosing not to stay on for the top-up year of the programme. Again, the important issue to recognise here is that this particular critical moment can only be fully understood in regards to its context and the available resources to which Danny had access. His initial feelings on hearing that he had inherited this sum are indicative of this fact:

DANNY: It was good, I was like 18 and it was ... just like 'fuck me that is like some people's wages for a year!' And um, yeah I go ... and pretty much because I had the money I was not wanting to get a job or go [to] college.

Neither Danny nor his family had ever had access to such a substantial amount of money, and he was encouraged to do with it what he wanted, with advice limited to 'treat it wisely'. The money lasted Danny a year, and the regret expressed during the interview for his lack of economic prudence was palpable:

DANNY: We was told to, like, look after the money. Treat it wisely. None of us did which was stupid. I could have gone to university or done something or gone further in education and put some of that money in my future. It sucks. It makes me feel sick now.
SR: What did you do with it then?
DANNY: Um, I decorated my room. I got a whole brand new room out of it. I think I got a couple of tattoos, I bought my mum a cooker, and bought her a few things ... Going out a lot, and I would splash my cash on other people. I was going out with a girl at the time. Fucking, fucking hate her, right, seriously. One of my friends said to me, she [the girlfriend] said 'well I'm sorted now'. You know what I mean? I bought her a lot of stuff! I wish I didn't.

Here again, Danny's actions were driven by what seemed appropriate. In his mind he was able to change his life, treat himself (and his mum, his girlfriend, his friends) to things that were previously out of reach. After 'not treating it wisely', as with Rob, Danny posits his situation purely as an issue of individual failing. Indeed, he was only able to retrospectively situate the inheritance as a negative critical moment for his educational disengagement and any potential future engagement. His understanding of the relationship between finance and further/higher education is explored in greater detail below. For now, it is clear Danny's lack of material resources combined with an apparent lack of cultural capital in regards to 'the right thing to do' (in middle-class terms) with his money and college course hugely influenced the direction of his educational engagement.

These three examples illustrate 'the extent to which different young people have access to the requisite resources to enable them to respond constructively to events and changing circumstances' (Thomson et al., 2002: 350). The significant point here is that as ordinary, unproblematic young men, they were still constrained by differentiated access to various forms of cultural and material resources. Understanding this is an important first step towards recognising that the apparently active choices that such young people make in education and employment are not necessarily indicative of positive situations which require no policy attention. The increasing emphasis given to young people's agency in shaping school-to-work transitions (e.g. Wyn & Dwyer,

1999; Woodman, 2009) needs to be carefully considered alongside the way young people respond to such critical moments and the cultural and material resources available at the time.

Higher education: awareness, aspirations, ambitions

This final section considers how the participants viewed and understood the possibility and plausibility of engaging in higher education. The context for this discussion is composed of two strands: first, long-standing concerns, which continue through to the writing of this book, with 'the absence of men, particularly working-class men, from post-compulsory education and training' (McGivney, 1999: 1); and second, the then Labour government's policy target of obtaining an HE participation rate of 50% of young people. The main reasons for this policy initiative include a strong economic case for the benefit of both individuals and the economy, and also a range of important social consequences, such as redressing poverty, providing health benefits and enhanced social cohesion through active citizenship (Aston & Bekhradnia, 2003).

On the surface, these young men were prime candidates for policy initiatives designed to increase and widen participation. Their educational engagement to date, even for those who had dropped out, indicated they were not anti-education to the extent that they might automatically reject the idea of HE. Moreover, being men, they are potential targets for equalising participation rates between the genders. In fact, as they do at most levels of the educational system, young men have lower entry participation rates, higher rates of non-completion, lower rates of successful completion, and generally achieve a lower proportion of the best marks (Thompson & Bekhradnia, 2009). Being working-class and, in fact, non-traditional (potential) students, made these young men even more of an obvious target group for widening participation initiatives. This is because to date, regardless of recent rapid expansion and increasing participation, 'there has been a persistent, consistent and continuing tendency to recruit students from the middle-class' (Archer et al., 2003: 73; see also Furlong & Cartmel, 2007; France, 2016).

The idea that aspiration is the primary barrier to expanding participation is highly significant in the relevant policy drives. Aspiration is, however, a very problematic notion and presents something of a class-based conundrum. Walkerdine et al. (2001), Reay (2012), Roberts and Evans (2013), Bradley and Ingram (2013), and Stahl (2015), among others, have shown a number of ways in which class-based issues can be obscured by the rhetoric of aspiration. Principally, the expectation of educational success in respect to both high-graded and numerous qualifications tends to be normalised and embedded in middle-class values. In fact, studies have found that there is often little celebration in middle-class families of such expected levels of achievement – in stark contrast to working-class parents who often celebrate even relatively mediocre results (Walkerdine et al., 2001). Similarly, the comprehension that many working-class parents had in regards to their child's present and future education has been shown to be very influential, with the importance of a good education often acknowledged, but existing alongside a lack of access to knowledge about educational processes and practice, which adversely affects working-class parents' ability to insert themselves into the prevailing discursive system (Reay, 2006; Crozier et al., 2011; Roberts & Evans, 2013; Walkerdine et al., 2001). There is often also a strong sense of legitimised condescension towards working-class parents by teachers, with their attempts to communicate concerns and ideas about their child's education being overlooked, while the high symbolic value attached to the employment of the parents of the middle-class pupils, alongside strong levels of experience and knowledge of the educational system, can mean they are often considered to be voices of 'authority' in regards to their children's education (Walkerdine et al., 2001). From this perspective, aspiration cannot be positioned simply as an issue of individual responsibility. However, the prevailing government objectives of raising aspiration do just this by further reinforcing the idea that cultural and material difference does not amount to particular social disadvantage for individuals.

This is not to say that research and policy have fully ignored such barriers. Research has shown how current available finances and material circumstance and/or future projections of personal debt form a central part in deciding whether to study locally and live in the parental home or to move away – or indeed whether to go into HE at all (e.g. Walkerdine et al., 2001; Archer et al., 2003; Abrahams & Ingram, 2013; Callender & Mason, 2017; Reay, 2017). Furthermore, Harrison et al. (2007) show how increasing access to bursaries has led to improved completion rates. Financial barriers tend to be the primary focus, yet they are not the only factors that require consideration. For example, Ball et al. (2002) illustrated that young people with access to particular types of social, cultural and economic capitals are likely to be 'embedded choosers', where entering HE is deemed to be part of a normalised process of transition and a necessary bridge between education and employment. Alternatively, young people from less advantaged backgrounds can only make decisions about engagement with HE after giving due consideration to overcoming various barriers.

A major limitation of this type of research is that it tends to base its findings on the responses of those who are involved in higher education, rather than on those who have never enrolled (Gorard et al., 2006). This gap in our understanding was the key driver for a major piece of research conducted by the University of Southampton as part of the Economic and Social Research Council Teaching and Learning Research Programme. This involved qualitatively researching 'networks of intimacy' (Heath et al., 2008) to better help understand patterns of non-participation in the available large-scale data sets. It also sought to understand non-participation through employing the concept of ambivalence as a mediating position between perceptions of HE as simply either advantageous or disadvantageous.

Non-participation is different from dropping out, therefore my participants' accounts offer fresh insight to this body of work. More importantly, given they have never attempted to engage with HE, they are a much closer reflection of the 'white working-class men [who] are both a threat to lifelong learning policy and its prime object of concern' (Quinn et al., 2006: 736), and who make up the group least likely to participate in HE (Crawford & Greaves, 2015).

The sample was sharply divided between those who had never considered university as an option, and those whose interviews contained several references to HE without ever spelling out firm plans of enrolling. Indeed, after the full seven-year research period, none of the remaining participants had engaged in HE. Tim, for instance, talked about how, even after dropping out of two FE courses, he had 'a year's worth of grades at AS level,[6] and I think that is still eligible to get into uni'. In regards to their non-participation to date during the first sweep of data collection, the themes were largely consistent. As with some of the research mentioned above, issues relating to finance featured strongly:

TIM: It didn't [put me off at first] but when you hear of people being in 18 grand of debt or something after a 3 year course ... terrible.
CHRISTIAN: I didn't think I'd be able to afford to do it to be honest ... At the time, I was learning to drive so I wanted to be able to afford, I wanted to be able to work to have money to get a car and things like that.
DANNY: I needed money, I needed a job, I couldn't stay on without no money ... to pay rent, like to help my mum, that's the way it is. I was put off of going to college or uni because of my mum needing rent to be honest.

As illustrated by Christian, some of the young men considered HE in an 'either/or' fashion where participation would result in them relinquishing or deferring items of consumption that were important to them now. Indeed, Carl, who spent a great deal of his wages on modifying his car, said he knew people at uni who 'didn't even have cars' and who often 'had to be the passengers! [laughs]'. Here we have another instance where my respondents seemed unaware of their own financial disadvantage – many middle-class students would, of course, be able to afford to both study and engage in their chosen leisure pursuits. In some circumstances though, as with Danny, finance was of even bigger concern, as attending HE would have negatively impacted his contribution to the family household income. The other central issue was potential debt. However, this cannot be viewed in isolation as concerns about debt were bound up with, first, what one could get in return when entering the labour market at the end of HE and, second, a complete lack of awareness of systems of financial support and bursaries.

The implications of this lack of awareness are vast. A major report into barriers into HE participation by the Office for Fair Access around the time of the interviews (Callender, 2009) drew attention to the positive difference bursaries can make to completion rates among non-traditional students. A lack of awareness of these bursaries was also highlighted, but significantly, this report drew its sample almost entirely from current students (or their parents). The lack of awareness of financial aid among my participants presents a significant challenge to engaging them in the first place, and poses serious questions about how to get this information to those who need it. The present method of using colleges, universities and HE advisers as bearers of knowledge in this regard might not suffice because non-participants are already likely to deem such places off limits.

This lack of awareness in regards to HE finance was also combined with a general lack of awareness of the processes involved in applying at all:

ADAM: All I know is that you gotta do a UCAS or something.[7] I don't wanna do UCAS. I remember people struggling at school, and I remember opening an account online at home and I was like what does this mean? What do I do here? And I had no one to talk to about …

CARL: I wouldn't know even how to start thinking about going to uni or anything like that, like I wouldn't even know what qualifications you might need.

JOHNNY: How the fuck would I know? You know what I mean? I ain't ever been, nor has my mates or my family. Loads of people do it though.

A final significant feature, which was overwhelmingly apparent in participants' discussions of HE, was the instrumental nature with which anybody's HE participation was viewed. This was clear whether participants talked about themselves or others:

JAMES: There is no point in having a degree for the sake of having a degree … one of my mates from school, just come back from uni, got a degree but he's come to work at Marks and Spencer 'cos he doesn't know what to do … what's the point? He could have been at Marks and Spencer for four years earning cash.

CHRISTIAN: If there was a career that I was set on, but at the moment sort of, I'm not really … The way I perceive it is that they want to do a certain thing and that's why they go into the route …

TIM: If people have got the money to blow on it then yeah … if you are gonna go to uni for three years and at the end of the course you can't really go into anything, like you know they have just brought in an exercise science course that you can do at uni but that doesn't lead into anything so you have got to do more years of uni and then at the end of the uni course you could go and work in fucking *Blockbusters* [the now defunct DVD hire store].

These comments suggest the respondents conceptualised a direct parallel between the subject one might pursue in HE and one's occupation of choice.

Only one respondent commented on the inherent value of education, and even this reflected the traditionally working-class vocational value of learning 'welding and fabrications just 'cos that's something I enjoy doing and I wouldn't mind to learn how to do it properly' (Mike). More crucially, none of the respondents saw any longer-term value in a degree or considered HE an opportunity to develop transferable skills. This understanding was consistent across the sample, and can therefore be deemed highly significant in young people's decisions around HE. Even on the few occasions when respondents considered the lifestyle benefits of being a student, they were soon dismissed in the name of occupational instrumentalism and/or fears about debt, as Bobby so aptly reveals:

BOBBY: The only other reason I would really go to uni is the partying. It sounds stupid, but I know uni is very good partying. I wouldn't want to go and get myself that much loans to go and do something I didn't wanna really do.

The connections drawn by the young men between instrumentalism and HE participation, in ways that were not present in their discussion of school or fee-free post-compulsory education, is telling. Unlike other avenues for post-compulsory study, it is neither a cultural nor numerical norm. Indeed, HE participation is seen as an investment risk; with a high risk of educational failure, and in a context in which they are required to transform their identity and commit to a difficult, often impossible, transition from struggling to successful learner, the attitudes and apprehensions exhibited here are understandable (Reay, 2017).

Aspiration is therefore not the key barrier to participation. The limited access to information is as significant as any perceived poverty of aspirations. This is especially telling since Berrington et al. (2016) have demonstrated that more than half of this 'problem group' of white working-class men aspire to go to university in their teens but only about 35% ultimately participate. Additionally, it should be clarified that in seeking answers to such matters, my questions needed to be quite deliberately focused. The overwhelming feature emerging in my interviews when first discussing HE was a sense of ambivalence. Comments such as 'I dunno' (Pat), and 'I'd not really given it much thought' (Christian), dominated initial discussions and only through 'digging deeper' were specific responses in regards to advantage and disadvantage of HE elicited. This ambivalence aligns with the alienated instrumentalism that the young men have generally held as a frame of reference through their educational engagement, and, as per Heath et al. (2008), seems to have been transmitted through existing social relations or through individual actions and experiences in education. Alienated instrumentalism and ambivalence, then, form a mutually favourable means of theorising and illuminating one another, whilst also reinforcing the idea that middle-ground positions and frames of reference need to be better understood.

We can implicate masculinity here, but we must not situate masculinity as centrally informing non-participation (cf Archer et al., 2001). Certainly, at the aggregate level of participation rates, and on the basis of my informants' responses, working-class masculinity has not simply been going through a process of catching up with the demands of the globalised, technology-led world (Marks, 2003). The gendered notion that 'women learn and men earn' (McGivney, 2004) was not conveyed by my respondents, but there was a strong sense in the interviews that HE pathways made little sense relative to upward social mobility. This is construed by interviewees as a rational decision, one that is not – in their understanding – gendered. Rather than seeing university non-participation as a form of masculine resistance perpetuating a counter-culture, it seems more pertinent to characterise these young men's ambivalence through the lens of 'partial penetration' as outlined by Willis (1977). Whereas Willis identified partial penetration of the myths of meritocracy as leading to an outward rejection of education and hyper-masculine performance among the schoolboys he studied, here the HE route is understood as being a risk at both the psychic and economic levels. This chimes with Bourdieu's (1990: 64) argument that aspirations are shaped by 'the accessible and the inaccessible', such that here the respondents' pessimism about HE participation as a route to higher-wage employment leads them to see it as both undesirable and inaccessible (see also Bourdieu & Passeron, 1990).

Nonetheless, the influence of a hegemonic ideal is observable, as the prescribed track for young men is one that prioritises achievable economic returns, and minimises related risks. This was never expressed explicitly, but it was underscored by the various ways they rationalised their rejection of HE. Yet even here we must avoid implicating working-class masculinity as problematic, per se. The men still operate along the lines of the ideal self-responsible, neoliberal subject, making good of the skills and qualifications they have whilst striving to maximise earnings. In other research this has been aligned with the need to sustain a masculine identity premised on being a wage-earner or 'breadwinner' (Archer et al., 2001; Connell, 1995). The work undertaken here suggests this is a conceptual overstretch. However, the orthodox masculine need to be a breadwinner is not central to these young men's lives; there is simply a recognition that one must earn to make one's way, to live, survive or thrive in the capitalist world. Similarly, in my participants' accounts there is no sign of an 'unwillingness to "give up" locally powerful masculine identities and enter into an arena of middle-class men's power' (Archer et al., 2001: 445). The answer to the question about why relatively fewer working-class boys engage in HE continues to be elusive, but the assumed rejection of the education system as being a feminised one is a vast oversimplification. Instead, greater attention must be paid to how 'men's disadvantaged positions within interconnecting power relations renders participation a less feasible and realistic route' (ibid.: 446).

Conclusion

Entering the new millennium, Louise Archer and colleagues (2001: 433) reminded us that many academics have engaged with 'public and media concerns that young working-class men are "anti-school", or prevented from achieving by their "laddish culture" [...] and their male peer group'. They also confirmed that, as suggested in Chapter 2, academic work has often conceptualised working-class boys as:

> highly resistant to schooling, associating education with 'femininity' and 'middle-classness' and as incompatible with working-class discourses of 'hard' masculinity. Instead, it has been suggested that male peer groups determine and deride softness and effeminacy and 'reward the macho qualities of being cool, hard and risk taking'.
>
> (Archer et al., 2001: 33)

The ways academics conceptualise working-class masculinity can be especially problematic. There are exceptional and deeply sympathetic portrayals of working-class young men's engagement with and negotiation of education spaces, notably Diane Reay's (2002) 'Shaun's Story' and Nicola Ingram's (2009, 2018) writing on working-class boys' schooling success. Yet, even academic work that attempts to disrupt negative media portrayals tends to produce a narrative of education as a key production site of (often problematic, or at the very least premised on resistance and counter-cultural practice) classed masculinities.

Power in the educational setting may be acquired either through achievement and subscribing to institutional values, or by attempting to obtain alternative forms of power through resistance, detachment and anti-school positioning (Keddie, 2007). However, this chapter shows that the pursuit of power is not necessarily central to working-class young men's lives. As per Brown (1987), for the most part my participants 'just got on with it', or practised non-dominance characteristics symptomatic of working-class traditions (Stahl, 2015). Therefore, it is my view that boys' and young men's pursuit of power is given disproportionate attention in research on the school environment, reinforcing short-sighted theorisations of working-class boys and men – and by extension working-class masculinity – as the principal problematic.

These young men's stories did not support the argument that they are especially influenced by Connell's process of hegemonic masculinity. There was some preference for sports over and above academic work but, for the most part, the young men enacted masculinities that are neither hegemonic nor necessarily marginalised. It is possible they benefited from the operation of power that facilitates men's profiting from a gender dividend, and they may have even exercised power in relations with female students (this did not emerge in the data). They certainly did not talk about challenging hegemonic norms. Yet, the participants expressed little support for hegemonic ideals or admiration for boys espousing them, and very little resistance to education. While this aligns with Connell's (1996: 220) position that 'the majority of boys learn to negotiate school discipline with only a little friction', it also undermines claims that boys need to 'acquire or retain status, mark difference and to gain pleasure', such that violence, sexual harassment, toughness, aggression and spectacular disengagement 'becomes central to the making of masculinity when boys lack other resources for gaining these ends' (ibid.).

The Bourdieusian reading of class was used to explain why many young men do not reject education entirely, but invoke an alienated-instrumentalist orientation. The working-class habitus is often posited as central in working-class boys' resistant or disengaged attitudes. However, despite 'facing an educational competition they cannot win' (Reay, 2009: 27), the habitus I observed in the data underscored that alienated-instrumentalist attitudes and middle-ground orientations are essential parts of working-class young men's 'unconscious schemes of perception and appreciation' (Bourdieu, 2001: 5). Accordingly, while the habitus celebrated within the school context was incompatible with their working-class habitus, the young men in my study by and large simply got on with their compulsory schooling, neither hugely excelling, nor overtly failing.

Similar messages prevail beyond compulsory schooling. Despite clear connections to masculine subject choices, theories of masculinity largely cannot capture an overwhelmingly normative attitude towards post-compulsory education participation. Bourdieu's notion of habitus, combined with his lesser-used concepts of *doxa, illusio* and *social gravity*, help in analysing the power of these norms. Post-compulsory participation, for at least some time, was an embedded idea, a *doxic* norm: something done 'by people like them' that made sense as an artefact of their habitus.

Despite being engaged in the educational process, though, this middle-ground attachment started unravelling for some during their post-compulsory years. Increasing anxieties around employment and finances saw the prospect of earning rather than learning, and the ways in which specific courses might enhance earning in various sectors, come to the fore. This is most evident in the disinterest in pursuing HE, which, even for those with the requisite qualification profile, was seen in wholly instrumental terms – most often as a risky pathway that might harm earning potential. This attachment to earnings could be assumed as imbricated with traditional working-class masculine ideals. Yet the next two chapters will show this assumption to be unfounded. While theories of masculinity can contribute to understanding the gap in attainment between working-class boys/men and girls/women, gender has a smaller impact than social class or race.

My last point is that we should theorise young men's educational histories and contemporary perceptions in ways that emphasize diversity among populations. The study's participants belong to a specific generation who grew up under certain economic, social and political conditions, and they are members of the working class. However, generational structures are marked by diversity and heterogeneity. This can be addressed through Mannheim's (1952) concept of 'generational units'; i.e. the different groups within a generation who 'work up the material of their common experiences in different and specific ways' (Mannheim, 1952: 304). These 'units' should not be read as distinctions on the basis of class (Mannheim, 1952), although it is not uncommon for this to be the case (France & Roberts, 2015). Class, like generation, may present researchers with a method for analysing differences between groups, but the lived reality, revealed at the level of qualitative research, is that working-class men's experiences are heterogenous. Here, too, we can perhaps think of 'units' or sections of the working class as different to one another. However, the crucial point is that we need to remain wary of overstatement and error in what we *perceive* to be modal patterns among a class or generation.

My study's participants are part of a generation with higher university participation rates and which is better qualified than the generations of young people preceding them. These signifiers, though, are indicative of a (significant) generational minority. Relatedly, a lack of HE participation among my sample and working-class men generally does not point to disinterest and disengagement. So, even in similar class locations, different articulations of masculinity can emerge. Unfortunately, reductive accounts of a particular and negative young working-class masculinity remain stubbornly influential.

Notes

1 For details see http://dera.ioe.ac.uk/27199/1/CDP-2016-0151.pdf
2 The UK qualification exam for each subject, undertaken by 16-year-old secondary school students.
3 Denotes 'Advanced-level' qualifications in the UK. These are generally required for university entry, and are achieved through exams in the final two years of secondary education.
4 Vocational training, not university.
5 Business and Technology Education Council vocational diploma.
6 Advanced Subsidiary (AS) levels are both a stand-alone qualification and a marker of the end of the first year of A-levels.
7 UCAS refers to the Universities and Colleges Admissions Service, the organisation that operates the application process for British universities. Here, Adam is referring to filling out the application form as 'doing a UCAS'.

References

Abrahams, J., & Ingram, N. (2013). The chameleon habitus: Exploring local students' negotiations of multiple fields. *Sociological Research Online*, 18(4), 1–14.

Anderson, E. (2009). *Inclusive masculinity: The changing nature of masculinities*. New York: Routledge.

Archer, L., Pratt, S., & Phillips, D. (2001). Working-class Men's Constructions of Masculinity and Negotiations of (Non)Participation in Higher Education. *Gender and Education*, 13(4), 431–449.

Archer, L., & Yamashita, H. (2003). Theorising Inner-city Masculinities: 'Race', class, gender and education. *Gender and Education*, 15(2), 115–132.

Ashley, M. (2009). Time to confront Willis's lads with a ballet class? A case study of educational orthodoxy and white working-class boys. *British Journal of Sociology of Education*, 30(2), 179–191.

Aston, L., & Bekhradnia, B. (2003). *Demand for Graduates: A review of the economic evidence*. Higher Education Policy Institute, accessed 18 August 2017 from: www.hepi.ac.uk/downloads/3DemandforGraduatesAreviewoftheeconomicevidence.doc.

Atkinson, W., Roberts, S., & Savage, M. (2013). *Class Inequality in Austerity Britain*. Basingstoke: Palgrave.

Ball, S.J., Reay, D., & David, M. (2002). 'Ethnic Choosing': Minority ethnic students, social class and higher education choice. *Race Ethnicity and Education*, 5(4), 333–357.

Beck, U. (1992). From industrial society to the risk society: Questions of survival, social structure and ecological enlightenment. *Theory, Culture & Society*, 9(1), 97–123.

Berrington, A., Roberts, S., & Tammes, P. (2016). Educational aspirations among UK Young Teenagers: Exploring the role of gender, class and ethnicity. *British Educational Research Journal*, 42(5), 729–755.

Bourdieu, P. (1977). *Outline of a Theory of Practice*. Cambridge: Cambridge University Press.

Bourdieu, P. (1990). *The logic of practice*. Redwood, CA: Stanford University Press.

Bourdieu, P. (1998). *On Television*. New York: The New Press.

Bourdieu, P. (2001). *Masculine domination*. Redwood, CA: Stanford University Press.

Bourdieu, P., & Passeron, J.C. (1990). *Reproduction in education, society and culture*. Sage: London.

Bradley, H., & Ingram, N. (2013). Banking on the future: Choices, aspirations and economic hardship in working-class student experience, in *Class inequality in austerity Britain*. London: Palgrave Macmillan, pp. 51–69.

Brown, P. (1987). *Schooling ordinary kids; inequality, unemployment and the new vocationalism*. London: Tavistock.

Brown, P. (1990). The 'third wave': Education and the ideology of parentocracy. *British Journal of Sociology of Education*, 11(1), 65–86.

Callender, C. (2009). *Awareness, take-up and impact of institutional bursaries and scholarships in England: Summary and recommendations*. Bristol: Office for Fair Access.

Callender, C., & Mason, G. (2017). Does Student Loan Debt Deter Higher Education Participation? New Evidence from England. *The ANNALS of the American Academy of Political and Social Science*, 671(1), 20–48.

Cassen, R., & Kingdon, G. (2007). *Tackling low educational achievement*. Joseph Rowntree Foundation.

Connell, R.W. (1995). *Masculinities*. Cambridge: Polity Press.

Connell, R.W. (1996). Teaching the boys: New research on masculinity, and gender strategies for schools. *Teachers College Record*, 98(2), 206–235.

Connolly, P. (2004). *Boys and schooling in the early years*. London: Routledge.

Crawford, C., & Greaves, E. (2015). *Socio-economic, ethnic and gender differences in HE participation*. Accessed 29 July 2017 from: www.gov.uk/government/uploads/system/uploads/attachment_data/file/474273/BIS-15-85-socio-economic-ethnic-and-gender-differences.pdf.

Crozier, G., Reay, D., & James, D. (2011). Making it work for their children: White middle-class parents and working-class schools. *International Studies in Sociology of Education*, 21(3), 199–216.

Department for Children, Schools and Families (DCSF) (2008). *Departmental Report, May 2008.* London: HMSO. http://webarchive.nationalarchives.gov.uk/20130 321050457/https://www.education.gov.uk/publications/eOrderingDownload/DCSF-AnnualReport-08.pdf.

Department for Education (2016). *Revised GCSE and equivalent results in England: 2015 to 2016.* ONS. www.gov.uk/government/statistics/revised-gcse-and-equivalen t-results-in-england-2015-to-2016.

France, A. (2007). *Understanding youth in late modernity.* London: McGraw-Hill Education (UK).

France, A. (2016). *Understanding youth in the global economic crisis.* Bristol: Policy Press.

France, A., & Roberts, S. (2015). The problem of social generations: A critique of the new emerging orthodoxy in youth studies. *Journal of Youth Studies,* 18(2), 215–230.

France A., & Roberts, S. (2017). *Youth and social class.* Basingstoke: Palgrave.

Friedman, S. (2016). Habitus clivé and the emotional imprint of social mobility. *The Sociological Review,* 64(1), 129–147.

Frosh, S., Phoenix, A., & Pattman, R. (2002). *Young masculinities: Understanding boys in contemporary society.* London: Palgrave Macmillan.

Furlong, A., & Cartmel, F. (2007). *Young people and social change.* London: McGraw-Hill Education (UK).

Giddens, A. (1991). *Modernity and Self-identity: Self and Society in the Late Modern Age.* Cambridge: Polity.

Gorard, S., Smith, E., May, H., Thomas, L., Adnett, N., & Slack, K. (2006). *Review of widening participation research: Addressing the barriers to participation in higher education.* Bristol: HEFCE.

Hage, G. (2012). Critical anthropological thought and the radical political imaginary today. *Critique of Anthropology,* 32(3), 285–308.

Harrison, N., Baxter, A., & Hatt, S. (2007). From opportunity to OFFA: The implementation of discretionary bursaries and their impact on student finance, academic success and institutional attachment. *Journal of Access Policy and Practice,* 5(1), 3–21.

Harrison, N., & Hatt, S. (2012). Expensive and failing? The role of student bursaries in widening participation and fair access in England. *Studies in Higher Education,* 37(6), 695–712.

Haywood, C., & Mac an Ghaill, M. (2013). *Education and masculinities: Social, cultural and global transformations.* London: Routledge.

Heath, S., Brooks, R., Cleaver, E., & Ireland, E. (2009). *Researching young people's lives.* London: Sage.

Heath, S., Fuller, A., & Paton, K. (2008). Network-based ambivalence and educational decision-making: A case study of 'non-participation' in higher education. *Research Papers in Education,* 23(2), 219–229.

Heidegren, C., & Lundberg, H. (2010). Towards a sociology of philosophy. *Acta Sociologica,* 53(1), 3–18.

Hodkinson, P. (1998). Career decision making and the transition from school to work. *Bourdieu and Education: Acts of Practical Theory,* 89–104.

Hodkinson, P., Hodkinson, H., & Sparkes, A.C. (2013). *Triumphs and tears: Young people, markets, and the transition from school to work.* London: Routledge.

Ingram, N. (2009). Working-class boys, educational success and the misrecognition of working-class culture. *British Journal of Sociology of Education,* 30(4), 421–434.

Ingram, N. (2018). *Working-Class Boys and Educational Success: Teenage Identities, Masculinity and Urban Schooling.* Basingstoke: Palgrave Macmillan.

Ingram, N., & Abrahams, J. (2015). Stepping outside of oneself: How a cleft-habitus can lead to greater reflexivity through occupying 'the third space', in *Bourdieu: The Next Generation*. New York: Routledge.

Jackson, D. (2003). Beyond one-dimensional models of masculinity: A life-course perspective on the processes of becoming masculine. *Auto/Biography*, 11(1), 71–87.

Jenkins, R. (1983). *Lads, citizens, and ordinary kids: Working-class youth life-styles in Belfast*. London: Routledge.

Jones, S., & Myhill, D. (2004). 'Troublesome boys' and 'compliant girls': Gender identity and perceptions of achievement and underachievement. *British Journal of Sociology of Education*, 25(5), 547–561.

Keddie, A. (2007). Games of subversion and sabotage: Issues of power, masculinity, class, rurality and schooling. *British Journal of Sociology of Education*, 28(2), 181–194.

Lareau, A. (2003). *Unequal childhoods: Race, class, and family life*. Berkeley, CA: University of California Press. Google Scholar.

Mac an Ghaill, M. (1994). *The Making of Men: Masculinities, Sexualities and Schooling*. Buckingham: Open University Press.

MacDonald, R., & Marsh, J. (2005). *Disconnected Youth?: Growing up in Britain's Poor in Neighbourhoods*. Springer.

Mannheim, K. (1952). The Problem of Generations, in P. Kecskemeti, *Essays on the Sociology of Knowledge: Collected Works*, 5. New York: Routledge, pp. 276–322.

Marks, A. (2003). Welcome to the new ambivalence: Reflections on the historical and current cultural antagonism between the working class male and higher education. *British Journal of Sociology of Education*, 24(1), 83–93.

McCormack, M. (2011). The declining significance of homohysteria for male students in three sixth forms in the south of England. *British Educational Research Journal*, 37(2), 337–353.

McDowell, L. (2003). *Redundant masculinities?: Employment change and white working class youth*. London: John Wiley.

McGivney, V. (1999). *Excluded Men: Men Who are Missing from Education and Training*. Leicester: National Institute of Adult Continuing Education.

McGivney, V. (2004). *Men earn, women learn: Bridging the gender divide in adult education and training*. NIACE.

Nayak, A. (2006). Displaced masculinities: Chavs, youth and class in the post-industrial city. *Sociology*, 40(5), 813–831.

O'Donnell, M., & Sharpe, S. (2000). *Uncertain masculinities: Youth, ethnicity, and class in contemporary Britain*. London: Psychology Press.

Quinn, J., Thomas, L., Slack, K., Casey, L., Thexton, W., & Noble, J. (2006). Lifting the hood: Lifelong learning and young, white, provincial working-class masculinities. *British Educational Research Journal*, 32(5), 735–750.

Reay, D. (2002). Shaun's story: Troubling discourses of white working-class masculinities. *Gender and Education*, 14(3), 221–234.

Reay, D. (2006). 'Unruly Places': Inner-city Comprehensives, Middle-class Imaginaries and Working-class Children. *Urban Studies*, 44(7), 1191–1201.

Reay, D. (2009). Making sense of white working class educational underachievement, in K.P. Sveinsson (Ed.), *Who cares about the white working class?* London: Runnymede Perspectives, pp. 22–27.

Reay, D. (2012). *Researching class in higher education*. British Educational Research Association.

Reay, D. (2017). *Miseducation: Inequality, Education and the Working Classes*. Policy Press.

Reay, D., & Ball, S.J. (1998). 'Making their Minds Up': Family dynamics of school choice. *British Educational Research Journal*, 24(4), 431–448.

Reay, D., Davies, J., David, M., & Ball, S.J. (2001). Choices of degree or degrees of choice? Class, 'race' and the higher education choice process. *Sociology*, 35(4), 855–874.

Roberts, S. (2011). Beyond 'NEET' and 'tidy' pathways: Considering the 'missing middle' of youth transition studies. *Journal of Youth Studies*, 14(1), 21–39.

Roberts, S. (2012). 'I just got on with it': The educational experiences of ordinary, yet overlooked, boys. *British Journal of Sociology of Education*, 33(2), 203–221.

Roberts, S., & Evans, S. (2013). 'Aspirations' and Imagined Futures: The Im/possibilities for Britain's Young Working Class, in *Class inequality in austerity Britain*. London: Palgrave Macmillan, pp. 70–89.

Rose, N. (1999). *Powers of freedom: Reframing political thought*. Cambridge: Cambridge University Press.

Sergeant, H. (2009). *Wasted: The betrayal of white working-class and black Caribbean boys* [online], available at www.cps.org.uk/publications/wasted-the-betrayal-of-white-working-class-and-black-carribean-boys/

Skeggs, B. (1997). *Formations of class and gender*. London: Sage.

Stahl, G. (2015). *Identity, Neoliberalism and Aspiration: Educating white working-class boys*. London: Routledge.

Thompson, J., & Bekhradnia, B. (2009). *Male and female participation and progression in Higher Education: Further analysis*. HEPI.

Thomson, R., Bell, R., Holland, J., Henderson, S., McGrellis, S., & Sharpe, S. (2002). Critical moments: Choice, chance and opportunity in young people's narratives of transition. *Sociology*, 36(2), 335–354.

Threadgold, S. (2017). *Youth, Class and Everyday Struggles*. New York: Routledge.

Walkerdine, V., Lucey, H., & Melody, J. (2001). *Growing up girl: Psycho-social explorations of gender and class*. Palgrave.

Ward, M. (2015). *From labouring to learning: Working-class masculinities, education and de-industrialization*. London: Springer.

Willis, P.E. (1977). *Learning to labor: How working class kids get working class jobs*. New York: Columbia University Press.

Woodman, D. (2009). The mysterious case of the pervasive choice biography: Ulrich Beck, structure/agency, and the middling state of theory in the sociology of youth. *Journal of Youth Studies*, 12(3), 243–256.

Wyn, J., & Dwyer, P. (1999). New directions in research on youth in transition. *Journal of Youth Studies*, 2(1), 5–21.

6 Young working-class men navigating the precarious world of work

Identity in and out of the labour market

Introduction

This is the first of three chapters looking at more dynamic data. In this case, the chapter considers the participants' labour market biographies and explores how various employment orientations, attitudes and situations have changed or stayed the same between the participants' first interviews at ages 18–24 and their final interviews at ages 24–30. A central question the chapter addresses is what kinds of implications do the challenges and changes during this period have upon the construction of an appropriate, socially approved manhood?

As per Chapter 2, since the 1970s, industrialised economies have evolved from being reliant on manufacturing and heavy industry, to becoming dominated by service sector employment. Previously, the male breadwinner model of the family and its concomitant gendered division of labour were central to notions of working-class masculinity. Paid work was *the* primary location for constructing a masculine identity and 'the main orientation point, in reference to which all other pursuits could be planned and ordered' (Bauman, 1998: 17). Employment usually required the demonstration of physical toughness, alongside solidarity against managers. Contrastingly, contemporary interactive service jobs require the performance of 'emotional labour' (Hochschild, 1983): that is, management of emotions, self-presentation congruent with employers' expectations, and efforts at inducing an emotional state in customers. Such behaviours have been theorised to be antithetical to normative working-class and/or protest masculinity (Connell, 1995), and are often argued to make service work unattractive to young men (Leidner, 1993; McDowell, 2003; Nixon, 2009). Beyond the changing *content* of work, the contemporary post-Fordist economy, underpinned by a neoliberal political consensus that facilitates ever increased flexibilisation, presents working-class people with significant challenges in respect of the *relations* of work: nowadays, 'the service-sector jobs that young men and women can realistically obtain ... are routine, subservient, low-paid and often insecure' (Gunter & Watt, 2009: 527; see Roberts, 2013, for further critique).

Some research indicates that men reject involvement in service work, even when unemployed (e.g. Lindsay & McQuaid, 2004; Nixon, 2009). Yet, despite contrary assertions that service work, subsequent customer interaction, and attendant deference all make entry-level service sector roles unpalatable, 'many working-class men find themselves in such jobs' (Lupton, 2006: 117). This is even more likely the case for *young* working-class men. Academic writing on this matter has often suggested that men in such positions adopt strategies to ensure their masculine identities are not compromised (e.g. Bagilhole & Cross, 2006; Lupton, 2006; Simpson, 2004), or opt for more obviously masculine roles in warehousing, distribution or 'shelf stacking' over jobs that necessitate customer interaction (Milkman, 1997). This is because embodied masculinity, physically working hard and 'grafting', has been the particular form of labour that working-class men have used to establish a positive and respectable discursive position in relation to women and middle-class men (McDowell, 2003; Nixon, 2009).

These ideas were core to my exploration of the young men's experiences of and aspiration for work, and the first section of the chapter features their responses at the time of their first interview in 2009, when all 24 men were employed in front-line, customer-facing service work. The chapter's first key message is that these young working-class men are not hostage to the traditional predispositions held by their counterparts from previous generations. They embrace service work and its attendant demands, and do not present a masculinity that is out of step with the contemporary economy; rather, such attitudes represent a 'new normal' for young working-class men. I explain their ease with the demands of service work is symptomatic of, in Bourdieu's terms, a social practice and as such is evidence of a coherent working-class masculine habitus. Their capacity for emotional labour has implications for men's emotions in other domains. In the second part of the chapter, the participants' employment biographies over the seven years of the study are explored. Here I emphasise that, even after exiting service work in search of higher wages, they mostly continue to hold relatively precarious, low-paid work. Despite evidencing a more inclusive version of masculinity that is required of them to successfully integrate into the contemporary work, they are far from able to engage in significant upward social mobility. Having dispositions that make emotional labour possible, even enjoyable, does not offer a 'silver bullet' solution to unemployment, underemployment, or low-pay, low-skill work. That is to say, that even though such gender performances make them broadly more employable, it has limited effectiveness in this realm.

Despite their reluctance to describe life as a struggle, this has little to do with having to remain composed or strong in a typically masculine fashion, and instead is balanced against an understanding that uncertainty, change and minor 'turbulence' are the reality of the world of work. The chapter closes with an exploration of how uncertain employment biographies strain the relationship between paid work and identity. It shows how some of the men invest in other activities in a search for status but also to develop a coherent 'sense of self'. While often typically masculine endeavours, I argue that this is not at odds with the more inclusive masculinity shown in the acceptance of service work. These pursuits of dignity and respect that occur in relation to hobbies, charity fundraising or work on the body, are observed especially in times of economic uncertainty.

Embracing service work: the new normal for young working-class men

Given a high proportion of young men work in retail in sales or elementary service-based positions in the UK (Roberts, 2011), we might assume one of two things: masculinity does not necessarily pose a threat to engaging with such employment, or men in these jobs have little other choice and consequently perform them under duress, perhaps seeking to reconstitute their roles to re-cast them in more appropriately masculine terms. These two positions can interweave in some ways, resulting in what Bradley (1993: 17) called 'infiltration', where 'a few individual men enter a women's occupation, sometimes for reasons of personal inclination, sometimes because of lack of other employment opportunities'. The infiltration hypothesis speaks to a complexity of agency and structural issues, but largely implicates men's motives as being against the interests of women, such that 'the occupation will probably remain defined as a largely female one; but men will often exploit their masculine attributes to maximise their career chances with it, while working alongside women' (Bradley, 1993: 18). Evident in my participants' accounts was that service work is not anathema to young men, and as becomes clear below, they did not exploit 'masculine attributes' to garner better career outcomes.

When discussing the most enjoyable aspects of their job, they emphasised that *customer interaction was central* to their employment satisfaction, as demonstrated here:

DAMIAN: ... it's mainly the interaction with customers, that's why retail is quite keen for me, it's like, you know, I like talking to people.
ADAM: If you have a nice customer and you can have a good chat and you help them buy what they want, I enjoy that and I enjoy talking to people. Like, we got some regulars and I'll have a chat with them, I enjoy the banter if they remember who you are.
CARL: I like having conversations with the customers and everything. I find it quite easy to just get a flowing conversation going, especially with older ladies as well, they laugh at anything. So it is quite easy to get a conversation flowing.
MIKE: I get a buzz from helping people, especially customers ... When they go 'ah thanks' and shake your hand and say 'you've really helped me', it makes me feel so good.

In focusing on the positives of customer interactions, we might perhaps interpret an effort at demonstrating status or import, of indicating some degree of mastery in typically masculine ways. However, the crucial thing is that these were responses to a question about what they enjoy in their jobs. The very basic tenets of service work, so disparaged and feminised in previous research findings, were negotiated with ease and even held up as being among the thing they most enjoyed. This in itself is an important starting point, given the research literature emphasises that '[c]ustomer-service work is gendered as female, largely due to the emotion management content' (Pettinger, 2005: 463).

A close second to their enjoyment of engaging in emotional labour was, for many of the young men, preference to be physically busy. This time in more conventionally masculine ways, the young men often talked of enjoying 'working the stock', and customers 'making a mess' of the display often being a source of frustration. This set of attitudes sits at odds with some of the above sentiments, and somewhat reflects the emphasis made by working-class men to 'work with their hands' (Nixon, 2006, 2017). However, to re-assert, this was not a case of prioritising working with hands, but an extension of finding ways to alleviate the boredom. Being busy, one way or another, was the preference, and above all customer-focused work. The young men did, though, often make clear their dislike of working on the tills:

JAMES: [Tills are] really boring and I much rather do stock 'cos I feel like I'm actually doing something … if I work department for four hours, after two hours you can actually see what you've done.
TIM: I preferred working on the floor … there's just more to do, yeah, than when standing on a till all day. There is *actually* more to do [his emphasis].

These might reflect efforts at avoiding servitude, and perhaps we might deduce that this was in part due to the intangibility of the emotional work of the till. Indeed, these comments seem to indicate masculine preferences to be physically active and involved in labour which is visible, and so likely to be recognised and rewarded. However, after some probing this issue proved to be more complex:

TIM: No, you *can interact* with customers on the floor. You *can help* the customers on the floor. 'Cos if you're on the checkout and they ask you where something is or they ask you for your advice on something you can't leave your post and go and help them out, whereas on the floor you can show them where the thing is; you can talk to them about what they're doing [his emphasis]
CARL: … with tills you've got to socialise with customers who you are only like having five second conversations with … just to make the packing seem not so slow. But when you're out stacking you can have, like, proper conversations with customers on the shop floor and you can proper stand there for five minutes making them feel comfortable shopping in the stores.

These quotations highlight two key themes resonating across the sample. First, the respondents were very positive about customer service situations and constructed interaction as an important aspect of their work. Furthermore, they embraced more protracted interactions positively. Second, and importantly, however, the type of interaction they privileged was on 'the floor' rather than at 'the till'. This spatial differentiation perhaps reflects that the floor allows more physical and verbal freedom for the young men to not only assist customers but demonstrate their knowledge and expertise.

In some ways, these responses reflect ideas about how men reconstitute their jobs to pursue apparently more masculine activities (Leidner, 1993; Lupton, 2006; Simpson, 2004). However, importantly, these attitudes operate as a source of distancing themselves from the *routine* emotional labour of the till point, rather than emotional labour, per se. This is an important distinction that permits an understanding of both change and continuity in respect of the relationship between masculinity and labour, emotional or otherwise. Indeed, the rushed nature of interaction and heavy surveillance of scripted dialogues at the till point was the biggest frustration for the participants. This was part of their job they completed under almost Tayloristic conditions. As with Beynon's (1973) discussion of factory workers, this source of frustration was derived from a lack of autonomy, but *mainly enhanced monotony*. In essence, the till point is comparable to mechanical production lines, and, for these young men, it *prevents* a genuine service encounter. The rejection of till work, therefore, can be seen as reflective of this lack of autonomy and the presence of enhanced monotony, and the ways in which these issues are exacerbated by the need to engage in the 'lip service' emotional labour involved in quickly meeting and greeting customers. Beyond this, till work was also positioned as being physically tiresome because of a lack of physical movement, as Danny revealed: 'standing up on the till all day ain't fucking easy – it's hard work and canes your back.'

Service experiences are, of course, not exclusively pleasant. Leidner (1993: 199) suggests that service sector employment is 'incongruent with manliness' because it necessitates an ingratiating manner, taking orders and holding one's tongue. There is a great risk, then, that having to do so, to be talked down to and not defend one's own position or dignity, might evidence that one is 'not a real man' – a sentiment that, for Kimmel (2008), is fundamental to the formulation of masculinity. The prospect of encounters that lead to humiliation or a loss of face have been seen as central for the avoidance of such work (Nixon, 2009), with *older* men, especially, outrightly labelling retail and associated service employment as 'women's work' (Lindsay & McQuaid, 2004) on the basis of these very possibilities. For my participants, too, being belittled, undermined or berated was, of course, a negative experience. Yet, when these circumstances arose, the young men *did* 'hold their tongue' and instead retained an ingratiating manner:

JOHNNY: Sometimes people can be so fucking rude, to the point where you want to knock them out! But you don't, you know, you do your best to try sort stuff out. It's not like you'd go out of your way to piss someone off so, you just try and see where they are coming from and try make them happy.

LUKE: It's par for the course, really. Don't get me wrong, I hate it when people are totally unreasonable, but you have to [put up with it] … you still have to do your job.

TIM: … as soon as it happens you just deal with it in your own way. And deal with it in a responsible and respectful manner.

PAT: It's obvious that you can't just shout at people or turn your back on them. It's not nice when they have a go, but only a few of them are complete tossers.

Again, then, the service encounter is not one which the young men avoided, and even when it was negative they understood it as central to the job – an unenjoyable part, but an important part nonetheless. The capacity for emotional labour, to manage one's emotions, to empathise with customers who might even behave in hostile or unreasonable ways, is evident. There are important practical and theoretical implications here that move beyond a simple recognition that young working-class men do not reject service work as older men have been documented to do. As Cottingham (2017: 273) explains,

> Skills in effectively managing emotion – masking, pretending, or cultivating authentic feelings – also form part of one's emotional capital, itself combining with other types of economic, social, and cultural capital *within the habitus*'.

(my emphasis)

Of note here, the young men's capacity to manage their emotions corresponds with a Bourdieusian conceptualisation of cultural capital – although referred to here as emotional capital – and it can be deployed to help negotiate and succeed in the 'field' of employment (Bourdieu, 1996). Moreover, though, because of the entwining relationship between capital and habitus, the use and production of emotional capital informs the prospects of emotional literacy within the habitus, because through 'a process of embodiment, incorporation' capital becomes an 'integral part of the person' (Bourdieu, 1986: 48). This has important implications for emotions in other settings, because 'capacities to feel are also part of one's trans-situational emotional resources' (Cottingham, 2017: 273; see Chapter 8).

To clarify, I am not suggesting that the capacity for emotional labour emerges only as a result of engaging in employment where the skill is used and cultivated.[1] Rather, the young men's habitus, their set of dispositions toward service work, has its genesis in the economic and social shifts occurring since the 1980s. The scale of the transformation from a production- to a service-based economy should not be overstated, but the apex of the changing circumstances corresponds with a specific historical moment. These men entered the economy some 25 to 30 years after the process of de-industrialisation began. In the interim, they had not merely inherited older generations of men's dispositions towards and understanding of appropriately masculine work, as outlined by Willis (1977); that would be simplistic and reductive social reproduction. While service work proved a difficult transition for older men, for young men it is all they know, and as many of the participants suggested, 'all there is' in contemporary labour markets. The economic structure, every year filled with growing numbers of service-based jobs, and its attendant requirements manifest habitus through the dialectical interplay between subject and object. The result is a working-class masculine habitus that is not necessarily at odds with the contemporary service sector. And despite the influence of the family in early socialisation, the habitus will continue to adapt as a result of practical engagements with the world of work. This is all quite clear in Bourdieu's writing (see Bourdieu, 1990: 116).

Not every habitus is the same, of course, and some are more durable and unchanging than others. When researchers do find evidence of *young* men being unwilling to engage in service work on the basis of its demands for emotional labour, it is sufficient to interpret that such people's habitus is out of sync with the rules of the field. Such a habitus may have remained durable in the face of social and economic change and instead retained the character and disposition inculcated through family socialisation, as per the older reproduction of masculine norms long connected to the 'intergenerational transfers of knowledge from father to son' (Walker & Roberts, 2018: 8); yet, this is not strictly a 'working-class' masculine habitus. The large numbers of young men in frontline service work (see Roberts, 2011), along with the qualitative data here, indicate that a contemporary working-class masculine habitus is not necessarily at odds with service sector demands.

More nuance is found in wider discussions about the young men's attitudes to work. Other researchers have documented men's rejection of the idea that specific employment compromises 'maleness' (Cross & Bagilhole, 2002; Henson & Rogers, 2001). Here, participants assertively challenged the notion that their work made them subordinate or lesser in relation to typically conceived working-class masculinity. Moreover, in defending their own position they subverted traditional embodied masculinity and ascribed it a lesser status:

CHRISTIAN: There are arseholes that think that you've gotta be a labourer to feel like a man. But I mean, I don't, like, spend 8 hours at work and then check my shorts to see if I still got a cock. I know I'm a man, I don't need to drink beer and, er, treat women bad.
JEZ: People might be like 'I swear they're gay because they work in a shoe shop or a fashion shop'. And it's not the case. We just like fashion.

There's great advantages as well ... like really attractive women come in every day and you get to serve them, so that's a bonus!
JOHNNY: How isn't a job 'manly'? It's fucking stupid. Like everyone is gonna be a labourer? I know plenty of lads who labour and get laid off all the time, or don't have any work for ages. How fucking manly is that?
DAMIAN: If someone said to me 'well you have got a girl's job', it doesn't really offend me 'cos I'm like no, a job's a job and I'm doing a job that I love. It [used to be] seen as the men would go and be wearing the suits and ties and the women would be selling perfume or what not. I think it comes from that era. The way I would feel, me serving a customer, helping them out, I wouldn't feel ashamed of it because I would know that I have helped someone.

These responses might illustrate typically defensive discourses aimed at quashing accusations of feminine attributes, and they reflect a not entirely diluted masculine disposition, with their defensiveness and efforts at status building reflective of more traditional characterisations of masculinity. However, these comments were made specifically in relation to a potential attack on their identity, rather than an unprompted re-assertion of some form of masculine hierarchies. In such circumstances, rather than withdrawing the positive comments they had made about service interaction, they disparaged the undesirable elements of masculinity that 'other men' perceived to be appropriate.

Jez's remarks, which could potentially be read as homophobic and also underscoring an objectifying approach to women, need to be understood in the context of a discussion about why such jobs might be perceived as being 'unmanly'. Here we see that being subordinated by the *apparently* cultural ideal of masculinity is not inevitable (Coles, 2008). In fact, their responses make clear that the young men are not suffering from what Bourdieu calls 'misrecognition', or a form of 'hidden persuasion' (Bourdieu and Wacquant, 1992: 168) that results in social actors being unaware of, indeed, complicit in the symbolic violence they are subjected to. Rather than 'misrecognising' the arbitrariness of the established logic of the typical masculinity hierarchy, they challenge its legitimacy.

These responses might also be understood as a form of *heterosexual recuperation*, i.e. 'strategies boys use to establish and maintain heterosexual identities without invoking homophobia' (McCormack & Anderson, 2010: 846). But considering Damian's case in greater detail, we see that rather than a sense of masculinity, such work instilled an almost ungendered *sense of self*. Simultaneously, he also put into words what bubbled beneath the surface of much of what these young men talked about: things are not the same as for previous generations – they were cognisant of a change in attitudes, a change in what was acceptable, a change in what was *possible*, as per Inclusive Masculinity Theory (see Chapter 3). Their understanding of 'other lads' who might disparage them speaks to the possibility of fractures within the generation, with each set of dispositions characterising different 'generational units' among young working-class men.

It's clear that at the time of the first wave of data collection, the participants in this research did not conform to the rather fixed caricature of working-class masculinity presented by much academic work to date. These work identities and attitudes, freed in some respect from the constraints of gender 'appropriateness', were revisited with the young men seven years later when they were in their mid-twenties or early thirties.

Working-class young men's working lives

In the space of seven years, lives swerve in various directions, as was the case for the young working-class men in my study. I watched some of their trajectory unfold online via the two-year *Facebook* ethnography, but the fine-grained detail of their trajectories only became apparent through detailed accounts during their final research interview. For the most part, the common theme that united their employment experience was that it was marked by change and instability – precarious, temporary or fixed-term contract work was part of this, but 'precarity' and its consequences extend much further than contract status. Before moving to the detail of their work experiences, I start by exploring their views on the relationship between gender and service work seven years after their mostly positive articulations.

Reflections on service work, seven years later

One thing that had mostly remained the same compared to their first interviews in 2009 was a commitment to the *idea* (if not always the practice) that jobs are not/should not be thought of as gendered, and thus service work was not a threat to one's masculinity nor was unattractive on this basis. This was also supported in reverse such that rather than broadly thinking there were jobs that men can't or should not do, they held the same view that women could and should be able to do any job:

CARL: I still don't understand the question of how [a job] makes you feel like a man. It makes me feel like I'm contributing to society … There's only a handful of jobs men could do that women can't, like … sperm donor! There's no reason a woman can't do my job. Maybe it's 'cos hospitality is a more open-minded sector?

JEZ: [specifically talking about jobs in the military] No issue if [women] are able to do the job. I'm happy about [more women being in the military these days] as long as they, or anyone is able to do the job required of them it doesn't bother me at all.

Despite these positions, while some of the participants had continued in retail or front-line service employment for a few years after their first interview, all but three (Dave, Johnny, Jason) of the men had left this line of work by the time seven years had passed. In all cases where they had left, the major reason was to do with pay, and relatedly, in most cases, because of a perceived *lack of prospects* for career progress or wage rises and how this would hinder the transition to adulthood:

BOBBY: When you're a teenager and you first start working and get some money in your pocket it's alright for a few years. But you're not out there in the big bad wide world, facing the pressure, needing the money.

JEZ: I wanted a career, military was a good option. I was a supervisor at a shoe shop, but going nowhere, they pay low wages. Now in the military police, get paid better and get to see the world.

PAT: You can't get paid enough to even move out from your parents'. It's very tricky with the low wages and often part-time hours, so you look elsewhere.

These positions reflect previous research, such as Lindsay and McQuaid (2004: 303), who note that young men, 'whilst holding surprisingly few gender-related prejudices towards the service sector, consider many entry-level service jobs to be of low quality and "dead end", with few opportunities for progression'. Many of the young men were adamant that adequate pay would have meant that any job was suitable, as Bobby made clear in his instrumentalist observation:

BOBBY: If the money's alright then you just, you just take it on the chin and any job is a job. When you're going home to your own house and you're in your own car and eating your own food you think actually, yeah, it is a shit job, but look what I've got from it.

Even for those who stayed in the industry, pay was often a motivating factor to move jobs. Dave, for instance, noted that after three years with a respected retailer he took up his job in a phone shop 'because of the money, even though the holiday pay wasn't as good'. In one circumstance the pay was described as so low that it led to an instance of employee theft. As Mike explained:

MIKE: It's not something I like admitting too much, I was stealing money from them ... it wasn't much, enough to buy food at night, because I didn't have the money to eat. I was begging them for hours.

On the other hand, Johnny, who had the most stable work trajectory across the sample, had consistently remained in full-time, low-level customer-facing retail roles since his initial interview. His remarks overlap with the idea of progression, but not so much about pay:

JOHNNY: There's a lack of ambition on my part ... I'm not bothered about having a 'good' job, I don't get any job satisfaction as long as I can pay the bills ... I went from [shop] getting minimum wage, when I went into [other retailer] and they paid the city living wage which was, not a great different world, but it's more. I've got no issues, I mean me and [partner], she's on probably a few tenths more ... we can still afford to pay our mortgage off, pay the bills and have 2–300 pounds left.

As well as Johnny's self-professed lack of ambition, he had until recently lived with his mother, paying very little rent, and so was able to save a deposit to contribute to buying a house with his partner. Johnny's trajectory to a typical adult status, featuring many of the classic markers of adulthood such as stable, full-time work, a permanent partner and a home of their own, is one that many participants wanted but felt they could not achieve by remaining in the retail or hospitality sectors.

Contradicting these arguments, Tim was an outlier. He explicitly stated that low-level service work cannot offer pride or self-respect. This, however, was unrelated to subservience compromising masculinity, but instead about the relationship between identity and skill:

TIM: I don't think it's anything to do with wage personally. If I was on the same sort of wage I am now, transfer that to a supermarket, I still wouldn't work in a supermarket. The reason being is, you feel better about yourself having a specialist skill, knowing that you've put in all that time and effort learning a skill. You know that you learnt that, and you can then go along and earn money by doing it, much the same as a musician. So, yeah, for me, with all due respect, anyone can work in retail. Anyone can do retail. Being a trained skills person is something that takes years of dedication, and it's something to be proud of.

This conceptualisation of skill resonates with older versions of masculinity. For previous generations, *some* men were able to make a niche for themselves to achieve status and money that distanced them from both the cerebral requirements of middle-class work and the more mundane backbreaking features of classically working-class unskilled, manual labour (see Nixon, 2017). Interestingly, despite exiting retail about four years ago, Tim did not have a certified specialist skill, and was a glazing firm sales assistant, 'taking orders on the phone, but also helping out with technical information and eventually mostly editing the website'. He articulated his role to emphasise the dimensions that, for him, offered more status or evidenced his competitiveness. Yet, the markers of status most evident in Tim's account revolved around conceptions of *adulthood*, much more so than masculinity:

TIM: It was attractive because it was an office job, it wasn't retail. It was a job which was grown up. Proper Monday to Friday, full-time job, and it was my first ever full-time job, I felt so proud of myself. Lots people applied for it. And, I got the job, felt absolutely fantastic about it.

Going against the grain of the 'emerging adulthood' (Arnett, 2007) literature that suggests contemporary young people no longer valorise traditional markers of adulthood, Tim clearly characterised full-time work as an indicator of 'growing up'. He also made plain that he felt the job he was doing was not gendered:

TIM: The world we live in, it's not new that men and women can do the same job, it's been going on for decades. I didn't see any sort of sexuality [meaning gender] defining information in that role.

Despite Tim's story, for the majority of the young men, the motivation to exit front-line service work was pursuit of better income to finance the transition to adulthood independence. The context in which they pursued those avenues was the aftermath of the global financial crisis (GFC). This left the UK in economic recession until 2013, having a pronounced effect on the employment prospects of young people (France, 2016), and young men in particular (Lanning & Rudiger, 2012; McDowell et al., 2014), as described below.

Work trajectories in the aftermath of the GFC

As mentioned, seven years after the initial data collection, three of the 14 remaining participants stayed in front-line service work. Only one, Johnny, was employed in a conventionally full-time sales assistant role. Jason was predominantly now a stay-at-home dad (see Chapter 7), but worked part time in the evening and weekends as a sales assistant in a craft beer store, and Dave worked as an assistant manager in a small, independent mobile phone shop. Among the other men, their occupations at the time of the final interview included the military police, the UK border force, window sales, delivery driving, phone sales, manual work on the Underground network, 'computer fixing' and even mobile disc jockeying (DJ). As well as Jason, two others were also stay-at-home dads, securing part-time income in various ways.

Arriving at their present work destination had, for the most part, been a journey characterised by moving between paid work of various kinds, or 'churning' from low-paying jobs to occasional short stints of unemployment, and back into mostly low-paid jobs (see Shildrick et al., 2012). Only Johnny, who had just three job changes, but always sideways moves to very slightly better-paid retail jobs, had maintained an observable coherent narrative during this period. The lack of predictability of employment trajectories for all of the other young men seemingly locates them as being part of what Standing (2011) calls the 'precariat' – a social class in the making that is characterised by chronic job uncertainty and insecurity. I do not find this term especially useful as it often serves as a catchall for all those who experience seemingly precarious working conditions, implicating a rising tide of inequality for all. The access to a variety of social, cultural and economic capitals, though, can mediate the experience of precariousness, such that some people may even find it desirable or advantageous to have fixed-term work, especially in the context of greater mobility. It is these capitals, and the specific working-class context, that I have found interesting in understanding how the young men have navigated the precarious world of working-class employment in the last seven years.

The GFC was recognised by some interviewees as an explicit driver of job change – through being made redundant, for example – whilst others thought it hardly to have had any impact, explaining 'that jobs come and go anyway' (Billy). Here, we are reminded that precariousness has long been a feature of working-class lives under capitalism, something recognised long ago by both Marx and Engels (see Jona & Foster, 2016 for a brief overview). Despite this reality, the participants braved the prospect of difficult labour markets with surprisingly positive approaches. Rather than complaining, they instead described 'getting by' as central to their lives – making a virtue of necessity, as Bourdieu would have it. This approach, though, might perhaps have been facilitated by the fact that the young men had avoided extended periods of long-term unemployment, which has been shown to damage self-confidence and create a perpetual cycle of labour market marginalisation (Gregg, 2001; Cockx & Picchio, 2013). Here I offer some detailed case studies to explore the decisions made and job opportunities that came the young men's way.

'Going to get a career': Gavin, Peter, Jez

While some participants left their front-line service roles in pursuit of higher wages, this was most often thought about in terms of getting a better job. Gavin, Peter and Jez, however, all made sense of this in terms of wanting to establish a career. Stability, along with prospects for progress *as well as* better wages were therefore clear motivations for these three men, with these three ideals being seen as important for one day having any possibility for having a family. This perhaps speaks to the perceived 'mission' of working-class masculinity to 'be a provider of material resources' for family (Simpson et al., 2016: 86), though their motivations were expressed slightly differently (see Chapter 7 for fuller account of the subtleties of the provider rhetoric). Jez said he felt in a very general sense that a few years in retail left him feeling like he was going nowhere financially and unable to move out from his mother's home, and thus unlikely to be able to one day have a family; the military made sense for him in terms of saving money and being able to move out. Peter explained how his parents' life served as a role model, and that his dad had encouraged him to follow in his footsteps as a customs officer, and especially as 'part-time work in a supermarket meant [he] would never be able to start a family of [his] own'. He ultimately was accepted into the customs and excise assistant officer training programme in 2014. The significance of social capital must be recognised here. Jez's own motivation had pushed him to join the forces, but for Peter the possibility of customs as a career was on his horizon because of his dad's active protestations that the career was suitable, and the father's encouragement, advice and contacts – that is, social capital – ensured Peter was given an opportunity for an interview.

In contrast, Gavin's motivation for a course of action was somewhat different. Having already left his retail job after being made redundant because of the effects of the GFC, Gavin had taken up a job as a delivery driver for a distribution centre. In preparation for the arrival of his baby daughter in 2010 (see Chapter 8 for full details), Gavin decided to train himself for and eventually pass a Microsoft A+ test, that would certify him to take up jobs as an IT delivery analyst, or as he said, 'mostly helping fixing computers and systems'. This outcome was rooted in rather ironic and serendipitous origins:

GAVIN: I was in a pub [at age 16] and a guy sold me a copy of the *Matrix Revolutions* about 5 months before it was due to be released, I knew nothing about computers but needed one to watch the film so I bought a cheap one, figured out how to play the film ... [This] impressed me greatly, so from there I started to play with the machine more, over the years I learnt how to rebuild it and reinstall the operating system, then bought all the bits and built my own then I built, a mail server installed and file sharing etc., then I built a network. I did a simple online course and passed the Microsoft A+ exam, at the time I was working at [distribution firm] after being made redundant from [shop], hated the job but it was better than the dole.

Gavin explain that 'half drunk' he saw a job online and felt brave enough to apply. As well as feeling 'brave' he was also determined to give himself a chance at such work because of the pending arrival of his daughter:

GAVIN: through all of this going to get a career, the thing that drove me most was what will that little girl think of me ..., what sort of an example would I be setting for her. I remember thinking back comments made by friends regarding their parents not being able to provide the means for them to have all the things we deemed so important in our little social groups, I was determined not, right or wrong, to be a parent that couldn't provide the little important things.

In each case, there was a strong investment in the idea of 'family' such that it shaped what was possible and desirable. However, among these seemingly positive career-making approaches, job insecurity is present. Gavin, for instance, while not having any protracted periods of unemployment, had been made redundant twice in the six years he had held his qualification. This brings me to cases that exemplify a more obvious instability and its associated consequences.

The following cases, which characterise the majority of the sample, are united by a context of immediate financial pressures and turbulent employment biographies. As seemingly manageable 'bumps in the road' on their employment journey, this *turbulence* was not akin to the more deleterious impacts of regularly cycling in and out of temporary/agency work and unemployment (e.g. Furlong & Cartmel, 2004; Shildrick et al., 2012). Nonetheless, these were still relatively precarious working lives, even if a few rungs above those at the very bottom of the social and economic ladder. Shifts in work circumstances punctuated the narratives, from moving jobs, to becoming *under*employed, to becoming unemployed. Even after periods of apparent stability, it is uncertainty that marks their trajectories as the most observable pattern to date.

'What you doing for work, now?' – Bobby, Christian

Employment biographies for most of the working-class young men I spoke to and observed in my research were heavily focused on '*now*'. This is a small but important word that provides tremendous insight into the temporal and discontinuous nature of working-class work. The young men often wanted to maintain their current or even previous jobs, but there was a sense that employment change was the expected feature. This often became crystallised in discussions with the young men about their friends, especially those they hadn't spoken to recently. Several young men used the example of asking, in such circumstances, 'what you doing for work, now?'. This implicates the significance of work for identity. The only continuity in many of the accounts was both the *expectation* and *normalisation* of discontinuity – in the form of someone working in a different job than they had previously held – and that was reflected in their own working lives. Bobby's first reflection on the last seven years of his employment experiences captures this well (my emphasis in italics):

BOBBY: I've always been really *good at finding work* ... [but] there's still so much stress when you're in-between jobs and driving round and your car's got no petrol and you think, shit what am I going to do ... *it always seems to happen when you've got no money* and like you just take it for granted *when you've got money.*

The prospect of often *finding work* and the understanding that work can be taken away at any moment are born from personal experience (and observation of other friends and family). Paradoxically, though, this never prevented Bobby from taking work for granted. He explained that this was because 'you hope it lasts as long as possible, and usually [joblessness] comes outta nowhere'. This is made clear when considering the job changes he had undertaken since 2009.

By the end of 2010, Bobby had left service work for a night job laying railway tracks. While this was better pay, and off the books for the first two months thus allowing him to claim benefits for six weeks, it came to a slow end after about a year, with his hours being gradually reduced. The pay had allowed him to rent his friend's house, but this turned sour after he fell behind on his rent; a result of declining income, but also, he admitted, from spending too much money on gambling in efforts to plug the gap from insufficient wages. Bobby then moved to his parents' home and was unemployed for about six weeks, before taking up a job as a delivery driver. This was both a blessing and a curse. Unable to afford to move out, he stayed with his parents, but had to sleep in their shed:

BOBBY: it was either like go and stay at, well I didn't have anywhere else to go, it was either my car, or the shed …

SR: Wouldn't it have been easier to sleep on your mum's sofa or on the living room floor or something?

BOBBY: I was working at a erm, a delivery company and I was getting up at 4 o'clock in the morning and getting home at like 7 o'clock at night, and the last thing I wanted to do was sit with my mum and dad on the sofa for three hours waiting for them to go to bed so I could go to bed … But like, I put a little heater in there for the cold, and a TV … then I stayed there for about 18 months. When people say 'oh it's cold', you ain't been cold until you wake up with ice on your duvet where your heater's broken during the nights.

Bobby moved on from the family home to live with a partner, though this was short lived as a redundancy precipitated a relationship breakdown. A new driving job followed, again lasting for over a year, and around March 2015 he was again made redundant. Bobby said he was 'lucky' to quickly get work 'laying tracks' on the Underground network paying 'a fucking grand a week!', but no job security. When I met with him for his last interview he had recently been laid off from this job, which, as per Chapter 8, led to a bout of dishonesty with his partner as he struggled to cope with the sudden cut in his buying power. Since his last interview, he messaged to tell me he had again quickly found 'permanent' work for a fencing firm.

The permanent impermanence of Bobby's work life was reflected also in Christian's employment biography. At his first interview he had been working in an independent music and video store for a couple of years and had done other retail jobs before that. However, in 2010, he took a call centre job for an insurance company that paid better wages. He was tempted by this role because 'it was Monday to Friday and better money, which made it a bit more like a "proper" job', he explained. It was a job he didn't really enjoy, and after a year he shifted into a bar job at his favourite pub. He had done a couple of casual shifts at the bar after the manager noticed he was always there.

CHRISTIAN: I would just look at all [the attractive women] at the bar and think 'geez I would love to work here', so when they offered me a couple of casual shifts I jumped at the chance. Then the assistant manager got sacked and I asked if I could work there full time and they said yes, so I resigned from [insurance firm] the next day.

Christian positioned this job as a way out of being 'depressed on my way to work', expecting it to be short term, saying 'working behind the bar is, as much as it is a job, it is fun as well and it's a social job, so I kind of saw it as having a laugh and earning money for six months'. Rather than going back to 'more serious work or a career' so soon, Christian stayed in this job for four years. The 'serious work' was directly related to what Bourdieu (2000: 166) calls the 'search for recognition', but the 'esteem, recognition, belief and confidence of others' upon which we all rely in the symbolic economy can be found in seemingly contradictory locations. For Christian, there was a tension between the symbols implicated in having an 'unserious job', but which delivered social status in different, yet still valuable, ways:

CHRISTIAN: Part of me knew, yeah, like my dad he went to tech college and worked for British Petroleum his whole life, like a career, but the popularity you get ... I will be completely honest it was the busiest bar in town. Everyone knows ya, everyone you know, everyone likes a barman don't they? That's why I stuck it out for so long and why I enjoyed it, because it was fun. And I was good at it.

This evidence that there are different ways in which members of dominated (or working) classes can achieve status, even in the absence of the cultural capital (such as the education qualifications Christian refers to) that might facilitate access to conventionally higher status employment. Of note also is that the recognition that might be brought about by better wages and the symbolic capital of a serious office job is offset by the possibilities for the status that can be gained in bar work. The 'perceptions of others' (Bourdieu, 2000: 166) are a little more multifaceted and complex than we might first assume, and work to offer both recognition from some as well as function in ways that we are dominated by others. That is, in the wider field of power, or even in the wider 'field of men', the symbolic capital of the barman can be either positive or negative; it is not a universally positive signifier, but it did allow Christian to meet this esteem need, temporarily at least.

Christian worked his way up over the years, eventually becoming bar manager. This garnered greater status, but an eventual clash of styles with the establishment's new owner ground him down and he eventually left without notice after finishing his shift on a Saturday night. His status as bar manager at the most popular bar in town meant that 'getting bar work was easy', and within a few days he had picked up shifts and then a full-time job for the summer, from April to September, at another bar. Starting this new job,

Navigating the precarious world of work 137

Christian promised himself that he would only do it for a few months, and use the opportunity to move back into something more serious, in search as he was of more legitimate symbolic capital derived from a 'serious job'. He successfully applied to be a prison officer, and his training date coincided with the end of the sixth-month work at the bar, as he had planned.

The mechanics of recognition again come to light here, because it was his then-girlfriend's mother who initially applied for the job on his behalf. In addition, he expected the role would evidence something of his masculine character:

CHRISTIAN: Her and her mum both thought it a good job, like a respectable one, and I thought, for me to become the prison officer was kind of showing myself that I could be, that I could handle umm ... intimidating situations. I was bullied a bit when I was kid, but at the bar, I would jump straight in if there was any fights and that, breaking it up, so I thought I would be good at, because at this interview, we were all role playing and dealing with different situations and issues and I got the job.

After six weeks' training, Christian was to undertake two weeks in a prison shadowing another guard. But this all came to an abrupt end after the encounters of the first three days:

CHRISTIAN: There's so many violent occurrences. Two days before I started ... two prisoners stabbed a prison officer in the head, they'd set fire to different parts within the prison. On the Monday I'm clearing out these two prisoners' cells, then I went to the segregation unit and this bloody Polish guy ... he'd smeared shit all over himself and was screaming at everyone. I saw a prisoner getting wanked off by his girlfriend in the visiting centre [laughs] ... it's a hell hole.

Christian left on the third day and did not go back, ending up mostly unemployed for five months, save the occasional casual bar shift. At this point he was again offered the same full-time summer job in the bar he had held the year before. During the summer season, he joint-hosted a party with a friend, providing the music after realising that a DJ he had previously hired had put the software and a large collection of music onto his laptop. This changed the course of his employment trajectory.

CHRISTIAN: Everyone went nuts when the cheese came on. I thought to myself, no one does a night like this in [town] any more. So then I started 'Shameless Joy',[2] I dunno if you've seen it on my Facebook? Basically a 'cheese' disco night. I went to the biggest venue in town, and said I've got an idea for a night, I'm going to do it for charity ... it went very well, [so] I bought some equipment off a friend of mine, and started getting the odd gig. It then kind of really took off. I'd booked a load of gigs, and [seasonal employer] couldn't have a barman that couldn't work on a Friday or Saturday night, they weren't going to put up with that, so that's the decision that I had to make.

At his final interview, Christian was still a mobile DJ, and was booked in for every weekend for the foreseeable future, which would return him £500 a weekend. He noted that if there was an occasional cancellation, one paid gig per weekend every so often would still suffice to pay the 'bills', as this was his sole source of income. This was a precarious existence, of course, but he was very much focused on the immediate present in ways entirely consistent with the proximity to necessity that is a feature of working-class life (Atkinson, 2010; Skeggs & Wood, 2012). Both these case studies make clear the dynamic nature of working trajectories for young working-class men and the significance of understanding that what a participant does for work 'now' is very often time-bound.

A fundamental issue, from both practical and theoretical perspectives, is the significance of habitus. Dispositions and preferences, and the 'practical sense' the habitus develops all, of course, have bearing on how these young men negotiate the labour market, but the contemporary working-class masculine habitus is *not out of sync* with the needs of the contemporary service economy. There is much evidence in these accounts that the participants have moved on from the dispositions of previous generations of men reliant on 'independence, physicality and symbolic intimidation' (Willis, 1977: 75). Yet, inclusive masculinities do not become a capital resource that operates as a silver bullet for the policy problem of precarious labour markets and their expansion under neoliberalism (see Walker & Roberts, 2018). Crucial here is that supply-side initiatives and theories that focus on reconfiguring the dispositions of the working class fail to understand that young people, in many industrialised nations, grow up in and into economies where 'an overall shortage of jobs, not least good jobs … are the plain facts about current opportunity structures that need to be addressed, not young people making the wrong choices' (Roberts, 2009: 365).

Sources of identity beyond the sphere of employment

[F]eeling that you are a legitimate actor in the world, comes from the feeling that what you do, whether in concert with or oppositional to others, has value.
(Sennett & Cobb, 1972: 265)

Economic shifts have revealed identity to be contingent, rather than static. This is not necessarily a bad thing – as per Du Gay (1996: 3) the 'modern worker' identity had been largely 'constituted in relation to the subordination of women in the domestic sphere' – and there are now possibilities for different identity articulations. Nonetheless, the search for recognition is seen as an important human endeavour by many theorists, including Bourdieu, and the dislocation of identity from work leaves important questions, in part captured by the Sennett and Cobb quote above. Of particular interest in this last subsection of the chapter is how the young men went about constructing a legitimate identity and tried to achieve a sense of value now that paid work is no longer the *core* site of masculine identity formation.

Given some of the above data and case studies, it would plainly be wrong to propose that work no longer has any relationship with identity. Yet, it seems clear that precarious work and turbulent employment biographies are conditions in which the relationship between occupational narrative and a sense of self(-worth) might well have slackened. Indeed, Holt and Thompson (2004: 425) contend that as the chances of being a breadwinner diminish, 'men who have suffered pangs of emasculation in this new environment have sought to symbolically reaffirm their status as real men through compensatory consumption'. Significantly, consumption is argued to offer men more 'degrees of freedom in the symbolic cloak of autonomy' (ibid.: 426). The variety of sources afforded by these degrees of freedom include men's turn to food (Pascual Soler, 2018; see also Chapter 7), style (Barber, 2016; Ensmenger, 2015), home improvements (Moisio et al., 2013), or the making and use of 'man caves' (Moisio & Beruchashvili, 2016) to aid revitalisation of masculine identities.

In almost all interviews at both the start and the end of the data-collection period, participants were unified in their opposition to the statement 'my job defines me', with several offering variants of 'my job says nothing at all about me' (Luke, first interview). There were more subtle versions of this, such as Billy's admission that 'I like bikes and I work in a bike shop, but, you know, I *could* just work in [a] bike shop', and Luke's seemingly class-conscious assessment that 'why should I, or anyone, presume to enjoy the job they do?'. Alongside these disidentifications with employment, then, the men did engage in a wide variety of activity that could be interpreted as responses to Holt and Thompson's (2004) 'pangs of emasculation'. While the young men did often engage in typically masculine pursuits in their search for identity, such behaviour is more than an agentic response that signifies compensatory masculinity. Often, instead, the activities that they pursue are *perceived* as being simply, firstly, of interest. The data reveal that such activity also offers alternative avenues for pride and dignity where it is not obtainable at work.

I gained an insight into the detail of much of this activity first through *Facebook* observation, which helped build an understanding of the picture of themselves the participants curated and presented to their social media audience. I then took this broad picture into the final interview to investigate the importance of the kinds of activities that predominated. Most of the young men had some kind of detail relating to the name of their employer in observable *Facebook* profile, though sometimes these were out of date by some years, sometimes ironic or humorous, ranging from 'IT type wizardry' (Gavin) to 'Mordor' (Billy). The two men with the most stable (Johnny) and the most chaotic (Bobby) employment trajectories each had no details in the 'work' section of their profile. While not absent, paid work was rarely an issue that found its way into any participant's *Facebook* feed over the two years. When employment did appear as a subject of a status update, it was predominantly in the form of complaints about work or colleagues, or jokes about the weekend not coming soon enough. In addition, both requests for employment and alerting others to job opportunities at their place of work, as well as statuses reflecting the end or start of a new job, were occasionally evident. Only Gavin ever mentioned his employment in a way that could be perceived as evidencing his own mastery, with one or two of his detailed work-related posts being entirely incomprehensible to me given I have no knowledge of computer systems. The next closest thing related to work was Dave's occasional post about the kinds of deals on offer at his employer's mobile phone shop. In some ways this lack of work discourse may be unsurprising – social media, after all, are primarily about the *social*. The lack of discussion or any sense of pride, interest or happiness about work is an instructive reminder about the antagonistic relations of working-class work under capitalism, and further signals a disconnect between work and identity.

The *Facebook* ethnography revealed sharing practices related to a wide range of content, though these were most often geared around general social interaction or typically masculine pursuits such as sports (see Chapter 8). What I discuss here, though, is the content the men shared about themselves and particular activities they undertook and displayed with such regularity and often unmistakeable degrees of pride, that they can be understood as important identity sources. This took the form of posted photos, text-based status updates and 'check ins' at specific locations. While research shows that young adults are likely to present their 'real' self more than their ideal self and false self on *Facebook* (Michikyan et al., 2015), I used the collected data to form the basis of a conversation with the participants at their final interview.

The most observable identity work in these respects emerged in the *Facebook* activity of the three men who were stay-at-home dads. They qualitatively and quantitatively substantiated that parenting was central to the identity they performed on social media, with their posts featuring mostly their children alongside (details in Chapter 8). The fact that their parenting was evidently so central alerts that it is not necessarily the case that men need to invest in activity that 'revitalises' (Moisio & Beruchashvili, 2016) their sense of being men to construct a coherent identity. This point is worth bearing in mind, as I briefly point to some other cases where *Facebook* activity, and follow-up interviews, signalled something the participants felt was central to them as a person. Some of these are clearly more typically masculine endeavours, but mostly these are efforts at cohering a sense of self, and often a sense of feeling valuable, demonstrating autonomy. This, of course, might well be a masculine endeavour.

The first most notable identity source related to the body. In contemporary individualised western societies (Shilling, 1993), work on the body's surface is implicated in maintaining 'a coherent and viable sense of self-identity' (Gill et al., 2005: 40; Shilling, 1993). As Coffey (2016: 169) notes, this is an issue across gender categories, with men's concern for their aesthetic appearance being 'an important component of current embodiments of masculinity'. Other scholars have noted an explosion in the numbers of young British men sharing images of their worked-out bodies on social media, with Hakim (2016: 1) contending that this phenomenon 'is an embodied and mediated response to the precarious structures of feeling produced by neoliberal austerity'. He traces this to the GFC in 2008 and its attendant consequences. Men, in this reading, use the body in pursuit of being valued, perhaps having felt those 'pangs of emasculation' (Holt & Thompson, 2004).

Among my sample, only Gavin and Mike showcased their body on social media in this fashion, and only Gavin engaged in serious bodybuilding and relatively prolific photo updates of progress of getting bigger. For Gavin, this body work had started well before the period of the GFC. Indeed, he notes:

GAVIN: I suffered with 'manorexia' pretty much all of my life, pinpointing what caused it could be tricky, maybe the film stars, possibly my father and comparisons to him, I don't really know. I've *always wanted* to be bigger than I am. I started to train with a view to getting bigger but fell in love with the process, it's much more than what people think it is, anyone can lift weights and grow some, but to get beyond that becomes somewhat of an experiment in nutrition and your ability to push yourself somewhere beyond where you thought you could go ... Also I like being bigger than most people as it acts very much as a deterrent against idiots who are looking for someone to victimise.

Gavin's proud (yet perhaps unhealthy) assessment of his own longer-term efforts at body work is in keeping with the idea of emphasising hard work and autonomy among working-class men. However, it also aligns with research that shows that before the GFC men's bodies were already a site of potential value accrual through various modification practices (Gill et al., 2005; Crossley, 2005; see Coffey, 2016 for discussion). This is perhaps especially pertinent to working-class men's bodies, which were traditionally central in conveying one's class position and the associated pride derived from a body that was hard, marked, scarred and sacrificed in the labour process (see Nixon, 2017).

Additionally, Jez and Peter also emphasised a fit body as an important part of 'who I am, [and] what people think of me' (Peter). The major difference between these two and Gavin was their lack of gym-based social media posts. Both men were featured in photos that occasionally demonstrated their torsos or arms, but this was almost always incidental. In talking to them about the significance of the body, they independently talked about body confidence, rejecting the need to flamboyantly show images of their toned bodies online, but certain that 'a good body is important for me, whether I'm in the military, working in a shop or a banker' (Jez). In these ways they seemed to commit to a more general hegemonic ideal that men's bodies accrue value from being toned and hard any time during the economic cycle. As Brod wrote 30 years ago, 'the physical body ... provide[s] a concrete means of achieving and asserting manhood' (Brod, 1987: 14).

The split in the sample, and the relative absence of a commitment to the body project (Shilling, 1993) beyond these few men signals that 'normative masculinity is paradoxically disembodied' (Coffey, 2016). The paradox at work is one in which men are 'simultaneously compelled to both achieve culturally privileged male bodies at the same time that they are interpellated to maintain a functional, aloof, and distanced relationship to their bodies' (Norman, 2011: 432; cited by Coffey, 2016). The majority of the interviewees were more strongly aligned with the latter.

Some other investments outside of work are noteworthy, all of which could be theorised as efforts at control in difficult economic circumstances. First, Carl – who like many others, over the seven years, had several ups and downs in the employment market – seemed increasingly invested in European football. During the period of ethnography it became obvious that Carl had started attending football matches all around Western Europe. Every ten weeks or so, especially in 2015, he used the *Facebook* 'check in' function at airports on his way to and then at the location of football games in various international cities. Having interviewed him previously, and seen his more general discussion and statuses online, I was aware his team was a London club, so his new consumption was intriguing. While his general interest in football was a reproduction of his dad's habitus, and that of many of the friends in his community who were part of his secondary socialisation, this appeared to be something new:

CARL: ... after I got made redundant last time, they offered me another job in their sister hotel but they'd showed me a lack of respect, so dunno why, I just decided 'fuck it', and four weeks later I was in Bilbao watching a [Spanish] La Liga game. And now it's, er, just a thing that *I* do ... as often as possible.

Carl also explained that to achieve this 'hobby' he had to 'live like a recluse', affording nothing 'outside of having food and a roof over my head'. In talking about his enjoyment of the activity, and of being 'in the amazing home crowds', his motivation reflected literature that has emphasised 'the importance of football for enhancing the collective experience and offering stability in a rapidly changing environment' (Dixon, 2016: 13). In addition to enacting some form of control to do something he enjoys even in difficult financial and work circumstances, he drew on this activity as something 'different' that marked him out as an individual, bound up with some form of stability that he had created himself.

Another example of a similar theme is, again, Christian. As mentioned above, now a mobile DJ, Christian positions himself as having achieved a status that his office job could not give him. However, his dignity and his identity are wrapped more specifically in being 'that guy who does stuff for charity stuff'. Again, Christian's first foray into being a DJ was in organising a 'cheesy' pop music night called 'Shameless Joy'[2], with the door proceeds going to charity. While 'Shameless Joy' had become a staple of his new business as a DJ, as well as regular fortnightly slots at various pubs, in the two years I followed him on *Facebook*, he organised a series of 'Shameless Joy' nights aimed at fundraising for, sequentially, the baby loss unit at a nearby hospital, a profound physical and learning disabilities charity, the local lifeboat station, Breast Cancer UK, Prostate Cancer UK, a children's leukaemia and lymphoma charity, and the children's ward again at the local hospital. This investment in such fundraising activities also included in this two-year period a 'ladies' night' (with him and his friends featuring as 'full monty' strippers), a pub quiz, two sponsored walks of over 100 miles, dips in the cold sea on two separate Christmas Days, and a pub football match, where all sponsorships and proceeds again went to various local charities. This important part of Christian's life, though, was not born from pure altruism.

Christian had done some fundraising for Prostate Cancer UK a few times in the years before I started following his *Facebook* feed; this was because his grandad had died of prostate cancer. At the start of a massive upturn in the regularity of fundraising, though, he was 'well aware' that his first charity night as a DJ was potentially a 'launch pad to paid DJ nights'. Christian also casually quipped about 'the amount of women you get though haha', and then 'I like a challenge and it's a nice feeling helping people'. It was also clear that the charities he raised money for were not always related to his own experiences, and not random, but were often suggested by friends who held particular charities close to their own heart.

Paralleling Farrell's (2003) analysis of the 1997 hit British movie *The Full Monty*, it appears that Christian's efforts are related to his reaction to the risk of being a 'social castaway'. While not related to unemployment, such as the movie's protagonists, there is clear evidence in his account that Christian invests in the charity man identity with a view to building his status. The rewards he gained from this identity are both economic and social, and in the case of the latter relate to both the esteem in which he is held by his friends (in part for raising money for their chosen charity) and also by the sexual other (indeed, he met his current partner when he was DJing a charity night). In this sense again we might interpret this as *compensatory* of his labour market situation. The acceleration of the fundraising after he was unable to 'prove himself' in being a prison officer is no coincidence, and is in keeping with psychological research on the issue of charitable giving, which notes, for example, that 'men's helping efforts tend to be more public and conspicuous' (Van Vugt & Iredale, 2013: 3), and also that for men such activity can be 'the human equivalent of a peacock's tail' (ibid.; see also Arnocky et al., 2017).

Pursuing status and a desire to demonstrate and narrate autonomy, these young men appear to be adhering to the more conventional logic of

Hegemonic Masculinity Theory. However, this is not at odds with, and more importantly nor is it a response to, performing emotional labour and more obviously inclusive masculinity in service-work settings. Two points underscore this: first, not all men in the sample made such identity investments, including stay-at-home dads and also those with the most stable occupational trajectories (like Johnny, who remained in retail during the entire research period). Secondly, and relatedly, the primary driver of these masculine pursuits was not having to do service work, but employment biographies filled with low wages, turbulence, and uncertainty. That is, negative experiences were a starting point for the pursuit of status in more orthodox ways, but service work was *not* negatively experienced.

Conclusion

It remains the case that 'occupational professions are frequently categorized as suitable for one gender or another' (McDowell, 2015), and that this stems from the construct of the gender binary and the idea that particular work roles are positioned as suitable for men and for women. Nonetheless, it is also undeniable that working-class men 'are now employed in growing numbers in feminized jobs at the bottom end of the labour market, in sectors such as retail, hospitality and care' (McDowell, 2014: 34). Such sectors, often associated with low pay, poor conditions and underemployment, are likely employment locations for contemporary young working-class men as they transition into young adulthood (Roberts, 2011; Gunter & Watt, 2009). The implications of this are of significant interest for sociology.

There is a strong leaning towards an understanding that masculine gendered identity sits in conflict with 'women's work', highlighting how men claim to manage possible conflict by exhibiting characteristics associated with hegemonic masculinity or re-casting work in more 'manly ways' (Cross & Bagilhole, 2002; Bagilhole & Cross, 2006; Simpson, 2005). Some research postulates 'men in "women's" jobs' often self-report being judged as 'failing to measure up to a "real" man's role' and 'often seen to be homosexual' (McDowell, 2015: 274), though significantly this claim relies on references from research in the 1990s. In addition, others have claimed that '[m]uch less frequently observed is men reconstructing their identities and practices in-line with more feminine workplace cultures and practices' (Nixon, 2017: 51). This line of thinking is in keeping with the major studies of working-class men's transitions to adulthood of the last 15 years (see Chapter 2). Talking to and watching young working-class men as they transition in and often out of these jobs, my findings go against the grain of much of this literature.

While others have reported resistance to service work and the persistence of traditional and hegemonic working-class masculine norms, the men in my study positively embraced the demands of the service economy. A key difference is that many of the studies noted above focused, variously, on older or unemployed men, and/or data from 15 (and often more) years ago. In respect of unemployed samples, the maximum that such research can offer is a theorisation of why unemployed men reject service work; this is a very worthy research pursuit. Yet, despite such research focusing only on a very small section of the working class, or in social generations terms one narrow 'unit' of the generation, the findings are extrapolated to make claims about working-class masculinity more generally. Painting a picture of working-class masculinity in this way, as static and simply mirroring the masculinity of generations past, is damaging and offers a simplistic, almost victim-blaming, rendering of young working-class men's labour market difficulties in contemporary times. It also ignores the research from 15 years ago that highlighted a shift in the attitudes of young men towards retail work (Canny, 2002), for example, as well as research from around the same time showing poor wages, rather than the content of the work, as being off-putting (Lindsay & McQuaid, 2004). Ultimately, the idea that great swaths are 'struggling to adjust to a shifting gender order' (Nayak, 2006: 814) develops in part because the *experiences* of men in front-line service work remain relatively overlooked compared with *attitudes* towards taking up such employment.

Through the narratives above, I have illustrated that rather than being out of step with the contemporary economy, these young men have a habitus that predisposes them to accepting service work and being able to do it well. As 'a structuring structure, which organises around practices and the perception of practices' (Bourdieu, 1984: 170), the habitus on display signals a shift towards a more inclusive masculinity. The sharp industrial changes beginning in the 1980s have now firmly entrenched a service economy replete with low-level customer-facing jobs, and alongside decreasing levels of homohysteria and cultural homophobia (Anderson, 2009), an expanded repertoire of behaviours is *not only a possibility* for men, but is a contemporary 'practice'. That is, the capacity for and use of emotional capital being displayed in the men's accounts of service work are part of that 'mix of conscious and nonconscious ways of being and doing that become habitual and natural' (Cottingham, 2017: 273). Because emotional capital (and all cultural capital) is incorporated into the habitus and becomes part of 'longlasting dispositions of the mind and body' (Bourdieu, 1986: 47), this finding has wider implications than solely the domain of work. I explore this further in the next two chapters.

The major issue for young working-class men is not that they are unable to engage with service work or show the requisite levels of deference and docility, but that being at ease with such demands does little to create more or better-quality and higher-paid jobs. Even after being the kinds of men and performing the kinds of masculinity that policy makers, employers and even academics identify as being important to employment success in the contemporary economy, their labour market positions over seven years most often were characterised by low pay, low status and few prospects. This context makes intelligible that, for some of the participants, the pursuit of status and a personal sense of value was deemed necessary and explains their efforts to do this in quite eclectic ways. While this finding in some ways hints at both continuity as well as profound change, it challenges the prevailing logic of hegemonic masculinity.

Notes

1 Although, informal and experiential learning, as well as observing others, at work is shown to be important for teaching men customer service skills (Roberts, 2013).
2 Name changed for confidentiality.

References

Anderson, E. (2009). *Inclusive masculinity: The changing nature of masculinities*. New York: Routledge.
Arnett, J.J. (2007). Emerging adulthood: What is it, and what is it good for? *Child Development Perspectives*, 1(2), 68–73.
Arnocky, S., Piché, T., Albert, G., Ouellette, D., & Barclay, P. (2017). Altruism predicts mating success in humans. *British Journal of Psychology*, 108(2), 416–435.
Atkinson, W. (2010). The myth of the reflexive worker: Class and work histories in neo-liberal times. *Work, Employment and Society*, 24(3), 413–429.
Bagilhole, B., & Cross, S. (2006). 'It never struck me as female': Investigating men's entry into female dominated occupations. *Journal of Gender Studies*, 15(1), 35–48.
Barber, K. (2016). *Styling Masculinity: Gender, Class, and Inequality in the Men's Grooming Industry*. New Brunswick, NJ: Rutgers University Press.
Bauman, Z. (1998). *Work, Consumerism and the New Poor*. Buckingham: Open University Press.
Beynon, H. (1973). *Working for Ford*. Harmondsworth: Penguin.
Bourdieu, P. (1984). *Distinction: A social critique of the judgement of taste*. Harvard University Press.
Bourdieu, P. (1986). The forms of capital, in J. Richardson (Ed.), *Handbook of Theory and Research for the Sociology of Education*. Greenwood Publishing Group, pp. 280–291.
Bourdieu, P. (1990). *In Other Words*. Stanford, CA: Stanford University Press.
Bourdieu, P. (1996). *The state nobility. Elite schools in the field of power*. Cambridge: Polity Press.
Bourdieu, P. (2000). *Pascalian Meditations*. Stanford, CA: Stanford University Press.
Bourdieu, P., & Wacquant, L. (1992). *An invitation to reflexive sociology*. Cambridge: Polity Press.
Bradley, H. (1993). Across the great divide: The entry of men into women's jobs, in C.L. Williams (Ed.), *Doing Women's Work: Men in Nontraditional Occupations*. London: Sage.
Bridges, T., & Pascoe, C.J. (2014). Hybrid masculinities: New directions in the sociology of men and masculinities. *Sociology Compass*, 8(3), 246–258.
Brod, H. (1987). *The Making of Masculinities: The New Men's Studies*. Boston, MA: Allen & Unwin.
Canny, A. (2002). Flexible labour? The growth of student employment in the UK. *Journal of Education and Work*, 15(3), 277–301.
Cockx, B., & Picchio, M. (2013). Scarring effects of remaining unemployed for long-term unemployed school-leavers. *Series A: Statistics in Society*, 176(4), 951–980.

Coffey, J. (2016). 'I put pressure on myself to keep that body': 'Health'-related body work, masculinities and embodied identity. *Social Theory & Health*, 14(2), 169–188.

Coles, T. (2008). Finding space in the field of masculinity: Lived experiences of men's masculinities. *Journal of Sociology*, 44(3), 233–248.

Connell, R.W. (1995). *Masculinities*. Cambridge: Polity Press.

Cottingham, M.D. (2017). Caring moments and their men: Masculine emotion practice in nursing. *NORMA*, 12(3–4), 270–285.

Cross, S., & Bagilhole, B. (2002). Girls' jobs for the boys? Men, masculinity and non-traditional occupations. *Gender, Work & Organization*, 9(2), 204–226.

Crossley, N. (2005). Mapping Reflexive Body Techniques. *Body and Society*, 11(1), 1–35.

Dixon, K. (2016). *Consuming football in late modern life*. London: Routledge.

Du Gay, P. (1996). *Consumption and identity at work*. London: Sage.

Ensmenger, N. (2015). 'Beards, Sandals, and Other Signs of Rugged Individualism': Masculine Culture within the Computing Professions. *Osiris*, 30(1), 38–65.

Farrell, K. (2003). Naked nation: *The Full Monty*, working-class masculinity, and the British image. *Men and Masculinities*, 6(2), 119–135.

France, A. (2016). *Understanding youth in the global economic crisis*. Bristol: Policy Press.

Furlong, A., & Cartmel, F. (2004). *Vulnerable young men in fragile labour markets: Employment, unemployment and the search for long-term security*. York: Joseph Rowntree Foundation.

Gill, R., Henwood, K., & McLean, C. (2005). Body Projects and the Regulation of Normative Masculinity. *Body and Society*, 11(1), 37–62.

Gregg, P. (2001). The impact of youth unemployment on adult unemployment in the NCDS. *The Economic Journal*, 111(475), 626–653.

Gunter, A., & Watt, P. (2009). Grafting, going to college and working on road: Youth transitions and cultures in an East London neighbourhood. *Journal of Youth Studies*, 12(5), 515–529.

Hakim, J. (2016). 'The Spornosexual': The affective contradictions of male body-work in neoliberal digital culture. *Journal of Gender Studies*, 1–11.

Healey, G. (2016). Proving Grounds: Performing Masculine Identities in Call of Duty: Black Ops. *Game Studies*, 16(2) [online], http://gamestudies.org/1602/articles/healey

Henson, K.D., & Rogers, J.K. (2001). 'WHY MARCIA YOU'VE CHANGED!' Male Clerical Temporary Workers Doing Masculinity in a Feminized Occupation. *Gender & Society*, 15(2), 218–238.

Hochschild, A.R. (1983). *The Managed Heart: Commercialization of Human Feeling*. Berkeley, CA: University of California Press.

Holt, D.B., & Thompson, C.J. (2004). Man-of-action heroes: The pursuit of heroic masculinity in everyday consumption. *Journal of Consumer Research*, 31(2), 425–440.

Jona, J.R., & Foster, J. (2016). Marx's Theory of Working-Class Precariousness. *Monthly Review*, 67(11) (April) [online], https://monthlyreview.org/2016/04/01/marxs-theory-of-working-class-precariousness/

Kimmel, M. (2008). *Guyland: The Perilous World Where Boys Become Men*. New York: Harper Collins.

Lanning, T., & Rudiger, K. (2012). *Youth unemployment in Europe: lessons for the UK*. Institute for Public Policy Research.

Leidner, R. (1993). *Fast food, fast talk: Service work and the routinization of everyday life*. Berkeley, CA: University of California Press.

Lindsay, C., & McQuaid, R.W. (2004). Avoiding the 'McJobs' unemployed job seekers and attitudes to service work. *Work, Employment and Society*, 18(2), 297–319.

Lupton, B. (2006). Explaining men's entry into Female-Concentrated occupations: Issues of masculinity and social class. *Gender, Work & Organization*, 13(2), 103–128.

McCormack, M., & Anderson, E. (2010). 'It's just not acceptable any more': The erosion of homophobia and the softening of masculinity in an English state school. *Sociology*, 44(5), 843–859.

McDowell, J. (2015). Masculinity and Non-Traditional Occupations: Men's Talk in Women's Work. *Gender, Work and Organisation*, 22(3), 273–291.

McDowell, L. (2003). *Redundant masculinities?: Employment change and white working class youth*. London: John Wiley.

McDowell, L. (2014). The Sexual Contract, Youth, Masculinity and the Uncertain Promise of Waged Work in Austerity Britain. *Australian Feminist Studies*, 29(79), 31–49.

McDowell, L., Rootham, E., & Hardgrove, A. (2014). Precarious work, protest masculinity and communal regulation: South Asian young men in Luton, UK. *Work, Employment and Society*, 28(6), 847–864.

Michikyan, M., Dennis, J., & Subrahmanyam, K. (2015). Can you guess who I am? Real, ideal, and false self-presentation on Facebook among emerging adults. *Emerging Adulthood*, 3(1), 55–64.

Milkman, R. (1997). *Farewell to the Factory. Auto Workers in the Late Twentieth Century*. Berkeley, CA: University of California Press.

Moisio, R., Arnould, E.J., & Gentry, J.W. (2013). Productive consumption in the class-mediated construction of domestic masculinity: Do-It-Yourself (DIY) home improvement in men's identity work. *Journal of Consumer Research*, 40(2), 298–316.

Moisio, R., & Beruchashvili, M. (2016). Mancaves and masculinity. *Journal of Consumer Culture*, 16(3), 656–676.

Nayak, A. (2006). Displaced masculinities: Chavs, youth and class in the post-industrial city. *Sociology*, 40(5), 813–831.

Nixon, D. (2006). 'I just like working with my hands': Employment aspirations and the meaning of work for low-skilled unemployed men in Britain's service economy. *Journal of Education and Work*, 19(2), 201–217.

Nixon, D. (2009). 'I Can't Put a Smiley Face On': Working-Class Masculinity, Emotional Labour and Service Work in the 'New Economy'. *Gender, Work & Organization*, 16(3), 300–322.

Nixon, D. (2017). Yearning to Labour? Working-class Men in Post-industrial Britain, in C. Walker, & S. Roberts (Eds.), *Masculinity, Labour, and Neoliberalism: Working-Class Men in Perspective*. Springer.

Norman, M.E. (2011). Embodying the Double-Bind of Masculinity: Young Men and Discourses of Normalcy, Health, Heterosexuality, and Individualism. *Men and Masculinities*, 14(4), 430–449.

Pascual Soler, N. (2018). *Food and Masculinity in Contemporary Autobiographies: Cast-Iron Man*. Basingstoke: Palgrave.

Pettinger, L. (2005). Gendered work meets gendered goods: Selling and service in clothing retail. *Gender, Work & Organization*, 12(5), 460–478.

Roberts, K. (2009). Opportunity structures then and now. *Journal of Education and Work*, 22(5), 355–368.

Roberts, S. (2011). Beyond 'NEET' and 'tidy' pathways: Considering the 'missing middle' of youth transition studies. *Journal of Youth Studies*, 14(1), 21–39.

Roberts, S. (2012). One step forward, one step Beck: A contribution to the ongoing conceptual debate in youth studies. *Journal of Youth Studies*, 15(3), 389–401.

Roberts, S. (2013). Gaining skills or just paying the bills? Workplace learning in low-level retail employment. *Journal of Education and Work*, 26(3), 267–290.

Sennett, R., & Cobb, J. (1972). *The hidden injuries of class.* New York: Vintage.

Shildrick, T., MacDonald, R., Webster, C., & Garthwaite, K. (2012). *Poverty and Insecurity: Life in Low-pay, No-pay Britain.* Bristol: Policy Press.

Shilling, C. (1993). *The Body and Social Theory.* London: Sage.

Simpson, R. (2004). Masculinity at work: The experiences of men in female dominated occupations. *Work, Employment and Society*, 18(2), 349–368.

Simpson, R. (2005). Men in non-traditional occupations: Career entry, career orientation and experience of role strain. *Gender, Work & Organization*, 12(4), 363–380.

Simpson, R., Hughes, J., & Slutskaya, N. (2016). *Gender, Class and Occupation.* Basingstoke: Palgrave.

Skeggs, B., & Wood, H. (2012). *Reacting to reality television: Performance, audience and value.* London: Routledge.

Standing, G. (2011). *The Precariat: The Dangerous New Class.* London: Bloomsbury Academic.

Van Vugt, M., & Iredale, W. (2013). Men behaving nicely: Public goods as peacock tails. *British Journal of Psychology*, 104(1), 3–13.

Walker, C., & Roberts, S. (2018). Masculinity, Labour and Neoliberalism: Reviewing the Field, in *Masculinity, Labour, and Neoliberalism.* Palgrave Macmillan, pp. 1–28.

Willis, P.E. (1977). *Learning to labor: How working class kids get working class jobs.* Columbia University Press.

7 Contemporary working-class masculinities and the domestic sphere
The diminishing significance of 'the man of the house'

Introduction

Continuing the dynamic analysis of the young men's production and performance of masculinities as they transition to adulthood, this chapter details the participants' attitudes towards housework and domestic duties, including childcare. These arenas have, of course, been regarded for considerable time as highly gendered domains, underpinned by ideas that gender is emergent in social situations (West & Zimmerman, 1987), such that 'women display their femininity through homework while men demonstrate masculinity by avoiding what has traditionally been seen as "women's work"' (Van der Lippe et al., 2017: 3; see also Coltrane, 1989). Aligned with arguments made by Coltrane (1989) almost 20 years ago, the findings I present in this chapter speak to the idea that the organisation of household labour presents the possibility of not only expressing and confirming gender but of transforming it. Indeed, what follows shows that the young men in my study have taken up this possibility, and illustrates how working-class masculinity is already transformed in this respect.

The next section of the chapter attends to some of the important literature on the issue of gender and domestic labour over the last 30 years, highlighting positive shifts as well as the current relative plateauing of these changes – that is, what Hochschild called the 'stalled gender revolution'. This is a somewhat unusual approach for a findings chapter, but this literature, in conjunction with the theoretical discussion outlined in Chapter 3, serves as an effective way of contextualising the data from my study. The chapter then reports the young men's generally egalitarian outlooks and attitudes when I first interviewed them in 2009, and then turns to an analysis of whether and how these attitudes were realised or, in some cases, became modified as the men journeyed through their twenties.

In both cases, as young men looking toward imagined futures, and then as young men living those futures as slightly more 'established adults', the evidence suggests that these working-class young men performed masculinities at odds with the dominant portrayals. The main finding is that though there are 'provinces in which women traditionally have been recognised as the experts'

(Courtney, 2009: 66), this is being challenged, both in relation to household chores and childcare. However, some stubborn gender patterns remain, with some contradictions occurring in the men's espoused ideals and the actuality of the precise division of labour. At times there is some evidence of a reconfiguration of masculinity, such that certain equality behaviours can be easily reconciled with the participants' ideas of 'being a man'. This suggests that there is still greater need to consider how to produce possibilities for 'undoing' gender (Deutsch, 2007). However, most observable is a shift that should not be understated, with efforts to reclaim being a man only ever occurring in the context of explicit discussion (either with the research or with friends or strangers online) about whether one's sense of manliness is compromised.

The most crucial point I wish to make in this chapter specifically relates to class. Where mostly middle-class, well-educated men have been seen as being the vanguard of positive changes in contemporary masculinities, the evidence drawn from my study, alongside other recent research, presents compelling evidence that it is working-class young men who veer towards more equal divisions of domestic labour, and authentic equal partnership approaches, and at the same time find no need to avoid such activity to consolidate their masculinity.

Domesticity, gender roles and social class

The archetype of hegemonic masculinity, for much of the 1900s, was underpinned by the male breadwinner model of the family, which emphasised a relatively rigid division of men and women into, respectively, public (i.e. employment) and private (i.e. homemaking) domains. The unequal share of domestic labour that follows from this divide was, according to Becker's (1965, 1981) theory of time allocation, premised on a gender trade-off whereby men, as a result of their greater earning potential, usually spend more time in the labour market, and as a consequence women take up the majority of domestic work. This discourse of decisions about domestic labour, based on economic rationality, was soon challenged by a raft of evidence.

When women in industrialised countries began moving into the workforce, they were shown to work 'a double day' (Szalai, 1966) or 'second shift' (Hochschild, 1989), as they were also expected to undertake the vast bulk of domestic tasks once they returned home. While supportive of their partners' right to and need for employment, Hochschild (1989: 12) found that many men *expected* women to do the 'lion's share' of domestic duties because they were lacking a 'notion of manhood that encouraged them to be active parents and householders'. As a result, many married/partnered heterosexual women were working the equivalent of an additional entire extra month per year more than their partners. While statistical data in the United States and UK at the time reported that men were doing more in terms of childcare and homemaking than ever before, a large gender gap remained, and any reduction in the gap was mostly the result of *declining totals* of domestic work brought about by labour-saving technologies as well as a decline in hours committed to and available for such tasks (Gershuny & Robinson, 1988).

In the decades since this research, attitudinal support for the male breadwinner/female homemaker model has further diminished across western countries (Cunningham, 2008; Van der Lippe et al., 2017; Crespi & Ruspini, 2016). Indeed, the labour force comprises more women than ever (Hook, 2010). According to Becker's model, hours spent on domestic chores should become more equitable between the genders. However, while men are doing more than ever in the domestic sphere, the trend towards convergence is slowing down, with a considerable gender gap of between 60 and 100 minutes per day in English-speaking countries (and much higher in Italy and Spain, for example) (Altintas & Sullivan, 2016). In the UK, women continue to carry out an overall average of 60% more unpaid domestic work than men (ONS, 2016; Crespi & Ruspini, 2016). Moreover, Thébaud (2010: 333) reveals:

> ... although men who are dual-earners do more housework than they would if they were sole breadwinners, they do not increase it enough to create parity or to reverse a traditional gender division of labor ... [and] in couples where the woman earns considerably more money, spouses still often perceive his work to be more important than hers; under such circumstances, women typically do the majority of the housework.

Thébaud, among others, found the presence of gender retrenchment, where men who earn less than their partners reinforce their masculinity by *not* engaging in feminine activities, such as housework, to avoid further emasculation. Whitehead (2002: 84) calls this the 'essentialistic retreat', brought about by a refusal to accept a peripheral position. This is an observable trend also related to unemployment, with several studies in the last four decades clearly illustrating that more time, made available by a lack of labour activity, does not equate to men becoming more active in household labour (McKee & Bell, 1986; Morgan, 1992; Van der Lippe et al., 2017). Instead, with masculinity denied in the routine, and the subordinated nature of domestic work, men make greater efforts to assert a strong patriarchal authority as a form of compensation. Such a retrenchment of gender is far from one-sided, with research showing that women respond to unemployment by *doing more* domestic labour in order to underscore a respectable feminine identity (Bianchi et al., 2000; Lyonette, 2015; Van der Lippe et al., 2017).

Lyonette and Crompton's (2015) research in the UK found use of a similar compensatory mechanism, and, of significant interest, that middle-class and/ or higher-earning men contribute to this gender gap more prominently. In addition to this greater level of compensatory masculinity, this discrepancy is perpetuated through the outsourcing of paid domestic help. Research also finds clear evidence of what Usdansky (2011) argues to be important class differences in what men do, even when they report that they are 'sharing'.

Most notably, Usdansky (2011) finds that working-class men, while holding traditional values, conform to 'lived egalitarianism', whereas higher-class couples exhibit preponderance towards 'spoken egalitarianism', with men from lower-income backgrounds doing more domestic work. This echoes Lyonette and Crompton's (2015: 36) qualitative finding that for middle-class men '"sharing" was confined to what was left after both the wife and the cleaner had divided the majority of the housework between them'. In quantitative analyses, while not using an exact measure of class, Fagan and Norman (2016: 95) have illustrated that in the UK, 'fathers employed at lower occupational levels are more likely to share childcare [...] than are fathers in managerial and professional occupations'.

A further issue of interest is the division of domestic tasks. This is seen as a vital component of gender inequity, and holds greater import for spouses' perceptions of fairness than total time spent on housework (Hook, 2010). Women tend towards more time-inflexible, routine tasks (Coltrane & Shih, 2010; Hook, 2010) like cooking, or are more likely to do onerous tasks such as laundry and ironing (OECD, 2011). Men, conversely, are usually disproportionately responsible for tasks that permit discretion allowing for leisure activities to take priority (Hook, 2010). This division *within* domestic chores is vital because who does what is actually more important for spouses' perceptions of fairness than the total time spent on housework (Hook, 2010). In relation to childcare, further complexity arises. Men in western countries are increasingly 'expected to be emotionally present and involved in their children's everyday lives' (Gottzén & Kremer-Sadlik, 2012: 640), and they are more likely to participate in childcare than in routine housework (Roberts, 2013; also Crespi & Ruspini, 2016). Yet, breadwinning remains discursively connected to popular notions of 'good' fatherhood (Gottzén & Kremer-Sadlik, 2012; Fagan & Norman, 2016), while men's involvement is to some extent influenced by social policies and other institutional barriers that reinforce women's position as a primary caregiver (Crespi & Ruspini, 2016). These very factors have, for example, been understood by some fathers as being pivotal in explaining their more limited involvement in their children's education (Gottzén, 2011).

Breen and Cooke (2005) argue that only when a sufficiently high proportion of women in society have attained greater equality can men change their beliefs and subsequent domestic behaviour in a partnership. Furthermore, as increased level of education also leads to decreased support for the male breadwinner model (Cunningham, 2008), given their limited but not especially poor educational profiles, we might expect the respondents to hold traditional understandings of the gendered division of labour. While my sample is not statistically representative and also acknowledging my participants were discussing imagined futures rather than current realities, traditional gender ideology was not a prevailing feature of the respondents' projected domestic ideal.

Attitudes and imagined futures at age 18–24

Commensurate with other research (e.g. Henderson et al., 2007), my participants anticipated living with a partner – although not necessarily married – in the longer term and most forecast having children. Though discussing *imagined* futures, this section considers whether the participants might prioritise traditionally masculine ideals in respect of domestic labour within their prospective roles as fathers and partners in committed relationships. A rejection of such ideals is often associated with the concept of the 'new man', a constructed stereotype characterised by sensitivity, emotional awareness, respect toward women and an egalitarian outlook (Gill, 2003). Gill (2003) posits that a key index of 'newmanishness' is his contribution to domestic work. Although shown to exhibit non-traditional masculinity in respect of their educational values (Chapter 5) and attitude towards service work (Chapter 6), these young men still might be expected to reflect the attitudes of the 'new lad' – that is, interested in hedonism and anti-feminism, maintaining a primary interest in 'beer, football and shagging' and, especially, a commitment to the male breadwinner model of the family. Although often found to exist alongside varied, contradictory and complex ways of 'doing masculinity', this discourse permeates much commentary about contemporary working-class masculinities (e.g. McDowell, 2003; Nayak, 2006; Richardson, 2010).

In the interviews, domestic duties were considered at two discrete levels: housework (defined as routine and labour-consuming household tasks), and childcare and/or care for other family members (see Kan, 2008). In relation to housework, overwhelmingly the young men talked of an expected relatively equal division of household labour:

JAMES: It's part of being a couple, you know, because you love each other and because you are a team. Jobs need to be done; it's not necessarily fair to make one person do all the main boring jobs.

LUKE: I wouldn't expect her to cook more than me or clean more than me … It would be pretty unreasonable for me to expect a woman to go have a job and then come home and have this second 'wife job' as well.

CARL: It would be an equal share to be honest. It's just normal to share. If *she wants to do* all the cleaning and ironing then of course she can do it, but if it needs doing then I'll do it, no problems with that [my emphasis].

A strong egalitarian perspective emerges here, with, for the most part, emphasis on team-based, partnership approaches, and with Luke's clear reference to the unreasonableness of the iniquitous 'second shift' (Hochschild, 1989). Carl, too, articulates very illuminating ideas that rest on, first, sharing as normal, but secondly, as per research on the relationship between domestic work and feminine identity (e.g. Bianchi et al., 2000), that his partner *might* want to do the housework themselves. I return to this below when discussing the participants' lived realities in their later twenties.

Despite this apparent general equity, there was an interesting, very acute dimension in terms of the kind of tasks the participants imagined they might do. Running through their accounts was their understanding that cooking a meal might be a good and attractive compromise as part of the housework bargain:

JEZ: I'm not very good with the cleaning, but I'd do the cooking. So I'd come to some sort of arrangement with her that I'd be the cook, she can do the washing up and stuff.
DANNY: Fancy myself as a bit of a chef, so there ain't ever gonna be like an expectation that someone would make dinner for me and all that. It's something I'd be able to do if *I* was in a couple. I'd be up for that.
PAT: My girlfriend hates cooking. I'm more than happy to do it every night. She also hates doing the dishes too. But she has gotta do something!

These comments reflect the participants would undertake tasks they 'didn't mind doing'. This speaks to a gender power imbalance, such that the men imagined a negotiation that would leave their partners doing the less attractive tasks. Interestingly, the suggestion that they might spend more time preparing and cooking meals runs contrary to recent evidence which shows that men of all ages have barely increased their cooking hours at all across most western countries for around 50 years (Hook, 2010).

There are two potential interlinked explanations for this attitudinal shift. First, as much housing data show, an independent dwelling forms part of many young people's experience of living arrangements prior to living with a partner. In these situations, we can assume that such young people have at some point had to cook for themselves. Indeed, the present respondents who had not yet left the parental home talked of often preparing their own meals as they have got older. Cooking, then, is not necessarily a foreign or unexpected task. Additionally, an abundance of 'celebrity chef' and cooking TV shows have permeated primetime popular media in recent years. Research has shown that such programmes often being hosted by male chefs who present particularly orthodox, but somewhat different, masculine repertoires (e.g. Gordon Ramsay, Heston Blumenthal, Jamie Oliver), allows us to hypothesise that such role models may have 'de-feminised' the culinary world, meaning that the kitchen and cooking become sites that do not necessarily compromise masculinity (Steno & Friche, 2015). Moreover, such glamorising of cooking could contribute to a desire to cook among men, moving it beyond being a mundane, gender-neutral activity. Hollows (2003) explains how, in the case of Jamie Oliver, presenting cooking as fun and leisurely rather than an act of labour has permitted the task to become 'recognisably manly'. Relatedly, that male chefs are presented as having wider horizons than female chefs, such that they become recognised as experts beyond the domestic setting (in Oliver's case as a social activist) (Scholes, 2011), further facilitates the masculinising of the prospect of cooking. That said, other theorists have noted that men's cooking is part of the rise of men's increasingly 'care-oriented ways' (Szabo, 2014: 19).

Discussing other general cleaning duties, the participants often insinuated they simply were 'not very good at it', appealing to the myth of males lacking domestic competence (Lyonette & Crompton, 2015), or moreover that an untidy home was something that did not particularly bother them:

LUKE: I don't think that's a women's role, that a woman should clean up the house. The reality is I'm a lazy fucker and if I'm gonna clean up and cook my fair share it's 'cos someone is kicking my arse to do it …

PAT: I wouldn't say I'm an unreasonably untidy person. But my god I'm more untidy than my girlfriend. Actually, more untidy than any girlfriend I've had. Or any female housemate I've had. For some weird reason men seem to be less offended by mess, you know what I mean? Go and have a look where men live in comparison to women!

GAVIN: I'm pretty standard when it comes to cleaning up. I'll do it when it gets to the point where I think it needs doing, which, like, I suppose is a different time to what a girl might think is the time to it, or anyone else … I mean I don't have expectations about how tidy a place should be or anything.

Without explicitly referencing gender essentialism, the participants have clearly positioned themselves as different from women, who are more 'offended by mess'. This insight is important because much research that contemplates attitudes towards the male breadwinner model considers either rational bargaining theories or gendered ideology as key determinants of the division of household chores. There appears to be an additional factor to consider, and another layer of complexity when determining the impact of gender. Whilst these responses can be linked to gender-appropriate behaviour, to suggest that the young men expect women to tidy up after them is incorrect. Further, their attitudes run contra Jones's (1995: 69) assertion that working-class boys stay at home until the domestic role their mothers account for can be taken up by their wives or long-term partners. The ambivalence the participants directed toward their own mess is perceived as the attitude they will take into a partnership. Consequently, they do not expect women to tidy up because it is their job; instead, they believe, aligned with the research on the role of domestic labour and feminine identity, that women will do so because they are more 'offended' by messy living conditions. Whether this is deemed a 'natural' or a social construction means little in this sense – their attitude is underpinned by their own ambivalence and this problematises the understanding that men are inherent 'beneficiaries' of all forms of domestic labour (Adkins, 1995).

An array of international evidence concurs that although women still undertake the major share of childcare duties, men are more likely to participate in childcare than in routine housework (see Crespi & Ruspini, 2016;

Kan, 2008). The participants' attitudes towards the second component of domestic labour (i.e. caring duties) were, again, not consistent with male breadwinner ideals. Instead, only Carl and Peter were explicit in viewing the male breadwinner model as an ideal when a couple has children. This idea rested strongly on the notion of gender role complementarity (as critically discussed by Cockburn, 1983), a model both men observed in the parental home. Carl protested that, all too often, bringing up children is disparaged and 'should be seen as a good and really honourable thing, rather than something negative'. This, he claimed, did not undermine his support for an equal share of other domestic labour, and even a 'good share of nappy changing and feeding', sentiments echoed by Peter, who said, 'I think I'd work but help out like my Dad did'.

The other men explicitly outlined that they should and would share the burden of hard work, as well as the joys of raising children. Additionally, though, many identified how social policies and other institutional barriers reinforce women's position as a primary caregiver:

CHRISTIAN: Obviously, the mother gets the maternity [leave] and they spend a lot more time with the baby. But, um, I'd feel if I had a baby with someone, I mean if I was the one not at work I'd give it a good shot. I don't want kids or anything like that now, but at a later date I'd have no problem ...

PAT: Men usually earn more than women. That is shit in some ways, but that's what happens. Other than that, which is pretty massive, there's no reason why men shouldn't have equal share of baby feeding and stuff. They will probably be the ones at work, not always, but probably. But when two people are in the house it's a share. It's just a human thing to do.

JASON: It's [employment] set up for women to look after kids. They need time to recover after giving birth, though. Men don't get much time to spend with a new baby do they, like paternity leave is pretty rubbish. Will employers let me go part time to look after the kids? I can't see it. Generally the decent thing to do is to help each other out with all of these things.

In recognising the structural barriers that promote female primary care giving, these young men are perhaps complicit in maintaining the conditions that facilitate this. However, given general attitudes, this would seem unfair. Congruent with Crompton and Lyonette (2005: 610), the responses make clear that 'structural factors are at least as important, if not more important, than "attitudinal" factors in shaping the working arrangements of couples', and echo Fagan and Norman's (2016) statistical analysis of UK childcare patterns that shows the influence of parental leave and the gender pay gap, for example, in decisions about such domestic arrangements between the genders.

Following their positive attitudes to service work, we see a changing picture of masculinity. Although stopping short of representing some form of 'new man', their attitudes do not reflect the kind of gender-appropriate behaviour associated with their fathers' generation, or indeed the kind of behaviour still often associated with working-class masculinity. These participants largely imagined and wanted to share household chores with their prospective partners and saw childcare as part of an active partnership that is structured and destabilised by employment practices and social policies. The bargaining that would see them and their partners divide paid and unpaid labour was very much based on rational calculations, à la Becker, over and above gender ideology. This could be particularly significant given their low-pay positions in the labour market; at this stage in their life it was entirely feasible that their future partners may earn as much, perhaps even more (as was the case for many, see below).

While these attitudes at a relatively young age are not illustrative of a full-scale detraditionalisation of gender (Beck, 1992; Giddens, 1992), developing an attitude associated with a traditional, and (for working-class men) expected, gendered division of labour is far from ineluctable. Failure to commit to ideals that correspond with working-class masculinity of generations past does not appear to prevent young men from obtaining a culturally validated form of masculinity. Instead, as per the inclusive masculinity thesis (Anderson, 2009), a new set of behaviours, previously seen as off-limits for men, have emerged as now acceptable. It seems clear that these young men imagine a future in which, in terms of the division of routine housework, attitudes towards traditional gender ideology are somewhat attenuated (Roberts, 2013). Yet, whilst the respondents all seemed happy to do their share, they largely had preferences for cooking, suggesting it was something they enjoyed. Consequently, the tasks they most disliked were something they hoped their significant other would perform. Indeed, they suggested their ambivalence towards untidiness, relative to females' 'natural' cleanliness, would mean that women would most likely perform some tasks. As noted, in regards to childcare, the young men claimed to want to be involved with both the hard work and the joys of raising children, but recognised that institutional and structural barriers would often mean that their prospective partners would likely become primary caregivers for their children. The regularity of the use of rhetoric that signifies moves *towards* equality is unmistakable. The espousal of such attitudes raises a few question, though. Are such dispositions, spoken in this way, generative of commensurately egalitarian social practices? Are they transposable from 'imagined futures' to 'real life'? These are important questions, especially as the accepted wisdom on the matter seems to match this position offered by Whitehead (2002: 84):

> While many heterosexual men may say they would wish for an equal relationship with a woman, far fewer appear to like the actual consequences of this on a day to day basis, for it requires them to adopt a non centralist position ... a position where they exist not as central but jointly peripheral.

Contrary to this position, as I now go on to show, for the most part these promising attitudes are retained as genuine practices as the men have grown older and, in many cases, entered serious romantic relations. What follows then is evidence of a habitus constituted by egalitarian dispositions that are inculcated, structured, durable, such that this more (but not always completely) egalitarian approach in the domestic sphere has 'come to be seen as inherent in the nature of things' (Bourdieu, 1976: 118).

Walking the walk, not just talking the talk: gender dynamics in the home, seven years later

It is worth reiterating that these findings must be considered in light of the specific historical circumstances that inform the possibilities for masculinity construction. After decades of restructuring, employment content, titles and contract tenures all vary massively from those faced by the participants' parents' generation. Furthermore, the men's experience of work, as detailed in the previous chapter, has loosened the relationship between occupational narratives and identity construction. Here, then, I make clear how the participants' engagements with parenting and housework highlight other possibilities for young men to negotiate masculinity in a generationally specific manner. First, I consider the domestic arrangements in the lives of the men who were partnered but who did not have children, and then move on to those who had partners and children. These accounts are not meant to accurately portray the exact division of labour, but to highlight the men's lack of discursive distancing from the 'feminine' terrain that was often derided and avoided by previous generations of working-class men.

'She's probably more motivated to do certain bits' – Dave, Johnny, Christian

The major thread running through the young men's accounts of their domestic labour arrangements when now living with a partner was an echo of what they described when they were younger; they lived out their imagined futures almost to the letter. This included a strong engagement with domestic duties, such that the young men described them as fairly or evenly divided, but at the same time there were multiple traces of what they had previously described around women's 'motivation' or desire to have a generally tidier house, which resulted in a continuation of the kinds of gender inequalities that have been found in research on the types of tasks being undertaken and total time spent on household labour (van der Lippe et al., 2017). In the following three cases, we strongly observe this commitment to the domestic sphere, with the idea that it is a strictly feminine terrain seen as laughable and even incomprehensible.

Johnny's take on domestic labour has changed over the course of the research period. The belief that someone should not have to clean up after him remained intact, but his attitude towards mess not being a problem shifted between interviews. Johnny explained that this change is required when one moves in with a partner:

JOHNNY: I think when you first move in, you kind of, because you're so used to doing your own thing ... it takes I suppose a minute for you to start thinking okay, now I'm home ... when you have your time off you can't just, like for me, when I have a day off I can't just get up and game all day for ten hours straight. Now, you've got the house as well to look after, so you've got to think okay ... You have to have that mindset, yeah, no one likes it but you've got to change your mindset, it can't be just about doing [whatever you like], because it's about you and your partner.

He then went on to explain how owning their home, in addition to wanting to maintain living conditions his partner would find amenable, aided the change in thinking:

JOHNNY: I'm not the tidiest person but it's surprising once you own your own house how you want to keep the kitchen tidy, you want to do all the washing and all that. Talking in more detail about the changes he has made, he reflected that his commitment to domestic work comes about from a requirement to 'grow up', though does not necessarily encroach on his free time entirely:

JOHNNY: in all fairness if I'm putting the washing on, that's on for like an hour, I can game if I want to or I can do the rest of the housework, hoovering and cleaning the bathroom, it's priorities I think, because [Partner] works early on a Saturday so I get up with her and she's not back until about two so then I think in that time I can at least spend the first two hours of the morning, or two hours in the morning doing the garden, doing the washing up, doing the washing, getting it outside. And then afterwards, then you have your time, but you kind of have to grow up, like you haven't got your mum there doing all the work for you like, when you live at home.

With Saturday morning as his designated time to do household chores, this might imply that his partner undertook all other chores Monday to Friday. However, he made clear that 'generally during the week, we don't really do housework, we'll just do the washing up and that'. The basic and necessary domestic work such as cooking and clearing up after the fact was something that, in Johnny's mind, was subject to a division based on an agreed rationale:

JOHNNY: I get home later than [Partner], so what happens is that she cooks during the week, then when I'm off at the weekend, I do the cooking. But that's changed, [when] I [first] started [my current job] I used to come home before her, so I would get dinner ready and do it, *and I don't mind the cooking*, in all fairness I think I'm more inclined to do the washing up than she is because, because if I'm cooking, I'll start washing up the bits that I've done because it's having that mess there, once you kind of stop it never gets done, so I'm more inclined to get that done [when] I'm doing [dinner] because then I don't have to worry about it afterwards.

Beyond these general domestic duties, he noted that his partner was 'more motivated to get bits around the house done', specifically referencing the aesthetics of the house and minor maintenance issues, but moreover that 'she'll probably admit that she does more of the house stuff like getting it tidy or she's *more interested* in getting it done than me'. Here again are echoes of research that implicates a feminine identity is related to having a presentable home. This theme emerged strongly in all the other accounts (see below), where the young men saw themselves as undertaking tasks they 'didn't mind doing' as well as tasks they didn't enjoy – in Johnny's case, the cooking and the gardening, respectively – but they saw their partners as motivated to undertake tasks more keenly. Referring to the general tidiness of the house (*not* cleanliness), Johnny stated:

JOHNNY: I know it needs doing, but it takes me a little bit of time because I want to I see it as I work five days a week and at my weekends I should be able to do what I want.He followed up, though, with an important caveat about how this way of seeing the working week and the tasks is incompatible with life as a partner:
JOHNNY: But that, that mindset doesn't work because. For her. For us. Er, so I think we are very even, we split it quite well, she's probably more motivated to do certain bits than I am, and I'm probably like more bit more laid back. Yeah, like if I do the washing up or something, she'll dry or vice versa. On her day off she'll, if she wants to do other things she'll go and she'll do the hoovering and dusting or if she doesn't, when I'm off on Saturday, I'll spend an hour and I'll do it.

Like Johnny, Christian provided very similar descriptions of his life with his partner, with an egalitarian sentiment that swerves away from the stereotype working-class masculine ideal of a breadwinner/homemaker ideology. There was no strict demarcation of domains, and Christian keenly observed the importance of both people in a partnership doing household chores. Rather than detailing all the similarities between the two accounts, however, here I focus in more detail on a particular issue: his articulation of the idea that women desire or 'need' to tidy up more regularly and to a different standard than men.

In his initial interview, Christian, like almost all participants, placed a strong emphasis on an assumed equal division of domestic labour, noting fairness as being a central element of any prospective relationship. Seven

162 *Working-class masculinities and the domestic sphere*

years on, as this exchange shows, he could not recall this commitment to an entirely egalitarian ideal, but moreover explained that this ideal did not exactly play out in real life:

SR: You said at the time, if you lived with a girl, you wouldn't expect her to do particular jobs and you do other particular jobs, like you'd just share it all together? Now you've done that a couple of times, how do you think that plays out in real life?

CHRISTIAN: It doesn't play out in real life, because, for example, there's a bowl of washing up in the kitchen, and I'm very much like, I'll do it whenever because it's only me and [partner] in the house. We've got friends coming round tomorrow night for example, so I'll make sure the house is looking nice for when our friends come round. [Partner] wouldn't be able to sit, she wouldn't be able to sit down and relax, knowing the kitchen is a mess for example, whereas I quite happily would. Not that I'm a slob, but just because if there's a few plates in the bowl, so what?

There might be temptation to wryly smile when reading that their imagined sharing didn't pan out in real life – 'a-ha: we knew it – young men espouse big ideals but ultimately reproduce long established gender dynamics'. However, the theme of differentiated gendered standards and needs looms large. I return to this momentarily, but it is also worth noting how Christian discussed his *expectations* of his partner:

CHRISTIAN: She's got two jobs … Today, she got home at five, and was back out of the door at ten to six, to work at the pub. She's very hardworking, she's always on the go. She finds it hard to sit still. So I'd not expect her to do anything [in terms of domestic chores]. You know, she is working loads.

So, Christian did retain his imagined commitment to doing domestic chores, and he was fully aware of his responsibilities as a grown adult man to not expect his partner to do an unequal amount of household tasks equivalent to Hochschild's 'second shift'. Indeed, the idea of men's and women's domains seemed bizarre to Christian and he looked confused when we discussed if men *should* do less domestic labour than their female partners. However, that women cannot relax in the presence of mess, a theme also discussed when the men were younger, was something that again emerged as I probed on his partner's inability to relax when the 'kitchen was a mess':

SR: Do you think her not being able to leave the dishes, do you think that has anything to do with her being a woman?

CHRISTIAN: I don't know why, but I do think that's the case. I mean, [male friend's name], he would be the same as me. If he had a day off, like yesterday for example, [football] Transfer Deadline Day. He wouldn't interrupt watching that all day because there was a bit of washing up to do for example. For some reason, [Partner] wouldn't be able to just chill out tomorrow, knowing that there was housework that needed to be done.

The distinction that Christian makes between men and women, a distinction commonly made across the sample, is made sense of here as being related to gender in that he infers his friend would have a similar sense of priorities, and echoes Johnny's account, above, where he implicated his partner's motivation to be tidier as a key driver of housework iniquities. As I noted in respect of their attitudes seven years earlier, whether or not the men understood such differences as resting on essentialist differences or socialised foundations of gender was not clear; rather, the key issue seemed to be that they perceived women had a need for a clean home environment. In the initial interviews some of the young men talked about this in respect of standards, but Christian was keen to state it was not differences in standards per se, but differences in standards when there was no one else in the home:

CHRISTIAN: I think we *have got the same* standards, but like tomorrow we have got friends coming round for dinner, and there's no way I would let them come round with the house not looking as nice as it could look. And [Partner] is the same, so tomorrow so we'll both go round and do bits and pieces, making it look nice. But if over the next couple of days I know that there's not really much going on, and there's a bit of hoovering that needs to be done, or the dishes, [Partner] would have to do that before she relaxed, whereas I'd quite happily relax ... And if I'm going out on Saturday night and there's a particular shirt I want to wear, I make sure it's nice and washed, whereas [Partner] will do washing all week long.

Christian's perceptions are at odds with more than a theory of masculinity here. He, like his partner, he suggested, are equally house-proud when it comes to hosting guests; this makes a tidy house more than simply connected to feminine identity, and the joint production of 'making the house look nice' belies that he would expect his partner to achieve the standards so he might take equal credit for it. Men can still be the beneficiaries of this gendered approach, though. Christian's partner's desire to wash clothes throughout the week and to tidy more often was also understood as having benefits, but these were positioned as unintended benefits:

CHRISTIAN: ... I do kind of [gain from partner's approach to domestic labour], because she is like that, you do, without intentionally using her or taking the piss, but because I know that she probably is going to do the washing up, I probably do subconsciously think, oh it doesn't matter, it will get done.

SR: ... before you said, 'why does it matter if there are a few dishes in the bowl?' ...

CHRISTIAN: Because, like I said, if I lived by myself or, like before, just with my mates, I wouldn't have done the dishes until I wanted. But she is ready and wants to do it quickly, otherwise she can't relax.

The last point made here should be stressed. Christian and many men like him do gain from the ways that domestic labour appears to have been bound to feminine identity, but the rhythm and timetabling of domestic chores between men and women appear very different and have different impacts on the sense of self. This was captured by Pat – whom I discuss below – who reflected that 'the women I have lived with have always liked to come home to the bed being made, like actually enjoy it; I've never made a bed for myself 'cos I enjoy it'. Similarly, the two participants who lived with their parents at the time of this interview suggested their preference to 'get it all done in one go rather than a bit at [a] time' (Peter), and even 'blitz it when I'm ready' (Carl).

Lastly in this section, I discuss Dave, who again provided echoes of above sentiments in his account of his life with his partner of just over five years. They had been living together for just over two years, and were due to be married within months of the final interview. As a forerunner for his discussion about being a partner in the domestic sphere, Dave first stressed that central to his relationship was a wider sense of compatibility and partnership:

DAVE: ... it's not really changed. We seem to get on really, really well ... our film interests and that are exactly the same and, when we [inaudible] our taste in certain things, it's exactly the same, so it's really easy to live with each other. That's why we didn't really feel like we needed to rent or anything to get to know each other, to make sure we can work together and live together.

This foundation served as the basis for, in Dave's eyes, a largely equal division of domestic chores. Initially describing how tasks might be divided by type, he started to backtrack as it made no sense for him to think about household chores like this:

DAVE: So, where I do the cooking, which is quite nice. But then [Partner] it's the same sort of thing really, it's not one of those ones where ... we kind of just go ... like on my day off and that, I'll do all the washing and stuff and like do the hoovering and everything. And [Partner] will do that on her day off. But what has kind of helped as well is like ... our mate [Inaudible], he lived with us for a while ... he would shift in with bits.

Clear in Dave's account is that anybody who lives in a home with others should 'shift in' to help the workload, too; this appears unrelated to gender.

Also interesting is his enjoyment of cooking complementing the discussion above on the masculinisation of the kitchen through its associations with pleasure. As with Christian and Johnny, though, Dave did find a difference, noticing that his partner in fact attended to some things more and has a lower tolerance that 'motivates' her:

SR: So do you think you do as much as [Partner]? ... I wonder if she'd be like yeah he doesn't do anything or ...?

DAVE: [Laughs] I must admit ... She would go round and start doing the dusting, she will notice it. But I would say we do the same amount [overall] though ... When I was a kid I never thought I'd be this much like my dad. With him being quite house-proud and stuff. I always thought, 'what're you doing that for? It's boring'. But I found out I'm doing the same [as him].

The division of labour, then, can be seen as at the very least veering towards equal and having no impact on the participant's sense of masculine self. It's interesting to note here that Dave's father is implicated in instilling this attitude because he had himself been a man who commits to tidying up and was 'so house-proud'. Despite Dave's admission that his partner notices the dust and is more likely to do something about it, there is strong evidence here – and in the stories above – of an 'egalitarian habitus' (Stahl, 2015).

The last point I want to make about Dave is in respect of his further imagined future in relation to childcare, which serves as a segue into a discussion of the young men who did now have children. Dave, now age 30, reiterated ideas he had originally articulated in his first interview by providing a strong economic rationale for decisions about how the presence of a child would affect their lives. He and his partner had agreed, he said, to follow traditional gender lines, expecting that if they had a baby his wife would likely drop her hours to part time:

DAVE: [Inaudible] with the wedding, we have discussed stuff like that. I think we have discussed the thought of obviously, [Partner] doing the ... I suppose it's quite traditional like, she takes the maternity off, I have a few weeks off, and then go back to work. Because I think [Partner] then wants to go part time, rather than going back to full-time work, after we have a baby and that.

Dave ultimately offered a rather standard economic rationale for this, but not before also supposing that his partner wouldn't like to work all day with children and then come home to another child:

DAVE: She works at a nursery school at the moment with kids, so I think ... So I think she wants to go part time, and then not resenting coming home to a baby sort of thing. So, I think, I think as well it is because I earn more wages, but if I stayed full time, it's easier, because at the moment, I've got the higher paid job ... Yeah, if it was the other way round and [Partner] earned more money, I'd be quite happy to go and do what's she's doing and go part time and that.

SR: That's interesting ... obviously she'd need maternity leave and stuff, but do you think you'd be happy to be a stay-at-home dad, if it was what was necessary?

DAVE: So, I don't think there'd be an issue with that ... if she got offered a job in the next six months or year or so, and it was more money and she really wanted to do it, then I don't think I'd have a problem going part time.

Dave sees his partner as expecting to come home and take care of the baby. How these dynamics play out in actuality are central to our understanding of working-class men's lives, because while the 'interactional level' of dividing housework tasks is considered an important site for the possibility of both changes in gender consciousness (Sullivan, 2011) as well as resistance (Gatrell, 2005), 'it is the arrival of children that tends to scuttle any egalitarian ideals and press couples into even greater gender specialisation' (Treas & Drobnic, 2010: 5). Moving from intentions to relationship realities, next I discuss six of the seven participants who lived with a wife/partner and their children or stepchildren. As will become clear through a discussion of their domestic and employment situations, there are complex ways to assess this, but overall the men illustrate commitments to domestic labour that deviate from many of their fathers' generation, showing how they ought to be conceived as a particular generational unit who embody inclusive forms of masculinity and reflexively reject hegemonic norms.

Breadwinning and 'leaning in'– Jez and Tim

Contrasting to his 2009 job assisting in a shoe store, Jez is now employed by the Royal Air Force Military Police. In July 2016, he married his partner of three years, with whom he has four step-children and two biological children, both under age two. Until their marriage, he essentially lived alone 'on camp', travelling back to see his partner and children 'on weekends and whenever possible' since their first biological child arrived. The arrangement for housework until that point was complex given they lived separately, but since they all live together permanently on camp (permitted since they are married), there is apparent adherence to a breadwinner model labour division. Jez explains:

JEZ: It was tough before, when I commuted back and forth to see her and the kids, but it's a lot better now. But I'm still away about a quarter or third of every month ... I chip in [with housework] when I can, but if I am back before kids' bedtimes then my evening's mostly spent with them, and my wife – she runs the house.

SR: Anything you prefer, like when you chip in ...?

JEZ: Washing up, probably. And garden stuff! But obviously I help put the kids to bed; there's three small kids.Jez illustrated the only slightly blurry lines between being breadwinner and the role of maintaining the domestic setting. Yet, on the possibility of a role reversal, he states:

JEZ: I'd happily be a househusband! But I'm a crap cook and useless at washing clothes, so I best leave it to the wife!

Here, Jez veers toward essentialised notions that equate maleness to being 'crap' at domesticity, echoing some participants' initial interviews. He seemingly suggested that he 'helps' with his wife's job (Doucet, 2004). Yet, he also exhibits a degree of 'leaning in' (Friedman, 2013) to territory traditionally seen as 'unmasculine' and off-limits for the kinds of men who consider themselves 'completely masculine'. He also recognises the *need* to 'lean in' to assist. Too much attention to how he phrases this may disguise that he does, in significant ways, participate with childcare and certain chores, both 'conventionally feminine' tasks like washing up, and 'traditionally masculine' or gender-neutral tasks like gardening (Altintas & Sullivan, 2016).

Such 'leaning in' to support the primary caregiver was also evident in Tim's life. At his latest interview and for most of the last three years, Tim had been a sales-related web editor for a glazing company. Tim explained an overall similar situation to Jez:

TIM: I do tidy up, but not like she does. Like I don't mind being less, but her standard is much higher. I go to work Monday to Friday, she's a housewife; stays home and looks after our youngest ... She does most of the cooking. I cook once or twice a week. Yeah, weekends, I take control and we do lots of stuff together to make up for the time I don't see the boys. Like, we go out and do something all together. But like last time [when you had tried to call me for the interview], I also took [eldest son] with me to get the car service because I knew it would give [wife] time to just have one of the boys.

Although still geared towards 'assisting his wife', Tim inclined towards a team-based approach to breadwinning, childrearing and housekeeping. His assertion about taking control subscribes to a typically masculinist frame of reference, hinting how during the week he lacks control over getting to spend time with the children because of the imposition of paid work. His domestic time is dedicated not to the more onerous tasks his wife undertakes, but rather to more leisurely pursuits with the children (see Gottzén & Kremer-Sadlik, 2012). However, this can be further contextualised by considering that, after briefly taking up a new job for less than a month, Tim and his wife decided together that he ought to go back to his old job because the significantly longer commute and longer hours meant he could not see his kids as often as he liked, nor help his wife in the evening, making him 'depressively unhappy', and this was jointly considered more important than an additional 30% income for the family.

These approaches are more nuanced than the gendered division of labour that was central to the model of functional equilibrium that characterised the family in the 1950s and 1960s (Parsons & Bales, 1955). Despite only 'leaning in', and somewhat supporting the 'myth of male incompetence' (Tichenor, 2005: 41), the participants undertook some homemaking and childcare, and their lack of an overt rejection of the idea of such activity says something about the social knowledge developed for and by this generation of young men. These two are, however, the 'worst cases' in the sample. Much more egalitarian forms of practice were present and, indeed, dominant.

'The best is both' – Bobby

Bobby has transformed considerably since 2009, from predicting kids and family were unlikely, to having had three serious relationships, one producing a baby, and now living with his fiancée and his two step-children. His fiancée works full time for Sure Start, the early years child intervention programme. At his last interview Bobby had very recently been laid off from a job 'laying tracks on the Underground', where, as an independent sub-contractor, he enjoyed significantly higher than average wages of 'a fucking grand a week!', but no job security. Such a job might have likely seen Bobby withdraw from household tasks, or limit them in the ways described by Jez and Tim. But, in keeping with the spirit of the generational consciousness that has helped enormous reductions in (though far from eliminated) the gendered gap in minutes committed to housework (Altintas & Sullivan, 2016), Bobby's attention to being an equal partner is telling of the kind of masculinity that is possible, and not uncommon:

BOBBY: We share all housework. And I help with the kids as much as I can, e.g. picking them up from school and cooking dinner. The amount I do now obviously changed [increased] since I got laid off, because I used to go before 5 am and get back about 8 [pm] ... We share the cooking and the other chores. As much as possible.

In terms of contravening appropriate manliness, Bobby quickly dismissed this issue. But rather than being defensive or reconstituting his role in the domestic sphere to highlight the manly aspects, instead he casually noted:

BOBBY: No, I don't think about it. I just do it to make her happy and keeps me in the good books [smiles]. Plus *I want* to do it [his emphasis]. How can I sit on my arse all day whilst [partner] is at work and expect her to come home to a dirty house and cook the kids' dinner. It's a respect thing ... Also if I do it, it makes more time for us to be together, as a family but also for us two. The best is both [sharing the homemaking].

Bobby frames the domestic arrangements as a matter of respect and equality, corresponding with Inclusive Masculinity Theory (IMT), but also pragmatism (see Gottzén & Kremer-Sadlik, 2012). This pragmatism is hinted at by Tim and Jez, but became a reality when necessary for Bobby. Hegemonic norms that compel men to maintain distinctions between gendered spheres (Cancian, 1987) do not function for this generation as for previous generations. Such findings demonstrate that '[t]he interactional level – at which the allocation of domestic tasks is largely worked out between partners – is an *important site of potential change* to both gender consciousness and practices' (Lyonette & Crompton, 2015: 24, my emphasis). More inclusive masculinities can, then, be found in behaviours extending beyond those in the predominantly male-to-male interaction/attitudes-focused research to date (Anderson, 2011; McCormack, 2012; Roberts et al., 2016). I now explore this in further detail, referring to participants who had become primary caregivers.

'What matters is what works' – Mike, Pat, Jason

Three of the men remaining in the sample for the full seven years had become primary caregivers during the research. This may seem a surprising number but it follows the patterns in the qualitative data above, and also resonates with international trends (OECD, 2014). By deprioritising employment, they echoed sentiments from the original interviews, where participants expected to share domestic workloads where possible, but which seemed unlikely due to structural constraints given, 'it [employment] is set up for women to look after kids [...] [and] paternity leave is pretty rubbish' (Jason, initial interview), or that 'men usually earn more than women. That is shit in some ways, but that's what happens' (Pat, initial interview). For each of these three young men, becoming primary caregiver was a rational calculation, resulting in each of them undertaking the vast majority of all domestic duties, including cooking and cleaning as well as childrearing.

Pat left retail after his first interview, having found better wages working at a logistics depot. After several years in this industry, he held a supervisory role for a logistics company for about two and a half years. This job was much better paid and permitted further space for masculine capital building, as it involved 'telling the drivers where to go and giving them a bollocking if they fucked up' (Pat). In November 2015, Pat posted some photos of himself with his two young daughters (one aged two and one five months) on *Facebook*. His comments on the post highlighted that his wife was away that day, and so he had the children to himself. One image showed his eldest child climbing on his shoulder and face while he held the baby in the other hand and also took the photo simultaneously. I sent him a private message on

Facebook stating 'pic with the kids looks fun! and quite a handful!', to which Pat responded:

PAT: Yeahs all good. [Wife] is having a day off going to a Spa with her mum and a wedding tonight. I best get used to this cos we thinking of going to me staying at home after maternity finishes.
SR: Cool. Why do you think that will happen then?
PAT: Expensive childcare man, we can't afford to both work cos it'll cost more than one wage to pay.
SR: Oh right. How do you feel about giving up work to do it?
PAT: It's gonna be the easiest job in the world! What's not to like[?] She works ten mins away I travel over hour each way everyday and my commute is fuckkkking expensive. So when you take that out [wife] earns more money than me. What matters is what works yo.

The pragmatic necessity was very clear, although it was noteworthy that Pat possibly headed off any questions about masculinity by suggesting, 'What matters is what works'. At his last interview, we discussed his experience of being primary carer and stay-at-home dad, which by this point had been about seven months. Pat was quick to redress his earlier assessment that childrearing was easy, but not because of anything to do with his masculine identity:

PAT: I'm tired, man. It is tiring, like go go go. We are both tired though.
SR: I remember you told me that it's the easiest job in the world … [laughs].
PAT: It's easy – at first! Like for a few weeks then I *realised* it *is* tiring. Like I love being with my girls. As well, I have down time when they're napping. They don't always nap at the same time but once you get your routine, like there's sometimes time for me to play my PlayStation or watch movies or something. I have to tell [wife] that I haven't seen some stuff 'cos I get time to watch it in the day and I just pretend that I haven't when we watch it together! And then it's pretty much constant go, feeding, tidying up, which is waste of time actually 'cos they just make mess all the time, then entertaining them.
SR: So what do you think, like that idea, it's less manly for blokes … ?
PAT: I *don't care at all*. It's fucking stupid because doing anything else would be the wrong decision, we would have less money.
SR: Do you miss work at all?
PAT: It'd be hard for me now to be away from the girls, but it is quite difficult for me to not be anything other than a dad, like I don't have a social life, so when I had a few I had a blow out [got drunk] we had a massive argument … That's the thing, that's why it's hard whoever does it. When she has to have both kids it drives her crazy and she is all over Facebook saying 'can't wait for him to come home'. So it would be hard for anyone to do it and not have anything else.

The dominant theme, then, was one of a reshaped masculinity operating under the requirements of the contemporary economic realities, but also the generational knowledge that realms previously associated with the feminine do not threaten one's masculinity. Possible behaviours and roles are clearly opening up as per the IMT thesis (Anderson, 2009). These sentiments do not make Pat the antithesis of masculinity. There is clear tension in his identity construction, such that he reacts a little aggressively and assertively to the idea that it's somehow less manly to be a primary caregiver. The other two stay-at-home dads showed understanding that some people will question why they are primary caregivers. The following, though, highlights the tension of knowing that this hegemonic expectation in some way exists, but simultaneously is something that can be reflexively negotiated.

Mike has been primary caregiver for over two years so that his partner could take up an apprenticeship at an accountancy firm. This was a longer-term decision because, while in the immediate sense an apprentice wage would offer relatively little income, they were banking on his partner yielding larger wage returns than Mike could amass in the future. Rationalising this, Mike asserted it was his ability, being good at looking after the kids, that also played an important role in what made him good at the job, but he also very quickly – and without being asked – attended to the idea that some people question gender non-conformity:

MIKE: I'm not fucking blowing my own trumpet or anything, but I'm a good dad and I'm good at looking after the kids and stuff like that ... Anyone, I say to them, I'm a stay-at-home dad, it doesn't matter who they are, I get questions ... a lot of them are like, oh, what do you do for a living? I'm like, well, I sit at home and look after the kids and I play video games in the evening and that's pretty much it. I get the questions, 'oh, your missus works?' Well, yeah, she brings the money in. Oh, 'do you not feel like a woman?' 'Do you not feel like you're the housewife?', or – and stuff like that. I'm like, no, it makes me feel like more of a man, to be honest, because I'm stepping up for my kids and that's what matters. It doesn't matter whether I'm a man or a woman or what. I'm being a parent to my kids and they're my number one priority, so I don't care what people say ... Like, you're stuck in this paradigm where men have to be men and women have to be women and you have this certain job and that's the be-all and end-all. Whereas if you actually just let go of all that bullshit and just go with what works your life might be a little bit better.

This reflexive reconstruction of masculinity was also echoed by the third stay-at-home dad, Jason, whose wife worked in an administrative role for the local council. In fact, Jason echoed some of Mike's stance almost verbatim, arguing 'I am more of [a] man, because I'm providing for my family, being there, taking responsibility'. This responsibility was evident in the fact that Jason had to curtail our first attempt at his final interview after just five minutes because his son had woken up and his wife was sleeping, and secondly, in that when we conducted his final interview he was partly entertaining his son the whole time (similarly, Mike also watched his son play during the last interview).

Jason spoke fondly of dividing general household tasks, suggesting 'when we get the chance we divide and conquer!', but noted he did most domestic chores as his wife was in paid work more often. Being a stay-at-home dad, just like many of the men had suggested in their first interviews when projecting to the future, was an easy decision:

JASON: I've *always* been under the impression that it would be best for the family if the highest earner goes back to work? Because raising your child, you need as much money as possible. So whoever has the highest wage would go and work full time [emphasis added].

Jason's articulation about the rational trade-off being something that he always presumed would be the deciding factor again highlights that this way of thinking is an ingrained disposition; it was an important part of the habitus of all of these young men. He also explained that being a primary caregiver also necessitated being a part-time worker, and since his wife returned to work after her maternity leave Jason negotiated with his boss to get hours that worked for the family:

JASON: I go in at five o'clock, an hour and a half after the evening shift would normally start, and start work then. It's just about manageable, but with the cost of living and everything else, you need to do what you can. We could barely survive on my wife's income, we would be living paycheque to paycheque.

As with Mike, there was a discernible recognition that sometimes people question the man's role when hearing that they are primary caregiver. Jason explained how he was proudly defensive against any maligning comments, frowns or questions in this regard:

JASON: Actually it's harder, because it's hard work and constant and on top of that sometimes people look at you and you can tell they think you shouldn't be doing that, like changing a diaper or something ... [But] Erm, to me, being a man is actually being able to take responsibility for your family, it doesn't matter which role you take. It's taking responsibility for your family. I cook, I do the cleaning, I just do general stay-at-home stuff. It's what's got to be done.

In this account, and those of the other stay-at-home dads, there is a clear absence of the loss of status felt by fathers documented in previous research at the turn of the millennium (e.g. Doucet, 2004). In Jason's case, part of the mitigation for loss of status, perhaps, was that he retained a part-time job where he could consolidate his masculinity (see Chapter 6). He did not reconcile this in his own mind but it is possible to determine that working with alcohol, showing his knowledge of the products, flirting with women and often objectifying them in chats with other colleagues (see Chapter 8) in his part-time job allowed Jason a form of masculine recuperation or compensation. It might also be evidence of the ways that men and masculinity can be chameleon like (Ward, 2015), such that men produce and enact different varieties of masculinity at different times (Jenkins, 1983; Ingram, 2018). Beyond this, another notable issue was that Jason was able to point to another man, who lived in the apartment below, who was also a stay-at-home dad. The two men had bonded, hanging out with their sons on 'playdates, usually swimming' two to three times a week. Jason described this man as his only friend, outside of work colleagues, and while he suggested they were an unlikely pair of friends given they would 'likely mix in different circles', the children gave them reason to become friends, gave them another man to talk to about 'the little one's development' and also helped reinforce for one another that 'I know that with the older generation it's still strange, but we think it's an acceptable thing'.

A last recuperation strategy, for Jason at least, was that he felt childrearing had 'unlocked [his] inner child'. This seemed to be especially the case given he had a son, and, while Jason talked of wanting his son to be whatever and whoever he wanted in terms of future occupations and romantic inclinations, he emphasised many typically masculine activities when discussing the time they spend together:

JASON: Yeah obviously I don't play football anymore, I've basically given up everything to have a happy family life. I've become a family man.
SR: Are you happy with that decision?
JASON: Yeah, because at the end of the day I go swimming with my little boy, and I take him to kinder gyms where he runs around and plays basketball, and I've unlocked my inner child. I'm kicking a ball around, I'm running around and playing, and I'm having fun with him. I'm teaching him the right way to be, and the way things go. I still do some fun stuff like play football, but I play football with him. And like we watch football and all that.
SR: Does he watch football with you? Is he a Tottenham fan?
JASON: [Boy's name], say 'The Mighty Spurs'.
(CHILD): [The Mighty Spurs!] The hardest thing for Jason, as with the other stay-at-home dads, was not its impact on their status as a man, but simply that it meant, in typically working-class circumstances of dual-earner households, that there was little time to spend with his partner:
JASON: We see very little of each other which is tough, but it's worked because obviously we see some parts of the weekend and most evenings together. Erm, yeah, to make the financial situation work, I've basically got to

work when she's not. So I do a Thursday day shift when she's working, and basically my in-laws have him, and we get the occasional staff holiday off together, but yeah, other than that it's very hard.

Each of the men who are now primary caregivers are, of course, consciously aware of the discourse of gendered expectations surrounding them, and they follow other research in expressing a lack of concern around the stigma (e.g. Rochlen et al., 2008), though this resistance for some might seem masculinist in itself. But as with all participants with children, emphasis is better placed on the reflexive search for pragmatic and inclusive ways to do what is right for the family and economic circumstances, with gender scripts holding significantly less sway. They represent an evident generational unit, who, under the same constellation of acquired social knowledge and social (and economic) circumstances, respond in similar ways. In the process, they are re-writing the rules of what it is to be young men (Woodman & Wyn, 2015).

Conclusion

Gill (2003) argues that any accurate account of 'newmanishness' – that is, men's apparent change for the better – must factor in men's role in domestic settings. Well, women still do the majority of the domestic chores, whatever the level and direction of income inequality (Crespi & Ruspini, 2016). Gender essentialist attitudes do appear to retain their strength and a 'natural' dichotomy is sometimes adhered to, whereby housework is associated with feminine identities, whilst being a 'breadwinner' is central to men's sense of masculinity (Adkins, 1995; Coltrane & Shih, 2010). However, starting with their projected ideals in their late teens or early twenties, and moving through to their actualised practices in their mid- to late twenties or early thirties, what becomes clear is that housework and childcare are regular and normalised for contemporary working-class young adult men, such that adherence to older models is starting to fray. 'Leaning in' or fully sharing the load in this domain, and even becoming primary caregivers, presents additional ways in which masculinity has become reconstructed for this social generation (Woodman & Wyn, 2015: 1404).

This is, of course, still no gender egalitarian utopia. But the capacity to reflexively build the possibilities for modern male manhood in the ways outlined above point to a generational frame of reference that presupposes the possibility of some gender non-conformity, rather than attachment to traditional notions of a gendered domain in the home. This opening up of acceptable behaviours and reference points is consistent with the core tenets of IMT (Anderson, 2009), where the prospect of being 'feminised' invokes less cultural fear. The economic, social and political contexts that constitute part of the conditions under which this generational constellation has formed, mean that retaining gender-equal ideals from one's early twenties can and sometimes needs to be realised as the young men become partners and parents into their late twenties. It is increasingly likely that current young generations are not lacking a 'notion of manhood [that] encouraged them to be active parents and householders' (Hochschild, 1989: 12). This, I argue, is only enhanced by a working-class habitus, which, long infused with egalitarian dispositions (Stahl, 2015), has under the current conditions permitted working-class masculinity to have positively transitioned. A working-class habitus has dovetailed with a world influenced positively by both feminist gains and more negatively by the challenges of contemporary capitalism (such as precarious work and the need to establish a 1.5- or dual-earner household), producing a more empathetic 'practice'. The 'team' approach between men and women in heterosexual partnership is an important feature of navigating this new world. I make no such claims for all working-class men, but the evidence of change – for at least this generational unit – is unmistakable. Documenting these changes is the first step to more widely instituting them as entirely normative.

In the domestic arena more positive forms of masculinity can emerge *more freely* among working-class populations, as is the case within my sample, and which strongly resonates with recent empirical research findings that working-class men conform to 'lived egalitarianism', whereas higher-class counterparts exhibit preponderance towards 'spoken egalitarianism' (Usdansky, 2011; see also Lyonette & Crompton, 2015). Quantitative analysis confirms this, and situates economic factors as being *part* of the reason for this lean towards egalitarianism among the working classes (Fagan & Norman, 2016). Additionally, as Craig et al. (2015) discovered, it is young men in couple relationships in particular (versus those living with female friends or with parents), who are most likely to equally divide domestic duties. These realities are important to document as we proceed if we are to avoid a deficit approach to understanding working-class masculinity, and for establishing just how sizeable this generational unit is within their wider generation. They also present us with possibilities and frame of reference that speak to a more commensurate fit with Becker's time allocation theory of gender-neutral, rational economic bargaining in respect of domestic labour. We haven't yet achieved that, but young working-class men illustrate that it is something we can make strides towards. Documenting the kinds of approaches highlighted in this chapter will help to disrupt the idea that men could or should reinforce their masculinity by *not* engaging in feminine activities, such as housework, to avoid further emasculation in situations where they are unemployed or earn lower wages than their partners.

Having explained how working-class young men have transitioned from the masculinity of their fathers' generation in relation to school (Chapter 5), paid work (Chapter 6) and domestic chores, the final analysis chapter turns to more focused discussion of emotional expression.

References

Adkins, L. (1995). *Gendered Work: Sexuality, Family and the Labour Market*. Buckingham: Open University Press.

Alimahomed-Wilson, J. (2011). Men along the shore: Working-class masculinities in crisis. *NORMA*, 6(01), 22–44.

Altintas, E., & Sullivan, O. (2016). Fifty years of change updated: Cross-national gender convergence in housework. *Demographic Research*, 35(16), 455–470.

Anderson, E. (2009). *Inclusive masculinity: The changing nature of masculinities*. New York: Routledge.

Anderson, E. (2011). Inclusive masculinities of university soccer players in the American Midwest. *Gender and Education*, 23(6), 729–744.

Anderson, E., & McCormack, M. (2016). Inclusive Masculinity Theory: Overview, reflection and refinement. *Journal of Gender Studies* [online], 1–15.

Beck, U. (1992). *Risk Society: Towards a New Modernity*. London: Sage.

Becker, G.S. (1965). A Theory of the Allocation of Time. *The Economic Journal*, 75 (299), 493–517.

Becker, G.S. (1991 [1981]). *A Treatise on the Family*, enlarged edn. Cambridge, MA: Harvard University Press.

Bianchi, S., Milkie, A., Sayer, C., & Robinson, J.P. (2000). Is Anyone Doing the Housework? Trends in the Gender Division of Household Labor. *Social Forces*, 79, 191–228.

Bourdieu, P. (1976). *Marriage strategies as strategies of social reproduction*. Baltimore, MD: Johns Hopkins University Press.

Breen, R., & Cooke, L.P. (2005). The persistence of the gendered division of domestic labour. *European Sociological Review*, 21(1), 43–57.

Cancian, F. (1987.) *Love in America*. Cambridge: Cambridge University Press.

Cockburn, C. (1983). *Brothers*. London: Pluto.

Coltrane, S. (1989). Household labor and the routine production of gender. *Social Problems*, 36(5), 473–490.

Coltrane, S., & Shih, K.Y. (2010). Gender and the division of labor, in J.C. Chrisler & D.R. McCreary (Eds.), *Handbook of Gender Research in Psychology, vol. 2: Gender Research in Social and Applied Psychology*. Springer, pp. 401–422.

Courtney, J. (2009). Real men do housework: Ethos and masculinity in contemporary domestic advice. *Rhetoric Review*, 28(1), 66–81.

Craig, L. (2006). Does father care mean fathers share? A comparison of how mothers and fathers in intact families spend time with children. *Gender & Society*, 20(2), 259–281.

Craig, L., Powell, A., & Brown, J.E. (2015). Gender patterns in domestic labour among young adults in different living arrangements in Australia. *Journal of Sociology* [online].

Crespi, I., & Ruspini, E. (Eds.). (2016). *Balancing work and family in a changing society*. Basingstoke: Palgrave, pp. 83–98.

Crompton, R., & Lyonette, C. (2005). The new gender essentialism – domestic and family 'choices' and their relation to attitudes. *British Journal of Sociology*, 56(4), 601–620.

Cunningham, M. (2008). Changing attitudes towards the male breadwinner, female homemaker family model: Influences of women's employment and education over the life-course. *Social Forces*, 87(1), 299–322.

Deutsch, F.M. (2007). Undoing gender. *Gender & Society*, 21(1), 106–127.
Doucet, A. (2004). Fathers and the responsibility for children: A puzzle and a tension. *Atlantis: Critical Studies in Gender, Culture & Social Justice*, 28(2), 103–114.
Fagan, C., & Norman H. (2016). Which fathers are involved in caring for pre-school age children in the United Kingdom?: A longitudinal analysis of the influence of work hours in employment on shared childcare arrangement in couple households, in I. Crespi & E. Ruspini (Eds.), *Balancing work and family in a changing society*. Basingstoke: Palgrave, pp. 83–98.
Friedman, S. (2013). Men: win at work by leaning in at home. *Harvard Business Review*, April 22 [online], https://hbr.org/2013/04/men-how-to-win-at-work-by-lean.
Gatrell, C.J. (2005). *Hard Labour: The Sociology of Parenthood*. Maidenhead: Open University Press.
Gershuny, J., & Robinson, J. (1988). Historical changes in the household division of labor. *Demography*, 25(4), 537–552.
Giddens, A. (1992). *The Transformation of Intimacy: Sexuality, Love and Eroticism in Modern Societies*. Cambridge: Polity.
Gill, R. (2003). Power and the production of subjects: A genealogy of the new man and the new lad, in B. Benwell (Ed.), *Masculinity and Men's Lifestyle Magazines*. Oxford: Blackwell, pp. 34–56.
Gottzén, L. (2011). Involved fatherhood? Exploring middle-class fathers' educational work. *Gender & Education*, 23, 619–634.
Gottzén, L., & Kremer-Sadlik, T. (2012). Fatherhood and youth sports: A balancing act between care and expectations. *Gender & Society*, 26(4), 639–664.
Henderson, S., Holland, J., McGrellis, S., Sharpe, S., & Thomson, R. (2007). *Inventing Adulthoods: A Biographical Approach to Youth Transitions*. London: Sage.
Hochschild, A. (1989). *The second shift: Working parents and the revolution at home*. New York: Viking.
Hollows, J. (2003). Oliver's twist: Leisure, labour and domestic masculinity in The Naked Chef. *International Journal of Cultural Studies*, 6(2), 229–248.
Hook, J. (2010). Gender inequality in the welfare state: Sex segregation in housework, 1965–2003. *American Journal of Sociology*, 115(5), 1480–1523.
Ingram, N. (2018). *Working-Class Boys and Educational Success*. Basingstoke: Palgrave.
Jenkins, R. (1983). *Lads, citizens, and ordinary kids: Working-class youth life-styles in Belfast*. London: Routledge.
Jones, G. (1995). *Leaving Home*. Buckingham: Open University Press.
Kan, M.Y. (2008). Does gender trump money? Housework hours of husbands and wives in Britain. *Work, Employment and Society*, 22(1), 45–66.
Lyonette, C. (2015). Part-time work, work–life balance and gender equality. *Journal of Social Welfare and Family Law*, 37(3), 321–333.
Lyonette, C., & Crompton, R. (2015). Sharing the load? Partners' relative earnings and the division of domestic labour. *Work, Employment and Society*, 29(1), 23–40.
McCormack, M. (2012). *The declining significance of homophobia*. Oxford: Oxford University Press.
McCormack, M. (2014). The intersection of youth masculinities, decreasing homophobia and class: An ethnography. *The British Journal of Sociology*, 65(1), 130–149.
McDowell, L. (2003). *Redundant masculinities?: Employment change and white working class youth*. London: John Wiley.

McKee, L., & Bell, C. (1986). His unemployment, her problem: The domestic and marital consequences of male unemployment, in *The experience of unemployment*. Palgrave Macmillan UK, pp. 134–149.

Morgan, D. (1992). *Discovering Men*. London: Routledge.

Nayak, A. (2006). Displaced masculinities: Chavs, youth and class in the post-industrial city. *Sociology*, 40(5), 813–831.

OECD (Organisation for Economic Co-operation and Development) (2011). Cooking and caring, building and repairing: Unpaid work around the world, in *Society at a Glance*. Paris: OECD, pp. 9–27.

OECD (Organisation for Economic Co-operation and Development) (2014). Balancing paid work, unpaid work and leisure. *OECD Gender Equality*, March 7 [online], www.oecd.org/gender/data/balancingpaidworkunpaidworkandleisure.htm.

ONS (Office for National Statistics) (2016). Women shoulder the responsibility of 'unpaid work'. *ONS Digital* [online], http://visual.ons.gov.uk/the-value-of-your-unpaid-work/.

Parsons, T., & Bales, R.F. (1955). *Family, socialization and interaction process*. Glencoe, IL: Free Press.

Richardson, D. (2010). Youth masculinities: Compelling male heterosexuality. *British Journal of Sociology*, 61(4), 737–756.

Roberts, S. (2013). Boys will be boys … won't they? Change and continuities in contemporary young working-class masculinities. *Sociology*, 47(4), 671–686.

Roberts, S. (2014). *Debating Modern Masculinities: Change, Continuity, Crisis?* Basingstoke: Palgrave Macmillan.

Roberts, S., Anderson, E., & Magrath, R. (2016). Continuity, change and complexity in the performance of masculinity among elite young footballers in England. *British Journal of Sociology* [online], 1–22.

Rochlen, A., Suizzo, M., McKelley, R., & Scaringi, V. (2008). 'I'm just providing for my family': A qualitative study of stay-at-home fathers. *Psychology of Men & Masculinity*, 9(4), 193–206.

Scholes, L. (2011). A slave to the stove? The TV celebrity chef abandons the kitchen: lifestyle TV, domesticity and gender. *Critical Quarterly*, 53(3), 44–59.

Stahl, G. (2015). *Identity, Neoliberalism and Aspiration: Educating white working-class boys*. London: Routledge.

Steno, A.M., & Friche, N. (2015). Celebrity chefs and masculinities among male cookery trainees in vocational education. *Journal of Vocational Education & Training*, 67(1), 47–61.

Sullivan, O. (2011). An end to gender display through the performance of housework? A review and reassessment of the quantitative literature using insights from the qualitative literature. *Journal of Family Theory and Review*, 3 (March), 1–13.

Szabo, M. (2014). Men nurturing through food: Challenging gender dichotomies around domestic cooking. *Journal of Gender Studies*, 23(1), 18–31.

Szalai, A. (1966). Trends in comparative time-budget research. *American Behavioral Scientist*, 9(9), 3–8.

Thébaud, S. (2010). Masculinity, bargaining, and breadwinning. *Gender & Society*, 24(3), 330–354.

Tichenor, V.J. (2005). *Earning More and Getting Less: Why Successful Wives Can't Buy Equality*. New Brunswick, NJ and London: Rutgers University Press.

Treas, S. & Drobnic, J. (2010). *Dividing the Domestic: Men, Women, and Household Work in Cross-National Perspective*. Stanford, CA: Stanford University Press.

Usdansky, M.L. (2011). The gender-equality paradox: Class and incongruity between work–family attitudes and behaviors. *Journal of Family Theory and Review*, 3, 163–178.

van der Lippe, T., Treas, J., & Norbutas, L. (2017). Unemployment and the division of housework in Europe. *Work, Employment and Society* [online].

Ward, M. (2015). *From labouring to learning: Working-class masculinities, education and de-industrialization*. London: Springer.

West, C., & Zimmerman, D.H. (1987). Doing gender. *Gender & Society*, 1(2), 125–151.

Whitehead, S. (2002). *Men and Masculinities*. Cambridge: Polity.

Woodman, D., & Wyn, J. (2015). Class, gender and generation matter: Using the concept of social generation to study inequality and social change. *Journal of Youth Studies*, 18(10), 1402–1410.

8 Emotional disclosure online and offline

Changes and continuities in forms of intimate expression among working-class men

Introduction

My participants' negotiation of education, the paid economy and the domestic division of labour says much about the changing nature of working-class masculinity, but attention to more overtly affective domains also offers considerable insight. This chapter focuses on how young men emote, and how this contrasts to the oft-depicted archetype of working-class 'manliness' in popular and academic representations. While not part of their youth transitions experience, per se, the style and meaning of emotional conveyance is related in important ways to what I have set out in the previous chapters. As working-class young men change the way they perceive and enact masculinity in education, work and the domestic sphere, what are the correspondences with a wider repertoire of emotional displays?

That men are not 'emotionally honest' is a long-standing stereotype, and is part of the package of activity associated with performing appropriate, socially sanctioned masculinity. This performance, as highlighted in various theories (see Chapter 3), rests upon the avoidance of *particular* emotional expressions, captured by Brannon's (1976) suggestion that boys and men must engage in 'no sissy stuff' and 'be a sturdy oak'. Vulnerability, sadness, fear, emotional (and physical) pain, and even love and affection must remain restrained and hidden (Courtenay, 2002; Bennett, 2007), as these convey 'weakness' (Seidler, 1994). This represents the antithesis of manliness, with one correlate of manhood being to remain 'in control' (Kimmel, 1994: 125). This approach to emotional repression is argued to deliver poor mental health outcomes and has been described as a 'cost of masculinity' (Messner, 1997) in other realms, such as 'intimacy with women, their capacity for nurturant fathering, their friendships with other men, and for themselves' (Pease, 2012: 128). Other forms of emotion – such as anger, rage, competitiveness – are seen as *central* to men's performance of masculinity. These emotions are (often) precursors to violence and/or are linked to displays of power; and power, of course, is seen by many theorists as central to masculinity. Aggression, then, as a reaction to being made to feel humiliated, is theorised as a response based on a man's efforts to maintain status. Other emotions may further flow from, or with, such actions – for example, 'satisfaction, pride, even happiness, depending on the context' (de Boise & Hearn, 2017: 785) can emerge from, or be co-present with violence.

The idea that men remain emotionally inarticulate is, though, challenged by theorists suggesting that appropriate 'manly emotion' is better understood as a combination of emotional expression alongside self-control (Shields, 2005). As Walton et al. (2004: 413) contend, 'to experience emotions is human; to control their expression is masculine'. Central to such thinking, though, is how emotional inarticulacy is produced by, and reproduces, gendered power relations (Pease, 2012; de Boise & Hearn, 2017). Inexpressiveness, then, according to Pease (2012), is not simply a result of adhering to a limited gender role, but functions to actively aid men's ability to oppress others and to inflict pain without needing to emotionally manage or process the consequences; it is about avoiding vulnerability and maintaining power.

Counter to these representations of men being unable/unwilling to (strategically or otherwise) demonstrate their emotions, a significant amount of new research has used Inclusive Masculinity Theory (IMT) to make sense of a remarkable transformation in the ways that emotional display has moved from being oppositional to masculinity (Bird, 1996; Kimmel, 2000; Connell, 1995), to becoming central to appropriate masculinity (Anderson & McCormack, 2016; Scoats, 2017; see also Chapter 3). Not only has this research documented a growth of men openly admitting in interviews or surveys that they engage in various forms of tactility, including cuddling, kissing, or dancing with other men (Anderson et al., 2012; McCormack, 2012; Anderson & McCormack, 2015); Scoats's (2017) semiotic analysis of 1,100 *Facebook* photos of heterosexual undergraduate men's interactions with their peer group highlights these very same activities and meanings in a wide range of settings. This latter piece is especially relevant for the present chapter.

The issue, then, is not whether men actually *feel* emotions, but whether or not they display or act on some emotions and not others, and with what consequences (see de Boise & Hearn, 2017; Pease, 2012 for discussion). These displays, born from constructed gender ideals, have a relationship to structures of power, such that the stoic and 'rational' approaches most often adopted by men (compared to women and other genders) are seen to give them privilege in, for example, the economic sphere. Neither the display nor absence of emotional expression should be taken as automatically signalling any transformation or, necessarily, even maintenance of the gender order. However, the durable association of particular types of emotional display with masculinity, and with others discursively signalling a lack of masculinity, means that any deviation from the previously dominant cultural script is inherently of interest for scholars of masculinity.

With this in mind, in this chapter I explore a range of different forms, and locations, of emotional expression. Using evidence from the *Facebook* ethnography combined with *Messenger*- and interview-based discussion with the respective young men about the material I observed, the chapter provides a data-heavy 'thick description' of talk *and* (discursive online) action in respect of family, friendships and romantic and/or sexual relations. Sadness, pride, anger, happiness, vulnerability – the full gamut of emotional content is regularly evident in the collected data such that the chapter presents considerable evidence that this contemporary generation of young adults, like the generation they precede (see Anderson & McCormack, 2016), are rejecting traditional ideals, with orthodox narratives about what constitutes appropriate manliness being questioned, subverted and overturned. The accounts I present here give credence to the idea that emotional display, as 'a mix of conscious and nonconscious ways of being and doing that become habitual and natural' (Cottingham, 2017: 273), forms an integral part of contemporary working-class men's habitus.

In line with the IMT thesis, acceptance of gay peers, colleagues and others more widely, is a prominent feature of this expanded emotional display; so too is increased tactility and emotional closeness with other men. Both this transformation of intimacy and a wider set of readily expressed emotions than routinely documented in literature outside of IMT research, though, requires critical scrutiny. Talk and action related to emotional expression, then, is not deemed as inherently positive, and the material I detail here is considered critically, but ultimately positioned as reflecting an expanded set of behaviours that constitute a new, and less-policed, normal. However, further interrogation of men's homosocial intimacy draws attention to the ways that remnants of orthodox masculinity remain prominent. In particular, the participants exhibited complex relationships with homophobia and misogyny, discursive traces of which co-existed alongside notably progressive approaches to same- and opposite-sex friendships and romantic relationships. The contradictions that emerge in accounts are explored, highlighting notable inconsistencies around homophobic and misogynistic language. Sometimes this inconsistency relates to the presence of others outside of a specific group of friends, such that the young men's use of discriminatory discourse is reduced to 'insider banter'. The men argue that such objectively problematic and often offensive language is used in subjective ways to evidence and enhance intimate bonding, considering it as having benign intent, and importantly, having *no prospect* of wounding. McCormack's intent-context-effect matrix provides a useful frame for understanding this behaviour. I also explain how the more identifiable misogyny (relative to homophobia) present in various parts of the data, even if somewhat attenuated compared to previous generations, remains congruent with working-class masculine habitus that has undergone significant transformation.

Emotion in abundance: an unexpected observation?

> Thinking of how men cry at football matches, gigs, births or funerals, among other situations, it is possible to see how the display of even supposedly 'unmasculine' emotions, in specific settings, becomes socially accepted.
>
> (de Boise & Hearn, 2017: 787)

This quote from de Boise and Hearn reminds us that men do engage in and display emotions, despite masculinity being traditionally thought to police and teach men to avoid such an outpouring. This occurs in specific conditions and settings, and as such it should come as no surprise that following a group of men for two years on social media would reveal all kinds of emotions related to those kinds of masculine settings or occasions. A range of expressions of both joy and sadness in relation to sports results, for example, was unquestionably present in the men's statuses, comments and so on. But of interest for this chapter is the last few words in the above quote – i.e. that which is now 'socially accepted'. As I will illustrate, the social acceptance of emotional displays goes vastly beyond the few settings and themes articulated in the quote. As per the IMT thesis, now free(r) from gender policing, the men in my study have largely embraced the opportunity to perform an expanded set of behaviours, and the evidence for this was overwhelming, both in the ethnographic data related to their social media activity and also in their interviews. I agree with de Boise and Hearn (2017: 788) that we ought not to automatically position 'particular emotions, as inherently progressive or regressive for men', and must instead consider if the emotionality we observe ties into the maintenance of gender power. Equally, we must state when it does not. I start, then, by thinking about the ways the young men share emotive content with me as a researcher.

Sharing emotional content in research interviews

The literature is somewhat split on the role of gender in interviewing. There has been a long-standing position that highlights the advantages women researchers have in achieving higher levels of emotional disclosure from men (McKee & Bell, 1986; Broom et al., 2009). Some have highlighted that where bonding between male researcher and male participants occurs, sexist and masculinist behaviour can be supported or even re-inscribed (Skelton, 1998; Vanderbeck, 2005; Pini & Pease, 2013). Nonetheless, others, such as Flood (2013: 67), note how their 'experience of qualitative interviewing men has not borne out this depiction of male non-disclosure'. My data correspond with Flood's (2013) inasmuch as instances of humour and reflection abounded. There was also deep and profound discussion of feelings of loss, shame, pride, joy, etc., and emotional disclosure was a central feature of the interviews with these working-class young men (cf. Simpson & Richards, 2017 on older working-class men). What follows leads me to seriously question the tendency in masculinity research to ponder or even assert that being middle class and tertiary educated may positively shape the possibilities for free and open disclosure practices (e.g. Flood, 2013).

My intention here is to briefly illustrate the breadth and depth of emotional content that emerged in interviews and message exchanges. The act of sharing stories with indisputable emotional resonances was illuminating in itself, but moreover the men regularly shared how they felt about such stories. In the initial interviews, for example, Billy talked about his difficult relationship with his step-father and how their being at odds led to him moving out of the family home. He unabashedly explained that he 'felt hurt' that his mother agreed he should move out. While not presenting an overly upset state, he was clearly sad as he reflected on what he felt was his step-dad's bullying of him and making his life uncomfortable by, for example, not letting them eat together as a family. In his first interview, Danny (see Chapter 5) talked about the guilt he felt after being given a fine that his mother had to pay. He also expressed a sense of shame that he had 'fucked up' his education, and exuded considerable anger reflecting on how a girlfriend had broken up with him after they had spent money together that he had inherited. Tim, in his final interview, talked candidly about struggling to come to terms with holding down a job as a retail assistant, with a period of unemployment at age 20 meaning, 'I just felt really lost and alone at that point'. He also freely recounted a troubling time when, five years later, after another change of job, the pressure of being the breadwinner and working a job he did not like felt crushing:

TIM: [I] didn't want to be there, and by ten, ten thirty, I was in the toilet crying. For no reason. I'd never experienced anything like that, I was just crying. Going to the toilet and crying every five minutes.

This same openness was clear in the confusing feelings Tim has for his second-born son. Around the same time as he was experiencing this breakdown he realised that he was conscious that he had not bonded well with this child, the opposite from how he had connected with his first son. The distress and sadness of this time were not shied away from, discounted or reconstituted in 'manly' terms in any sense. This goes, too, for Mike, who told me about the pivotal death of his friend. Killed on a train track in front of Mike's eyes (see Chapter 5), Mike remembered being 'hysterical', 'crying uncontrollably for weeks'. The more recent loss of his father to a heart attack, some four years before his final interview, also brought about a reflective and emotionally attuned response.

Another interesting discussion of overt emotions perhaps not usually associated with working-class manliness came in Bobby's interview. There are two particular examples that I draw attention to here: shame and love, both of which relate to his fiancée. Bobby spoke with gratitude when talking about his partner, expressing his love for her unabashedly. The strength of his love was, he felt, illustrated in a story he told me about going on another man's premarital 'stag' holiday with a group of friends. Bobby made clear that despite substantial and aggressive peer pressure from the stag group's 'best man', he actively (and successfully) resisted going to a strip club:

BOBBY: ... I've been on stag do's in the past and strip clubs weren't an issue and then, I meet my future wife and the thought of looking at someone else in that way actually makes me feel sick. 'Cos it's respect I think … respect for women … And erm, the fact that I'm crazy about her. And I wouldn't want anything to jeopardise what we can have in the future … A moment's pleasure for a lifetime of suffering – what's the point in that? Three other lads from the seven also didn't go [to the strip club]. We just went and had some food and a few quiet beers.

I make no claims about young men's changing (or otherwise) sex consumption practices; the point is that Bobby asserted love for his partner as being pivotal, over and above the hegemonic norms related to consuming or desiring the female body and the pleasure that might bring in the specified social situation. Masculinity is complicated, of course, and this is evidenced in another interesting disclosure that occurred about eight months after the stag tour.

Two weeks before Christmas 2015, Bobby was laid off from his job as a sub-contractor laying tracks on the London Underground. The following weekend, he decided to take his partner for a surprise romantic getaway, but his sudden loss of work resulted in cash-flow problems. I interpreted his decision to pay for this unexpected trip as linked to the job loss. His high pay – 'a fucking grand a week!' – had been a source of dignity and pride, and having this taken away seemed to initiate a course of action to show his value and retain his status in a typically masculine fashion. However, to pay for this trip Bobby had, without permission, taken £200 from their 'wedding savings' jar, money which had been a gift from his partner's mother. While planning to put the money back before anyone noticed, his partner realised the money was missing on New Year's Day. Rather than confessing, Bobby joined his partner in announcing their disappointment on *Facebook*, publicly expressing 'heartbreak' that one of their friends or family who had visited during Christmas 'must have betrayed and stolen from us'. Bobby continued this charade for two days, before his partner challenged that, by process of elimination, it could only have been him who took the money. On the third day, still trying to maintain some pride, and after arguing with his partner, Bobby left the home, with her wanting to call off the marriage.

Bobby explained how during this time several male friends asked what had happened and offered to help pay for their loss, but he doubled down, insisting he had been robbed, even speculating to his friends that 'perhaps it was another [lover] she hadn't told me about'. Eventually he confessed and after extensive apologies to friends and family, his partner forgave him. The reason I recount this story is both the masculinised approach to status that almost destroyed his relationship, but also because *he decided* to provide this account. The overwhelming emotion, for the whole process, was shame. Having felt ashamed of losing his job, he acted in ways that he felt, upon getting caught, were shameful, lying to his friends and family, and then, finally, relayed that shame in an interview setting, where there was no gain to be had from revisiting or admitting his feelings and action:

BOBBY: Honestly I was gonna put it back. I don't know. Just wanted to do something nice, it got out of hand. I was so ashamed. And embarrassed to tell my friends that I lied to them.

Finally in this subsection, I recount Gavin's case, where the majority of emotionally driven content was communicated via *Messenger*. After trying several times to organise a face-to-face interview, we eventually decided asynchronously answering questions by a message app was more timely. Gavin responded at considerable length in this format, more so than in face-to-face interactions. However, for the sake of brevity, I have reduced his extremely detailed accounts to a number of quotes in a manner that (I hope) does not reduce his emotionality to prevailing stereotypes.

Interestingly, it was only at the last interview, where Gavin was able to ponder the question and respond at his own pace, that he revealed the full extent of his history. He had not been especially quiet in the first interview in 2009, but, perhaps, having established a stronger degree of trust, he willingly provided much more detail. The emotional content was at times staggering. In one of these exchanges, we discussed the differences between himself and men of his father's generation at age 30, and why Gavin thought he was empathetic in ways his father was not. However, what followed was an unfolding train of thought that tailed in various directions of interest, illuminating issues of masculinity, and an array of explicitly emotional content.

He shifted to a description of his array of emotions when he learnt of his first daughter's conception:

GAVIN: what if i am a monster, what if the child didnt take to me, what if i was a horrible selfish parent that creates another broken person … i had decided that no matter what i do i would put right all the wrong things my parents had done to me for both my sanity and to make sure the child never felt all the things i had to.

He described his tumultuous childhood; microwaving his own dinners at age ten, being kicked out of his neglectful, emotionally abusive mother's house at age 12 and having to live with a father who worked long hours and a step-mother who blamed him for her childlessness. He then returned to the story of his first daughter: 'probably the hardest thing that has so far happened to me':

GAVIN: … i have tears in my eyes thinking about what im about to write … [Baby girl's name], was born on [date], she died on the next day … complications during birth … at 2 am i was told she was in labour, at 6 am i was told i was going to loose them both … i found myself on the floor, you never recover, ever.

He lamented that he 'was expected to be a robot during this whole thing, nobody asked me if i was ok', and described the struggle of dealing with his own grief while trying to 'stay strong' for his severely depressed partner. In an unprompted follow-up message he spoke of his intense love for his second daughter:

GAVIN: [the next pregnancy was] the most terrifying experiance of my life, [but Second baby girl's name] was born without any complications two days before new years, it was the first time in my life i has actually lost control of my bowels and physically shit myself, i have never before or will again probably never experience a love so overwhelmingly powerful, forget your parents, dogs, sex, drugs, not even close, on the flip side ive spent the last years of my life in constant fear of something happening to her ... people dont tell you about the fear that comes with loving something so much.

Since his second daughter's birth he also described leaving his partner and dealing with his own depression and suicidal thoughts, but ultimately he turned things around, 'gave up drinking and started back going to the gym, i filled my surroundings with only positive things ... nothing in this world could stop me from being the best father to my little girl'. He ended the message by saying:

GAVIN: Glad if it helps in anyway, I've been in a very much lighter mood since writing it, another bullshit way of thinking about real men not showing there emotions quashed I think, not that I'm saying I'm a real man or anything.

Oftentimes, in both academic and popular literature, 'men are said to be out of touch with their feelings and to need to express more emotions to allow them to be vulnerable' (Pease, 2012: 128). The material contained in Gavin's story is exceptional in its content relative to the sample, but undoubtedly the idea that working-class men do not emote is a myth that must be busted. The ways the young men talked about emotions, emotional content or experiences, and emotional display in an interview can, perhaps, be considered as a performance, where the interviewee says what the researcher 'wants to hear'. I doubt this to be the case, and if anything, I would suspect that a stronger masculine front might be present if any performance were to take place. Nonetheless, in the next subsection I draw on the *Facebook* ethnography to consider the kinds of emotional displays that happen outside of the interview setting, which on some level, aids moving beyond 'an assumed correspondence between language and action' (de Boise & Hearn, 2017: 783). In combination, I contend that there is little to suggest that these men are engaging in any kind of 'distraction from analysing their privilege and power' (Pease, 2012: 130; see also Robinson & Hockay, 2011).

Emotion-laden activity on *Facebook*

As a normatively used tool for online self-representation and communication (Hogan, 2010; Brooks et al., 2011), *Facebook* is understood as an important platform for the presentation of the emotions. Research has documented that *Facebook* might not necessarily present something that is a thorough and full representation of one's life. This indicates that positive rather than negative experiences and emotions are more likely to be shared via this medium. Thus, while considerable research has deployed Goffman's theoretical tools on impression management in analysing *Facebook* presentations of the self, Hogan (2010) has argued that social media activity is better understood as *curating* 'exhibitions', rather than *performances* in 'situations'. This is a subtle but important difference, with the latter relating to those interactions that happen between people in certain spaces, and the former being 'spaces where individuals submit artifacts to show to each other' (Hogan, 2010: 377). *Facebook* blurs the distinction between the two. But, as per Hogan, individuals curate their social media to account for the *possibility* that the audience is wider than in typical 'situational' interactions. The idea here is that because of the *possibility* that one's parents, children, wider family, colleagues, subordinates and/or superiors (etc.) might see the content – even if they are not the (primary) intended audience – these wider audiences shape and 'define the lowest common denominator of what is normatively acceptable' (Hogan, 2010: 383). What is *normatively acceptable* is important because it allows us to develop a sense of how masculine norms shape and produce particular online behaviours in this 'general online space' (Hogan, 2010: 383). Simultaneously, though, it does not preclude individuals who *might* use other niche sites or locations for presenting extreme views that are 'unambiguously questionable (nudity, violence, political extremism, racial epithets)' (Hogan, 2010: 383). I proceed here, then, to show that in an everyday and general sense, emotional content and emotional expression are a highly normalised aspect of men's presentation of self through their role as curator.

To begin, the postings and comments varied considerably in terms of content and regularity. The participants' *Facebook* activity varied hugely, from barely using the platform or mostly being tagged in statuses by their partners, to posting, sharing and commenting every two days, daily or in some cases, 5–10 times a day. While each person produced and shared different content, it often contained references to entertainment of various varieties. That is, the young men would predominantly 'share their location' when engaging in activities from the relatively mundane – but not 'everyday'. This included going to see a movie, gig or a theatre show, or going to a party of some sort, to more unusual and high-profile activities such as skydiving, or taking part in charity events. They would also share photos and content from when they went out drinking, attended or played sports, and often talked about online gaming, movies, TV shows, music. They shared jokes and (sometimes adult-themed) memes fairly regularly that were relevant to them and groups of friends. In almost all cases they shared more typically masculine videos of events that they thought were examples of hilarity or supreme skill in various activities (from professional sports, to amateur risk taking). Online communities like *LADbible* [1] were a major source of such material. Occasionally this material was plainly sexist, objectifying women or making jokes that draw on gender stereotypes.

Overt conventional political content was, for the most part, relatively absent. This was noteworthy because there is growing interest in the UK in understanding the alleged working-class turn to extreme right-wing political parties, such as Britain First. Other than in the months building up to the UK general election in 2015, and then to the European Union membership referendum in mid-2016, for the most part mainstream political issues were marked with ambivalence. There was some evidence of mixed sentiment on immigration, with both pro and anti views apparent, and occasional anti-elite content, shared from, for example, accounts related to 'Occupy' or 'the 99%' movements. Even more infrequently, I observed questioning of feminist logic that, in participants' minds, positions 'all men as rapists' and, even more rarely, some confusion around the use and politics of gender pronouns, albeit alongside other content that was often unmistakably pro equal rights for LGBTI people. All such content, mundane or otherwise, is of course inherently emotional – it was content that the young men had views on, that made them happy, sad, annoyed, bored, etc. This collection of everyday emotion co-existed alongside other forms of overt emotional expression that have in some of the literature been posed as being problematic for an authentic masculine self. Such material was not the most central feature of their *Facebook* behaviour, but it was very often a significant, and easily observable part of the rich amalgam that comprised their curated activity, as I now show with a variety of themed examples.

Family and children

As above, emotions poured out unambiguously through narrative interviews. In more subtle but equally notable ways, the young men's *Facebook* presence gave strong indicators of just how normal it is to display forms of care, love and sensitivity towards one's family members and children, whether their own or otherwise. Such expressions, indeed, were the cultural 'lowest common denominator' (Hogan, 2010), and thus a highly accepted norm. On one hand it may seem unsurprising that the men, for example, post photos with their children or young relatives, alongside comments that illustrate, among other emotions, a sense of pride. This was evident in many posts. It might suggest that the men curate their online presence in ways that garner praise or status for doing tasks that women often do without praise (Deutsch & Saxon, 1998; Gaunt, 2013), or reflect the presence of men in their children's lives in ways that are relatively novel (see Chapter 7). However, it may be 'at odds with the tenets of hegemonic masculinity and traditional fatherhood that detach men from reproduction and parenting' (Schmitz, 2016: 3). A reading of such images does not prove to be so clear. Yet, the disruption of hegemonic masculinity does emerge more readily in other images as we move on from the benign photos of the men hanging out with their children.

Peter posted photos of his nephews and nieces around five or six times a year, commenting 'Such a proud uncle x' or 'love these little ones'. While there is nothing *especially* progressive or different here, a conversation in the accompanying comments that involved another man enquiring 'No pictures of Grandad with them?', and Peter's dad replying 'That stuff is for wimps xx' is of interest. Note the ironic use of 'kisses' to soften the older man's policing of his own gender performance, as he distanced himself from Peter's somewhat attenuated masculinity. Beyond these fairly common types of commentaries, many of the young men (semi-)publicly professed their love for their family members, and did so in ways that disrupted the notion that men expressing intimacy has a negative, 'feminising' effect. A significant minority of Gavin's online footprint, perhaps unsurprisingly given the above statements, relates to his daughter. It is perhaps most immediately captured in a photo from 2016, which was captioned 'sometimes you just need to look up from what the problem is to realise what's important', and which depicted four pictures of his daughter and an array of drawings and cards his daughter had given him, situated above his work computer.

While many theorists view work and the public domain as the central site of masculinity, Gavin's words and actions here suggest his values and identity more closely align with the private sphere. He is of course making this statement very publicly to his *Facebook* 'friends'. He was unconstrained by orthodox masculine norms, not *just* because he rejects these norms, but because a different set of norms is expected and accepted in this general online space. These norms are also observable in a photo posted by Mike that depicted him walking his two older children to school for the first time, alongside his toddler. He declared his happiness at doing the 'smallest but most important things'. This was further demonstrated in Jez's postings about the photos he received via text from his wife and video calls while working away from home:

JEZ: Crap being away from my lil man and the girls, but FaceTime always manages to put a smile on my face! Such a happy lil man ♥ xx

These 'feminine' expressions of affection often extended to romantic partners – in ways so affectionate they would previously have been restricted to the private sphere – and even other people's children. For example, in 2015 Jez shared a viral video of hearing-deficient babies listening to their parents' voices for the first time. This video was accompanied by Jez's comment 'Heart warming and tears will get you'.

Emotion relating to death, sympathy, loss

As above, death – and especially funerals – is deemed among those specific contexts in which it is socially acceptable for men to show emotion (de Boise & Hearn, 2017). The way the participants conveyed their emotions in this respect is worthy of further consideration. The posts relating to loss of a friend or loved one, both of their own, or in sympathy with others, was most illuminating, and evidences more than the social acceptance of crying at a funeral. Instead, the following examples illustrate the participants' willingness to express their emotions in various ways and to extend comfort to others in a manner that might appear, by orthodox standards, 'unmasculine'.

As a starting point, all the men used *Facebook*'s sad face 'react' function for the deaths of various celebrities. Though a seemingly unremarkable fact, this signifies how a baseline 'sad reaction' is comfortably permissible. Beyond this, the young men often openly expressed their sadness in greater detail. For example, Tim expressed a deep sadness[2] about the death of Chyna, a WWE women's wrestler, lamenting both her early death and his own loss as a fan of her work. Further, in the same post he reacted angrily to the spreading of a leaked sex tape featuring Chyna, and lambasted those who had shared it. Unguarded outpourings also came about in 2015 when WWE men's wrestling 'legend' James Hellwig (stage name 'The Ultimate Warrior') died at age 54. Tim, Bobby and Johnny expressed disbelief and condolences in comments on public forums, while Pat posted a link to the news story on *Facebook* alongside the following comment:

PAT: I can't fucking believe it ultimate warrior has died !!!! ;(half my memories of my childhood were around him and the undertaker. Im devo. Feels like I lost family. Been tearful today :(xx

Participants responded similarly to the deaths of various actors, including Leonard Nimoy, Alan Rickman, and Christopher Lee. Interestingly, rather than being an individualised experience, they would often 'tag' friends in these comments and engage in collective nostalgia and mourning. However, responses to the loss of loved ones proved more revealing.

Somewhat echoing Gavin's story about the loss of his first child, above, Tim took to social media to share how he and his partner were coping with a decision to terminate a pregnancy at 12 weeks due to 'complications', having announced the pregnancy on social media in joyous fashion only weeks before. These social media posts conveyed his own sadness, as well as sensitivity towards his partner and an explanation about why she would be 'off social media for a while'. Love, respect, and various signifiers of vulnerability were entirely apparent. This emotional vulnerability was also present in Carl's posts about his late father. Every year on Father's Day and his dad's birthday, Carl wrote something in remembrance of his dad, such as this status: 'wants to wish my dad [dad's name] happy fathers day up in the big blue sky, love

192 *Emotional disclosure online and offline*

and miss you everyday'. Mike, who had lost his dad and witnessed a friend killed by a train in his late teens, reflected on a comment he found about a poem on *Reddit*:

MIKE: I've lost a lot of very close friends and family over the years, and this guys comment struck a chord very deep within me, so wanted to share here so others who have lost those close to them could read it, it's fucking poetry. It tears a hole through me whenever somebody I love dies, no matter the circumstances.

The comment Mike found on *Reddit* spoke to issues about grief, loss, anguish, about learning to 'wear and own scars' as a way of healing. The poem illustrated that one is lucky to have felt so connected to other people and to have loved: 'My scars are a testament to the love and the relationship that I had for and with that person.' Highlighting the sometimes contradictory nature of their online curation, though, a few months later Mike shared a meme stating 'avoid posting your personal problems; Personal problem require personal attention not social attention'.

Affection towards and about male friends

Scoats's (2017: 337) study of men's *Facebook* photos revealed homosocial tactility in terms of dancing, hugging and kissing to be the 'most thoroughly demonstrated behavior'. While not the majority, this type of material was fairly common in my study. Close proximity to other men was not a problem at all; photos of weddings, birthday parties, stag nights and regular nights out drinking all depicted the men engaging in a wide range of platonic touch. Two of the men, Dave and Christian, also each had photos of them naked with other men in settings that were not related to nights out. On some occasions this could be read as being ironic renderings of gender non-conformity (see Manago, 2013; McCormack, 2012), or even to attract the attention of women (Ralph & Roberts, 2018). Dave offered an example of this when on three different occasions he posted photos of himself and a group of friends naked together. In the new nude photos, one consisted of Dave and two friends standing naked side by side, cupping one another's genitals (not their own) to obscure the full nudity of their friend. Another image depicted Dave and four friends sitting naked on the floor in front of a sofa with their arms and legs entwined in ways that again hid their genitalia from the camera but made clear they were completely naked. The third image was a re-created replica of this group photo, but posted one year later, with Dave and his friends mocking themselves for how their bodies had changed. In Christian's photo, irony certainly was not initially at play. Instead he had posted a photo of him and his friend taking a shower together during a 140-mile charity walk, alongside a caption that jovially chastised the friend who had taken the photo:

CHRISTIAN: Posting this before bastard [friend's name]. Sneaky photo of me and [other friend] in the shower. He won't blackmail me for being naked!

Interestingly, Christian made no reference to the fact he was showering with his friend, and was more concerned about being seen naked by a wider audience. Another photo posted soon after, captioned '119 miles to go', showed the three men standing in a line, backs to camera, wearing nothing but their rucksacks. Here irony was overtly present as they built on the opportunity to promote their walk in a humorous fashion, in ways that garnered credit and notoriety from their friends.

Beyond images, though, the participants communicate with other men in textual formats that would likely be unrecognisable to men of their fathers' generation. The most notable manner in which this occurred was through the deployment of an 'x' or 'xx' (kisses) at the end of their responses to male friends. These 'kisses' are a commonly understood form of communication that, until very recently, would have been considered a feminine or romantic signifier. All except Jason, Gavin and Johnny semi-regularly did this to demonstrate platonic affection. For example, in the space of three months Peter shared four updates derived from *Facebook*'s automatically generated 'friend anniversary' photo montage. Sharing these updates, Peter also posted a comment that began with 'Aww' and proceeded to post a few words such as 'Aww mate emotional times! xx'. 'Kisses' also featured alongside birthday wishes, congratulations, condolences or other general enquiries or reminders to 'catch up soon' with other friends, both male and female. This expression from Mike to another friend [not actually his brother] was typical across the board: 'Here's to the best friend I could ever ask for. My brother. Love you man!x'

The textual 'kiss' also functions as a signifier of harmless or humorous intent when engaging in 'banter'. For instance, when teasing (or being teased by) their friends about football results, a harsh comment would be somewhat modified by the presence of a 'kiss'. There were, though, inconsistencies in the use of this rhetorical device. For instance, responding to a nice and considerably effusive comment by a friend telling him he loved him, Christian wrote back simply 'gay x'. However, this homophobic expression was deployed ironically and not an effort at policing the other man's gender performance (cf. Pascoe, 2007), as evidenced by Christian's deployment of this exact sort of affection with this man, and other men. I return to this below.

There was, then, abundant evidence of sharing emotional content and acting in unguarded emotional ways in the interviews and on social media. This diverges from the dominant narrative and fixed caricature of working-class masculinity, corresponding more closely to Anderson's IMT; behaviours once seen as unacceptable are now deemed possible. Yet, this may not be evidence of increasing agency that some researchers imply is open to individuals (see Anderson, 2009; Scoats, 2017) or even part of a generational subjectivity (Woodman & Wyn, 2015), per se.

A less 'homohysteric' culture can alter the possibilities for men's gender performance (Anderson, 2009), but I argue these men's emotional literacy is better understood as a function of habitus. Rather than *freer* to pursue inclusive forms of gender performance, the young men's emotions can be understood as *social practices*. As Scheer (2012: 193) notes, 'conceiving of emotions as practices means understanding them as emerging from bodily dispositions conditioned by a *social context*, which always has *cultural and historical specificity*' (my emphasis). The present socio-historical context is one of (not entirely) diminished homophobia, and it forms a habitus – the unconscious collective inculcated principle – at ease with, and productive of, the kinds of gender performance outlined in the IMT literature. Alongside an increasingly inclusive culture, and despite some obvious remnants of orthodox hegemony, the economic context, too, has a bearing here (see Chapter 6). The demands for emotional labour in the contemporary service economy – demands that surfaced at least 30 years ago and which are only increasing – have led to 'a shift in the masculine habitus to incorporate compassionate responses to others' (Cottingham, 2017: 278). For Cottingham (2017), this results from being monetarily incentivised, such that some men have adapted to new requirements. But for many (especially) young men, care, compassion, and emotional expression are a normalised feature of their practice because they are born from, and reflect, wider social structures. The emotional practices I highlight above, then, are entirely intelligible because they are 'both the product of past practices and the anticipation of new demands, including old and new caring moments' (Cottingham, 2017: 282).

This alteration in the readiness to be emotionally expressive must be considered critically. As de Boise and Hearn (2017: 789) remind us, 'simply describing how men talk about emotions' is insufficient as such talk might not necessarily be progressive. Accordingly, in the final major section of this chapter I explore how the young men explained elements of their friendship practices, in particular the ways that emotional closeness coincides with the use of homosexually themed language (McCormack, 2011) and the persistence of misogyny as a function for homosocial bonding.

'It's just between mates': making sense of misogyny and homosexually themed language

While many studies using IMT have noted the almost entire absence of homophobic language and also little to no overt misogyny among all male peer group cultures (see Chapter 3), my participants present a slightly more complex case. As above, the young men's physical behaviours observed in their social media footprint fit with those documented in dozens of pieces of research finding the presentation of inclusive masculinities (i.e. the total absence of the need to maintain physical distance from other men and the practice of ironic same-sex attraction). Yet, the social dynamics between the participants and their straight male peers allow for insights into the complex and slightly more problematic use of homosexually themed language as form of banter (McCormack, 2012).

Central is the presence of various qualifiers designed to moderate the language deployed. The most overt examples are that emotional closeness is requisite for using profanities and homophobic slurs as a form of *affection* or as terms of endearment; that homophobic slurs should never be used to genuinely insult; that saying 'gay' has a double meaning; that misogynistic commentary is never applied to friends' sexual partners; and, in all cases, the avoidance of using such language in the presence of those it might wound. What I go on to show here is that despite these rules of engagement oftentimes clearly being marked by double standards, the young men identify a 'discursive gap' (Magrath, 2017). The gap is between their actual views on women and non-heterosexual people and the ways they deploy language infused with problematic sentiment.

The multiple uses of 'gay'

McCormack (2012), studying men of various sexual orientations, has investigated and theorised the use of 'gay discourse' (cf. Pascoe, 2007 on 'fag discourse'). He notes that diminishing homohysteria leads to different forms and changing meanings of 'homosexually themed language' (McCormack, 2011). Most notable here is the phrase 'that's so gay' (McCormack, 2012). This phrase has evolved from one with ostensibly and irrevocably homophobic connotations to a commonly used and sexuality-neutral expression of frustration/annoyance. This was absolutely the case for the young men in my study. Examples of its use include Johnny telling me about his football team conceding a last-minute goal, Pat referring to a 'gay' hand in a card game, Billy having to change his plans for a night out because he could not get out of work, and Dave referring to a *Facebook* post of his friend that he described as 'so lovey dovey with his mrs; so I wrote "gay"'. Mike went on further to explain that the word was a 'catch-all':

MIKE: if I were to say to you, this interview is gay, that wouldn't be like a bad thing on gay people. It would just be something I'd say if I thought it was gay. I can't even explain it. It's just a catch-all phrase, like 'he's being a prick'.

Building upon Pascoe's (2007) work on boys' use of such discourses to police other boys' gender behaviour (rather than sexuality), McCormack et al. (2016) note that usage of this phrase amongst liberally minded heterosexual males with gay friends, as well as amongst gay men themselves, often complicates theoretical assumptions about the phrase's enduring homophobic underpinnings. Appealing for more nuanced evaluation, McCormack et al. draw on two strategies. First, they identify a marked generational divide in understandings of this kind of language (see Plummer, 2010). Second, they identify 'homosexually themed language that is used to bond people together in socio-positive ways or to demonstrate pro-gay attitudes' (McCormack, 2011: 672). To avoid positioning particular types of language simplistically as 'definitely homophobic', McCormack et al. (2016: 748) offer a more sophisticated understanding of the complexity of language through the concept of an intent-context-effect matrix:

> The interdependency of intent and context with effect [is] so strong that we reject using them as distinct variables, instead conceptualizing an intent-context-effect matrix. Highlighting the situated nature of this matrix, participants emphasized the importance of the existence of shared norms between those saying and hearing the phrase when interpreting such language.

Shared norms become an important part of how my participants used homosexually themed language. Beyond the double meanings behind the phrase 'that's so gay', the men sometimes deployed such language as a form of 'gentle' chastisement and banter, rather than meaning 'that's rubbish'. The *function* of this language was understood by the participants as facilitating socio-positive bonding (McCormack, 2011). However, this was understood as linked to group insider status, such that it was usually associated with 'bromances' (Chen, 2011; Robinson et al., 2017), characterised by tight emotional bonds:

DAVE: Gay slurs or anything are just in banter, never said in seriousness to someone. Only the group [of best friends] do it ... because everyone knows that everyone's there for each other. We greet by kissing and hugging, you know.

PAT: It's always about your good friends. Some of them, might just be a 'hey' and a hug, or will come in and be 'alright losers'. Other times they might even say, 'hello cunts'. It's all good 'cos it's love and respect.

CHRISTIAN: Because we're so close as a group ... If [friend's name] went, 'ah he's been a really good friend to me', and I went 'alright gay boy', ... he'd say something like, 'well you weren't complaining last night', and joke about it ... He would stand by what he said and we'd both know he meant it.

The closeness of the friendship groups, in almost all cases, determined the level of softness and harshness of the language used, with close-knit friendships free to variously use profanities, softer, more loving forms of greeting or even seemingly homophobic slurs. That these were all interchangeable complicates any analysis. Still, we must not assume that this translates into homophobia or policing other men's gender performance. The evidence of the required closeness is calcified in Christian's account of greeting another man who was a relative newcomer to his friendship group:

CHRISTIAN: I saw him out a couple of Saturdays ago, and I hugged him and I was like, 'hello mate?' and then [another close friend] turned around and went [quietly], 'here, you on fucking cock now?' and [the new friend] is completely different to [close friend], he would never dream of saying something like that. Not yet.

For many participants, using a homophobic slur with intent to wound was seen as completely unacceptable. This was especially the case in consideration of another gay man:

MIKE: If [gay] people are around, there's stuff I won't say in front of them, because I know they'll get offended by it. I have friends that are gay and [Partner's brother] is gay ... I hate homophobes with a passion.
CHRISTIAN: If there was a gay guy, or a straight guy, I would never in an argument go, 'you fucking gay cunt', never *ever* [his emphasis]. But if any of my friends walked in and they had a bright pink bloody t-shirt on or something like that, I would be like, 'alright gay boy', or something like that. They would know I'm just joking with them.
JASON: I'd be sitting in the pub and [gay colleague] would tell me that I have a mouth that was wasted on a straight guy. It's kind of lad's banter. He liked men of darker skin, and I would point them out and say, 'there's one for you', just laugh and joke. There was always a line which I knew not to cross ... he was out as gay, but I wouldn't ever be abusive towards him.

Shared norms facilitated ironic humour about same-sex desire and gay stereotypes, which acts simultaneously as an ironic 'recuperation' of straight men's heterosexual identities (McCormack, 2012), and even, as the last case, strengthened banter between straight and gay peers. This was not necessarily always in correspondence with entirely pro-gay attitudes, with contradictions appearing in some men's accounts about the contingent acceptability of being gay. For instance, in addition to espousing pro-gay sentiment, and talking up respect for gay colleagues, family members and friends, some non-heteronormative practices, and by extension non-heterosexual people, were 'othered'. The practice of authentic male-to-male interactions was commonly a theme of such 'othering', sometimes resulting in blatantly discriminatory perspectives (my emphasis):

MIKE: [talking about his partner's brother] he's horrendously gay. He's hilarious. I love him. He's brilliant. *Gays don't bother me, unless they're getting off with each other in front of me. That would probably bother me.*
CHRISTIAN: I know plenty of gay people that I get on with. I mean, there's [friend] I've known for years, he's gay, *but he doesn't throw it in your face, he doesn't mince around town.* That's what *I find uncomfortable* ... Not the actual being gay.

JEZ: [talking about a former tenant, now an acquaintance] I know I'm wrong for saying this ... knowing that [name] is now gay or bisexual, knowing that back then, I don't think I'd have lived with him, because I would have felt uncomfortable with him and his boyfriend in his bedroom, with me downstairs.

Such perspectives potentially problematise the use of gay discourse as a bonding mechanism between straight friends. It further highlights the complexity of contemporary working-class masculinity as it veers towards, but does not accomplish, an entirely inclusive form. Yet, the men's interactions never rested on the idea that being gay was, in and of itself, a subordinated masculinity (Connell, 1995). Across the entire dataset pernicious intent was almost entirely absent.

Beyond boy code: the young men's talk about women

While the participants' homosexually themed language was mildly inconsistent, there was plenty of *horizontal* homosocial intimacy (Hammarén & Johansson, 2014), characterised by inclusive attitudes and a high value placed on emotional intimacy. However, it was in the young men's discussion of women between men – especially between good friends – that limits to their progressivity was most overt. In some ways this should come as no surprise. The role of close emotional relationships, or 'bromances', has been seen in much literature as sites that sustain hegemonic masculinity (Hammarén & Johansson, 2014), such that heteronormative hierarchies are maintained to the supposed exclusion and derision of gay men (Chen, 2011), while women are cast as the objects and conduits through which homosocial bonds are strengthened (Sedgwick, 1985). This reflects the seminal writing of Rubin, who explains 'the use of women as exchangeable, perhaps symbolic, property for the primary purpose of cementing the bonds of men with men' (1975, cited by Sedgwick, 1985: 26). Kimmel (2008) has referred to such behaviour as being part of 'boy code', while Flood (2008: 355) contends that male homosociality in part generates *storytelling cultures* that emphasise:

> achieving sex with women is a means to status among men, sex with women is a direct medium of male bonding, and men's narratives of their sexual and gender relations [ought to be] offered to male audiences.

More recent literature highlights that homosociality, in times characterised by low cultural homophobia, can act as sites where 'emotional disclosure, and the discussion of potentially traumatic and sensitive issues', can occur (Robinson et al., 2017: 1). This more positive account of the productive possibilities that can manifest in homosocial situations is further evident in Thurnell-Read's (2012) ethnographic exploration of pre-marital 'stag tours'. Against the grain of the common preconceptions that align with the literature in the previous paragraph, Thurnell-Read (2012) highlights the co-existence of heterosexuality re-affirming language and activity, alongside largely non-competitive norms and, moreover, extensive evidence of expressions of intimacy and the valuing of group cohesion and togetherness.

While not universal, misogyny was more notable than homophobia. So too, however, was a general discussion of women, of sexual relationships, and of good and bad sexual experiences. Here, *close* friendships between working-class young men can be both a breeding ground for misogyny as well as sites of generating respect for women. However, more *casual* acquaintanceships sometimes facilitate less progressive attitudes towards women.

The *Facebook* ethnography revealed surprisingly little sharing of overt misogynistic, objectifying content. Thinking about the ubiquity of such material available on social media on the whole, the participants often asserted that sharing 'primal' and 'stupid' material was a preoccupation of older men:

MIKE: ... like memes with a woman with big tits or whatever, that's like the stuff old men like. You know, still reading *The Sun* [newspaper] looking for page three, [but] you know, [we've got] the internet. I can see tits when I want.

BOBBY: There's that generation who are cartoons with their tongue hanging out. So they might comment or share something really blatant. There's a lad who is about ten years older than me and he will, like, share jokes a lot that usually have a picture of a hot big-breasted barmaid, like it's the 1970s or something.

DAVE: It's kinda, like, primal. Some guys I used to play football with, like [now] in their fifties and sixties, they post stuff like a wink and nudge, really, a bit [what they think to be] 'phwoar'. I'm in a football [*Facebook* community] group, some dude shared a picture of a woman bending over, no knickers, like, with a bridge in the background and the caption is about the bridge. Nothing about football. Just stupid.

Easy access to pornographic material ensured that participants did not need to engage with sexualised content in *Facebook*'s quasi-public space. Attempts to do so were disparaged and/or seen as characteristic of older generations of men. That's not to say the men did not share woman-related and sometimes misogynistic content: examples include Carl sharing a meme of an image of a disembodied young woman's hands over the top of another young woman's breasts with the caption 'grabbing a pair of boobs decreases stress by 70% ... so grab away'; Billy shared a meme that depicted toilet doors with gender signs 'BLA' for men and 'BLA BLA BLA BLA BLA' for women, highlighting the perceived difference in how men and women talk to a member of the same sex in a bathroom. Others shared material with a political axe to grind against some feminist positions. Mike shared a meme of a white woman wearing her hair in braids with the words: 'claims to hate sexism; assumes all males are sexist.' More often, though, they shared material that was not sexist but politically incorrect or distasteful. For instance, Gavin shared a distasteful joke about the death of the actor Paul Walker, and Carl shared a meme mocking the presumed choice of dog meat among people from Asian backgrounds. Outright objectifying of women was present in the men's discussions with one another outside of the public gaze, but even this was highly variable.

Building upon the above social media content, I asked the participants to discuss the things they talk about and share with their male friends. All participants talked about having various *WhatsApp* or *Facebook Messenger* group chats wherein they shared content and discussed issues with particular groups of friends. For many participants this included at least one all-male 'lad's group', though the rationale for this varied:

PAT: I've got a WhatsApp chat with some lad mates. And [partner] has one with just the girls too. Because sometimes girls and boys wanna talk about different things.

TIM: I'll send a group message to loads of people if I'm trying to promote a gig or trying to rally people for a night out. And I've also got one which is about [playing] football, and I guess that's needed so [manager] can tell us the ground to go.

These all-male digital spaces were largely an arena for 'banter' and organising social events. This banter also included the sharing of controversial material, with pornographic video content featuring strongly, but in different ways:

JOHNNY: There's one mate who for some reason sends loads of videos and compilations of naked women, usually bouncing their tits around. I'm not kidding, no one else cares. It's like he is trying to be funny by not being funny.

PAT: Some good bromance stuff goes on in the lads' [chat] group! Looking out and talking about problems. And football chat and that. But also lots of absolute bollocks. Complete nonsense banter. Like someone might very rarely send a photo of them[selves] on the toilet. I don't [share sexually explicit content] but one or two do. It's fierce, kind of not for the sake of enjoying it, but because it's weird. [Friend] recently sent this horrible video of shit spraying out of a woman's arse all over the place.

Sharing explicit pornographic material was often done as a way of cementing bonds, and an effort at humour or to provoke disgust. This is, of course, still reliant on derogatory images of women, but their accounts do not fit squarely with the idea that 'friendship between men builds on and involves fantasies and experiences of having sex with women, as well as sharing memories of collective sexual harassments and sexual encounters' (Hammarén & Johansson, 2014: 2).

The young men suggested that, most often, sex stories were genuine and authentic accounts, as it was understood to be *safe* space for describing such encounters:

BOBBY: I sent my girlfriend's tinder profile photo, 'cos she is gorgeous and I wanted them to see how lucky I was ... nothing naked or anything! I think I have always sent face shots of girls I have been with and [SR: for approval?] ... not exactly approval, but because I'm interested [in what they say] and I know it's safe there.

PAT: I've told some graphic sex stories in there. Not to brag really, like I told them about a time when, unlike me, I was able to have sex for 30 minutes ... it was to tell them how unusual, 'cos they know I'm normally a 2 minute man! I wasn't being harsh about anyone. I've probably been harsh before, like one girl sent a few nudes without me asking and I put one into the group to show them how forward she was being. But it's never to be harsh about anyone ... that stuff will never get sent to anyone else.

CARL: I've talked about girls' bodies in chat groups. Sometimes I might be 'yeah sex is amazing, her body is rocking', or, I dunno, her 'tits are fucking amazing', but it's not the only thing. So for the rocking body one, I also said I really like her and want to see her seriously.

Among the sexist language here, it's important to stress that the participants conceptualised their sharing as praise and support. This is, of course, not harmless, nor without foundation in trading in the 'currency of women'. However, the kinds of dismissive and outright sexist, slut-shaming and/or abusive language that women report from men who are 'trolls' or who engage such tactics after being rejected (Powell & Henry, 2017), were not central to participants' 'trade' in women.

In terms of using women to build homosocial capital between men, there were several examples of how this pertains more to men who are one less familiar. Jason, for example, described how in his workplace he would talk about attractive female customers to his male colleagues. He did not socialise with these men outside of work, so the common ground was small and they thus resorted to 'having a laff' (Willis, 1977) using seemingly fantasised sexual encounters as the lowest common denominator:

JASON: ... we get a lot of young ladies in, so we talk about, once they're out of the shop and all that, what we thought about [their attractiveness], you know, as guys do ... But at work it's worse ... I know it will never get back to my wife, but it's worse because there's nothing else to talk about really. It's just the way we are. I interact with them like that and they interact with me like that.

This glimpse into the dynamics of male-to-male sociality was nuanced further when I asked Jason to compare his work interactions to his interactions with men he is closer to:

JASON: I don't actually hang out with many other men because I don't see my wife much so any time I get, I want to spend with her. But the other stay-at-home dad, he is my like only proper male friend here.
SR: Do you think you have that kind of 'laddy' banter like you would at work, or do you think it's different?
JASON: It's different, because we're around the children, so you, not just can't, just don't. It's not *necessary*. I save my lad banter for the guys at work [smiles]. Obviously we talk about the kids and what development they're having and everything else. We talk about obviously [my] work stuff, his work stuff.

This ease of movement from one discursive style to another speaks clearly to the ideas around fluidity, or chameleonising (Ward, 2015; Fisher (2009). The pervasive discussion of women in more objective ways among acquaintances, rather than close friends, was also present in the men's explanations of how they manage such discussion in interactions with relative strangers:

PAT: ... some men [you don't know] start by saying stuff about women because they've nothing else to say. It's awkward and weird when people do that to have something in common. But it happens and sometimes you go along with it like nod 'yeah yeah' sometimes.
DAVE: If a new bloke comes into our group and says something a bit disrespectful about women ... Erm, I'm not sure what the challenge would be, but I think it could be more that the lads might change the subject, or they might not really say anything to it. I don't think any of the boys ... say 'stop'.

The negative hegemonic norms described so vividly in some of the literature situating women as the currency in which men trade (Sedgwick, 1985; Flood, 2008) are still present here but in significantly more nuanced ways than has previously been documented. The function of hegemonic norms is to offer a common currency where there is no other; this thus occurs when men talk to relative strangers. A lack of ability to overtly challenge these norms – even when they disagree with the content of conversation – speaks to the process of dominative hegemony (Howson, 2006). However, among friends, there is a more complex dynamic. All-male friendship settings are *sometimes* arenas in which sexist and derogatory language is used, but, much like McCormack's (2011) take on homosexually themed language, the context and intent of this language often needs to be carefully analysed (McCormack et al., 2016). The data highlight how, very often, overt objectification is seen as inappropriate and less worthy of status. Explicit discussion of sex and women's bodies is part of a rich tapestry of meaning and intent that is sometimes in praise of sexual partners and sometimes about one's own sexual shortcomings – 'woman' is not held up as unitary other that the young men trade or discuss in a derogatory fashion.

There is no mistaking, however, that misogyny, even where somewhat attenuated, is more present than overt homophobia in the data. Yet, this position is in keeping with a Bourdieusian reading of the participants' more progressive habitus. In western societies, the structural location, bodily surveillance and dominant representation of women at the level of culture positions them as other, as object and, in many respects, as 'for' men, and 'as a man or woman [...] we have embodied the historical structures of the masculine order in the form of unconscious schemes of perception and appreciation' (Bourdieu, 2001: 5). This norm in the objective structure comes to be internalised such that the masculine habitus, even among relatively progressive men, generates a set of dispositions that permit men to think and talk about women as sexual pursuits in these particular ways. It is the self-perpetuating, but somewhat attenuated logic and practice of patriarchy in action. Not reproducing the exact norms as previous generations, but producing practices that remain problematic and tainted with sexism. This legacy of sexism, though, is not one that has a particular working-class character, as suggested in some masculinities research. Opposed to Ward's (2015) position that attending a strip club is part of 'older versions of traditional working-class culture', the sexism evident here, I would argue, is likely related with men across the class spectrum. Similarly, the ways that men show some progressive actions – such as *avoiding* strip clubs even when being pushed by peers to go – does not evidence a *working-class* masculinity but a masculinity in contest and being reconfigured.

Conclusion

This chapter considered whether the young men's more inclusive experiences and attitudes relating to the transition to adulthood translated into a wider set of more expressive and inclusive behaviours. Two dominant strands of literature featured as important backdrops whilst I was collecting and analysing the data. The first emphasises men's lack of emotional display as connected to the structures of idealised masculinity, or efforts at limiting and controlling emotional display as part of performing appropriate display of masculinity. Bennett (2007: 3), for instance, has observed that emotional weakness and not seeking help for health problems may be enduring themes considered important 'both by men born in the early twentieth century and by those born much later'. Others, such as Jackson (2006), suggest that talking about feelings is incompatible with a successful young masculinity. This might be the case for some men, even some young men, but it is *not normative* in the ways implied in the literature. The maintenance of orthodox formulations of masculinity that rely on the avoidance of expressing sadness or fear will and do continue to thrive in 'subcultural working-class worlds where machismo, crime, drug use and aggression are celebrated' (Daley, 2016: 139). However, the range of emotions so readily expressed in the above passages, both (quasi-)publicly on social media and in narratives provided in interviews, makes clear that these more 'mainstream' working-class men avoid neither emotional display nor intimacy.

The second set of literature informing my thinking and, indeed, expectations was the more critical accounts that centre on power and how emotional inarticulacy is produced by and reproduces gendered power relations, as captured here:

> Rather than thinking about emotions, or particular emotions, as inherently progressive or regressive for men, or indeed for women, it is equally important to consider how emotions fit into, and circulate within, neoliberal-capitalist, patriarchal frameworks as a way of maintaining inequalities.
>
> (de Boise & Hearn, 2017: 788)

There are important points here, but also some risks. I did not want to consider data showing emotions or their expression as inherently progressive or regressive, but we should also not underplay the theoretical significance of a wider set of emotional behaviour among young working-class men. The very presence of wider emotional repertoires, as articulated in this chapter and the IMT literature, disrupts the theory of hegemony and partially undermines the 'difference' so central to gender power.

Some have suggested that appropriation of a wider set of behaviours either fortifies hegemonic positions (Demetriou, 2001) or represents little but a change in styles of masculinity (Messner, 1993). Where this is not evidently the case, we should accept that the maintenance of patriarchy is often predicated on the perceived and essentialised differences between men and women. As these discourses of difference are challenged and altered, and the discursive distance and enacted differentiation between gender norms shrinks, they produce new possibilities for ameliorating gender power relations. 'Men expressing emotions does not necessarily disrupt gendered inequalities' (de Boise, 2016: 58), but it is a necessary step in the right direction towards better and more equal gender relations (cf. Duncanson, 2015).

That said, a more critical approach, as per the second part of the above de Boise and Hearn quote, would be to consider how emotions factor into power differences. The literature is clear here that the management of emotional expression has helped underscore men's iniquitous higher share of economic capital as well as positions of power and influence (Pease, 2012), and some have highlighted how men (often middle class and/or in offices of power) are praised as 'strong' or even 'more manly' when they express emotions, for example shedding a tear, when 'situationally appropriate' (Messner, 1993: 732). The aim in this chapter, then, was to think through the data in ways that did not disguise how emotional display might be connected to enactments of power and the maintenance of inequality. However, for the most part I found that young men's emotional repertoires are not connected to nefarious abuses of power even when I explicitly looked for it (see Moller, 2007), and the 'situationally appropriate' has expanded way beyond the handful of sites the literature (somewhat stereotypically) suggests. There was often an absence of conscious or subconscious motivation for the emotional displays documented, and instead I theorised the comfortable expression of vulnerability, sadness, happiness, shame, love and intimacy for children, partners and male friends as *practices* that make up the contemporary working-class habitus. These practices derive from the dialectical interactions between subjective agency and objective circumstances (Bourdieu, 1977; Scheer, 2012) that produce new paradigmatic situations (Bourdieu, 1990). There is thus a mutually constitutive instantiation where habitus is the 'embodied and axiomatic understandings and norms about feelings and their expression' (Gould, 2009: 10), and simultaneously, feelings and their expression are 'socially regulated, prescribed and learned as part of our pre/dispositions or habitus' (Colley, 2003: 6). Unequivocally, then, the emotional displays I have documented here are not 'the selective incorporation of elements of identity typically associated with various marginalized and subordinated masculinities and – at times – femininities into privileged men's gender performances and identities' (Bridges & Pascoe, 2014: 246). Neither are they simply acts of inherent agency manifesting as resistance to dominant, negative gender norms. They are bound up, produced by and productive of an increasingly less homohysteric culture.

Despite the shifts described, I am of course not suggesting that gender differences have been eliminated. The young men in my study still dress quite conventionally, and many of their *Facebook* statuses were conventionally gendered and 'manish' in their cultural attachments – characterised by posts about sport, cars and motorbikes, acts of physical strength, violent or action-based TV shows and movies, gaming, 'banter' based on humorous 'fails'. But the gap between what is deemed acceptable in the realm of emotions has diminished, with a clear break from the prevailing working-class stereotype. Even here, though, there are *remnants* of the long-standing idea that 'male misogyny and homophobia are, in part, forms of masculinity in disguise' (Reeser, 2011: 8). The remnants become most clear in homosocial bonding practices; though, as demonstrated, this is far more complex than simply homophobia and misogyny used to fortify male bonds. Authentic intimacy was present and alongside plenty of evidence of socio-positive practice, where discussion of sex lives included one's own inadequacies and praise of female partners. While some residual homophobia was apparent in some accounts, for the most part, as per McCormack et al. (2016), the intent, context and effect of homosexually themed language point towards largely socio-positive motivations.

Notes

1 LADbible is an organisation describing itself on its web presence as 'redefining entertainment and news for a social generation' with a focus on viral content and social video to 'provide news, entertainment and community to a global audience of young people'. It also stimulates campaigns, such as 2017 initiatives on both climate change and the issues of men's mental health. It has over 25 million followers on *Facebook* and its content accumulates well over 3 billion views per month as of 2017.
2 In this section I refrain from using direct quotes where the comments were posted on public *Facebook* pages because quotes are potentially searchable, thus compromising participant anonymity. Quotes on posts to a participant's own timeline remain intact. There are multiple texts on ethical best practice in such circumstances; my approach is informed by Townsend and Wallace (2016) and Snee et al. (2016).

References

Anderson, E. (2009). *Inclusive masculinity: The changing nature of masculinities*. New York: Routledge.

Anderson, E., Adams, A., & Rivers, I. (2012). 'I kiss them because I love them': The emergence of heterosexual men kissing in British institutes of education. *Archives of Sexual Behavior*, 41(2), 421–430.

Anderson, E., & McCormack, M. (2015). Cuddling and spooning: Heteromasculinity and homosocial tactility among student-athletes. *Men and Masculinities*, 18(2), 214–230.

Anderson, E., & McCormack, M. (2016). Inclusive Masculinity Theory: Overview, reflection and refinement. *Journal of Gender Studies* [online], 1–15.

Bennett, K.M. (2007). 'No sissy stuff': Towards a theory of masculinity and emotional expression in older widowed men. *Journal of Aging Studies*, 21(4), 347–356.

Bird, S.R. (1996). Welcome to the men's club: Homosociality and the maintenance of hegemonic masculinity. *Gender & Society*, 10(2), 120–132.

Bourdieu, P. (1977). *Outline of a Theory of Practice*. Cambridge: Cambridge University Press.

Bourdieu, P. (1990). *In Other Words*. Stanford, CA: Stanford University Press.

Bourdieu, P. (1998). *Practical reason: On the theory of action*. Stanford, CA: Stanford University Press.

Bourdieu, P. (2001). *Masculine domination*. Stanford, CA: Stanford University Press.

Brannon, R. (1976). The male sex role – and what it's done for us lately, in R. Brannon & D. Davids (Eds.), *The forty-nine percent majority*. Reading, MA: Addison-Wesley, pp. 1–40.

Bridges, T., & Pascoe, C.J. (2014). Hybrid masculinities: New directions in the sociology of men and masculinities. *Sociology Compass*, 8(3), 246–258.

Brooks, B., Welser, H.T., Hogan, B., & Titsworth, S. (2011). Socioeconomic Status Updates: Family SES and emergent social capital in college student Facebook networks. *Information, Communication & Society*, 14(4), 529–549.

Broom, A., Hand, K., & Tovey, P. (2009). The role of gender, environment and individual biography in shaping qualitative interview data. *International Journal of Social Research Methodology*, 12(1), 51–65.

Chen, E.J. (2011). Caught in a bad bromance. *Texas Journal of Women and the Law*, 21, 241–266.

Colley, H. (2003). Learning to do emotional labour: Class, gender and the reform of habitus in the training of nursery nurses, in *Experiential, Community and Work-based: Researching Learning outside the Academy, 27th–29th June 2003*, Glasgow (unpublished).

Connell, R.W. (1995). *Masculinities*. Cambridge: Polity Press.

Cottingham, M.D. (2017). Caring moments and their men: Masculine emotion practice in nursing. *NORMA*, 12(3–4), 270–285.

Courtenay, W. (2002). A global perspective on the field of men's health: an editorial. *International Journal of Men's Health*, 1(1).

Daley K. (2016). Becoming a Man: Working-Class Masculinity, Machismo and Substance Abuse, in *Youth and Substance Abuse*. Palgrave Macmillan, pp. 139–168.

de Boise, S. (2016). *Men, masculinity, music and emotions*. Springer.

de Boise, S., & Hearn, J. (2017). Are men getting more emotional? Critical sociological perspectives on men, masculinities and emotions. *The Sociological Review*, 65(4), 779–796.

Demetriou, D.Z. (2001). Connell's concept of hegemonic masculinity: A critique. *Theory and Society*, 30(3), 337–361.

Deutsch, F.M., & Saxon, S.E. (1998). The double standard of praise and criticism for mothers and fathers. *Psychology of Women Quarterly*, 22(4), 665–683.

Duncanson, C. (2015). Hegemonic masculinity and the possibility of change in gender relations. *Men and Masculinities*, 18(2), 231–248.

Fisher, M.J. (2009). 'Being a Chameleon': Labour processes of male nurses performing bodywork. *Journal of Advanced Nursing*, 65(12), 2668–2677.

Flood, M. (2008). Men, sex, and homosociality: How bonds between men shape their sexual relations with women. *Men and Masculinities*, 10(3), 339–359.

Flood, M. (2013). Negotiating gender in men's research among men, in B. Pini & B. Pease (Eds.), *Men, Masculinities and Methodologies*. Basingstoke: Palgrave, pp. 64–76.

Gaunt, R. (2013). Breadwinning moms, caregiving dads: Double standard in social judgments of gender norm violators. *Journal of Family Issues*, 34(1), 3–24.

Gould, D.B. (2009). *Moving politics: Emotion and ACT UP's fight against AIDS*. Chicago, IL: University of Chicago Press.

Hammarén, N., & Johansson, T. (2014). Homosociality: In between power and intimacy. *Sage Open*, 4(1), doi:2158244013518057.

Hogan, B. (2010). The presentation of self in the age of social media: Distinguishing performances and exhibitions online. *Bulletin of Science, Technology & Society*, 30(6), 377–386.

Howson, R. (2006). *Challenging hegemonic masculinity*. London: Routledge.

Jackson, C. (2006). 'Wild' girls? An exploration of 'ladette' cultures in secondary schools. *Gender and Education*, 18(4), 339–360.

Kimmel, M.S. (1994). *Consuming manhood: The feminization of American culture and the recreation of the American male body, 1832–1920*. Ann Arbor, MI: University of Michigan.

Kimmel, M. (2000). Masculinity as Homophobia: Fear, Shame, and Silence in the Construction of Gender Identity, in M. Adams, W.J. Blumenfeld, R. Castaneda, H.W. Hackman, M.L. Peters, & X. Zuniga (Eds.), *Readings for Diversity and Social Justice*. New York: Routledge.

Kimmel, M.S. (2008). *Guyland: The Perilous World Where Boys Become Men.* New York: Harper Collins.

Magrath, R. (2017). 'To Try and Gain an Advantage for My Team': Homophobic and Homosexually Themed Chanting among English Football Fans. *Sociology,* doi:0038038517702600.

Manago, A.M. (2013). Negotiating a sexy masculinity on social networking sites. *Feminism & Psychology,* 23(4), 478–497.

McCormack, M. (2011). Mapping the terrain of homosexually-themed language. *Journal of Homosexuality,* 58(5), 664–679.

McCormack, M. (2012). *The declining significance of homophobia.* Oxford: Oxford University Press.

McCormack, M., Wignall, L., & Morris, M. (2016). Gay guys using gay discourse: Friendship, shared values and the intent-context-effect matrix. *British Journal of Sociology,* 67(4), 747–767.

McKee, L., & Bell, C. (1986). His unemployment, her problem: The domestic and marital consequences of male unemployment, in *The experience of unemployment.* Palgrave Macmillan UK, pp. 134–149.

Messner, M. (1993). 'Changing men' and feminist politics in the United States. *Theory and Society,* 22(5), 723–737.

Messner, M.A. (1997). *Politics of masculinities: Men in movements.* Lanham, MD: Altamira Press.

Moller, M. (2007). Exploiting patterns: A critique of hegemonic masculinity. *Journal of Gender Studies,* 16(3), 263–276.

Pascoe, C.J. (2007). *Dude, you're a fag: Masculinity and sexuality in high school.* Berkeley, CA: University of California Press.

Pease, B. (2012). The politics of gendered emotions: Disrupting men's emotional investment in privilege. *Australian Journal of Social Issues,* 47(1), 125–142.

Pini, B., & Pease, B. (Eds.). (2013). *Men, masculinities and methodologies.* London: Springer.

Plummer, K. (2010). Generational sexualities, subterranean traditions, and the hauntings of the sexual world: Some preliminary remarks. *Symbolic Interaction,* 33(2), 163–190.

Powell, A., & Henry, N. (2017). *Sexual Violence in a Digital Age.* London: Springer.

Ralph, B., & Roberts, S. (2018, forthcoming). One small step for man: Change and continuity in Australian young men's perceptions and enactment of homosocial intimacy. *Men and Masculinities.*

Rasmussen, M.L. (2004). 'That's so gay!': A study of the deployment of signifiers of sexual identity in secondary school settings in Australia and the United States. *Social Semiotics,* 14(3), 289–308.

Reeser, T.W. (2011). *Masculinities in theory: An introduction.* London: John Wiley & Sons.

Robinson, S., Anderson, E., & White, A. (2017). The bromance: Undergraduate male friendships and the expansion of contemporary homosocial boundaries. *Sex Roles,* 78(1–2), 94–106.

Robinson, V., & Hockay, J. (2011). *Masculinities in Transition.* London: Palgrave Macmillan.

Rubin, G. (1975). The Traffic in Women: Notes on the 'Political Economy' of Sex, in R.R. Reiter (Ed.), *Toward an Anthropology of Women.* New York: Monthly Review Press.

Scheer, M. (2012). Are emotions a kind of practice (and is that what makes them have a history)? A Bourdieuian approach to understanding emotion. *History and Theory*, 51(2), 193–220.

Schmitz, R.M. (2016). Constructing men as fathers: A content analysis of formulations of fatherhood in parenting magazines. *The Journal of Men's Studies*, 24(1), 3–23.

Scoats, R. (2017). Inclusive masculinity and Facebook photographs among early emerging adults at a British university. *Journal of Adolescent Research*, 32(3), 323–345.

Sedgwick, E.K. (1985). Gender asymmetry and erotic triangles, in *Between Men: English Literature and Male Homosocial Desire*. Columbia University Press, pp. 21–27.

Seidler, V.J. (1994). *Recovering the self: Morality and social theory*. London: Psychology Press.

Shields, S.A. (2005). The politics of emotion in everyday life. *Review of General Psychology*, 9(1), 3–15.

Simpson, P., & Richards, M. (2017). *Macho myth-busting: working-class men aren't all too tough to seek help*, accessed 10 November 2017, https://theconversation.com/macho-myth-busting-working-class-men-arent-all-too-tough-to-seek-help-85149.

Skelton, C. (1998). Feminism and research into masculinities and schooling. *Gender and Education*, 10(2), 217–227.

Snee, H., Hine, C., Morey, Y., Roberts, S., & Watson, H. (2016). *Digital Methods for Social Science*. London: Palgrave Macmillan.

Thurnell-Read, T. (2012). What happens on tour: The premarital stag tour, homosocial bonding, and male friendship. *Men and Masculinities*, 15(3), 249–270.

Townsend, L., & Wallace, C. (2016). *Social media research: A guide to ethics*. University of Aberdeen.

Vanderbeck, R.M. (2005). Masculinities and fieldwork: Widening the discussion. *Gender, Place & Culture*, 12(4), 387–402.

Walton, C., Coyle, A., & Lyons, E. (2004). Death and football: An analysis of men's talk about emotions. *British Journal of Social Psychology*, 43(3), 401–416.

Ward, M. (2015). *From labouring to learning: Working-class masculinities, education and de-industrialization*. Springer.

Willis, P.E. (1977). *Learning to labor: How working class kids get working class jobs*. Columbia University Press.

Woodman, D., & Wyn, J. (2015). Class, gender and generation matter: Using the concept of social generation to study inequality and social change. *Journal of Youth Studies*, 18(10), 1402–1410.

9 Conclusion
Changing the tune, but not changing the record: working-class masculinity in transition

Introduction

'Fuck Nuance': so starts and ends a recent provocative argument by Healy (2017) in *Sociological Theory*. One of Healy's chief concerns is that nuance 'blocks the process of abstraction on which theory depends' (Healy, 2017: 119), while he also laments how sociologists fall into nuance traps such as the 'strong tendency to embrace the fine-grain, both as a means of defense against criticism and as a guarantor of the value of everyone's empirical research project' (Healy, 2017: 121). Actually, I think there is much to be said for some parts of his overall argument. However, and paradoxically, the fine-grain detail of data I have offered in the preceding chapters has a necessary function. A main contention of the book is that masculinity theorising to date, particularly Hegemonic Masculinity Theory (HMT), has retained the abstraction on which theory depends, but has done so from a narrow empirical focus. This has led to working-class men being caricatured and has complicitly co-produced the myth making that pertains to working-class masculinity. Thus, in often depicting actual nuance in seemingly more generalised ways – as per the major studies of youth transitions and masculinity – a *partial* reading of contemporary working-class masculinity has emerged and retained hegemonic status. It might be more fruitful to proceed inductively rather starting with a rigid abstraction to which data should fit (McCormack, 2012).

Despite ambitions to present unheard voices, research has often privileged only those deemed 'newsworthy', with men's everyday or seemingly mundane actions not sufficiently featuring in HMT, beyond being recognised as complicit in support of hegemonic masculinity and the maintenance of patriarchy. This narrow selection of social actors also informs researchers' efforts to *understand* and *empathise with working-class men* who might feel lost in fast-changing and often hostile economic landscapes. Similar types of voices take centre stage, with the most marginalised and most disenfranchised being used as the basis for theory making. Such stories have been vital for theorising power relations between different masculinities and patriarchal domination. Yet, researchers of such topics have often not remained 'open to the possibility of discovering potential movements toward a redefined hegemony that contains the seeds of utopian visions of the gender order' (Hammarén & Johansson, 2014: 9). In part this is because, as a critical discipline, scepticism in regards to positive change is a *modus operandi*. We must, of course, remain guarded against the possibility of power relations being disguised, reconfigured or down-played in the process of social transformations. This is something that masculinities studies has done very well. Messner (1993: 725), for example, signalled some 25 years ago that while '"softer" and more "sensitive" styles of masculinity are developing among some privileged groups of men, this does not necessarily contribute to the emancipation of women; in fact, quite the contrary may be true'.

In the same paper Messner (1993: 733) called for a 'focus on the ways that marginalised and subordinate masculinities are changing'. However, driven by the search for 'particularly nefarious instances of masculinist abuses of power' (Moller, 2007: 275), research on young working-class masculinity has established the realities of working-class men's marginalisation, revealed their methods of response and resistance and their subversion of dominant norms, *but then* often implicated those responses as being mostly about the disempowerment, subordination and 'othering' of women and/or 'untypical' masculinities (cf. Walker & Roberts, 2018). Such symbolic boundary work was theorised as being a central plank of what became a rather monolithic representation of working-class masculinity. Somehow, academic work has inadvertently been complicit in representing working-class masculinity as being 'the lowest level of consciousness, the dumping ground for all the vestigial traits discarded by the middle class' (Ehrenreich, 1983: 136). Accordingly, middle-class men, given their access to institutional power, 'historically, have not necessarily been considered the most chauvinistic, homophobic, or "physically" powerful' (de Boise, 2015: 326); by implication these are then the characteristics of *working-class* men.

One mode of masculinity seems to be writ large. The representations of working-class young men conform to the narrow set of expressions often defined as orthodox masculinity (Anderson, 2009) – explicitly homophobic, avowedly anti-feminist and misogynistic, alongside a strong predilection for anti-feminine acting. Despite often occurring at the same time as more fluid, contested and contradictory modes of 'doing' masculinity, this is the kind of picture that emerges in much research about contemporary young working-class men (e.g. McDowell, 2003; Nayak, 2006; Ward, 2015).

These kinds of assessments have been closely aligned with the valuable feminist project of examining men's subordination of women, and correspond with the impulse in the critical study of men and masculinities to make gender visible in order to change men's harmful practice (Walker & Roberts, 2018). In this sense, it is clear why there has been a relative absence of studies of those masculinities beyond the hegemonic ideal. Yet, as a result, the difference between 'dominant', 'dominating' and other forms of non-hegemonic masculinities has received relatively little consideration. Understanding and distinguishing between these forms of masculinity is critical if we are to identify what Messerschmidt (2012: 73) calls 'equality masculinities' – similar, I suppose, to Anderson's (2009) inclusive masculinities – and encourage more benign, even benevolent attitudes and activities as an antidote to harmful manifestations of masculinity. This, too, is part of the project of critical masculinities research, and something I have tried to address in this book through a longitudinal study of young working-class men's transitions to adulthood.

Myth busting: the key findings

In 1996, Connell noted that 'second wave feminism has now influenced public thinking for more than two decades, and one of its long term consequences has been to unsettle traditional ideas about men and masculinity' (Connell, 1996: 207). In the two decades that have followed, this 'unsettling' of tradition has continued, as made clear by a large swath of research finding more inclusive masculinities among young adult men in a variety of settings (see Anderson & McCormack, 2016; also Chapter 3). My longitudinal data, comprising biographical and follow-up interviews over a seven-year period, and a two-year social media ethnography, with a group of working-class young adult men, adds to this body of work in a novel way by making transitions to adulthood a core focus.

Other studies have, of course, focused on working-class young men's transition to the labour market (see Chapter 2). Unique in my study is that it is the first to have considered three of the key domains of young adulthood research – education, the labour market and the domestic sphere – and an intensive investigation of wider practices of emotionality. It is also novel in using an eclectic theoretical approach and study designed to specifically consider and account for the possibility of reconfigured versions of working-class masculinity. I combined Inclusive Masculinity Theory with Bourdieu's theory of practice, and blended these with insights from social generation theory – with the concept of generational units especially useful for identifying possibilities for different 'clusters' of behaviour to emerge among class groups. Despite my misgivings about HMT's ability to offer a lens to understand social change other than in ways that directly related to the maintenance of hegemonic/patriarchal dominance, I did not discard the theory. Indeed, it has been useful for thinking through continuities that emerged alongside considerable change.

Before summarising these changes, I should stress that they of course do not constitute a gender utopia. Adherence to the gender binary and to gendered identities still proliferates globally, and the violence, subordination and discrimination that emerge as a result remain entrenched in most societies. Nonetheless, the key point is that the lives of the young men who are central to this book mark a departure from both recent and historical literature describing and theorising the process and practice of working-class masculinity.

First, in respect of their reflections on their educational trajectories, Chapter 5 argued that the binary model of the engaged or disengaged male student that permeates much education research overlooks that most boys and young men just 'get on with it', to greater or lesser extents. The dominant narrative in academic work is that education is implicated in the production of classed masculinities, and that very often these are problematic and/or premised on resistance and counter-cultural practice. However, disconnection, defiance, deficit, do not constitute working-class masculinity. My participants' school days were marked by distinctly middle-ground orientations to education; they were neither completely compliant nor mostly resistant, orientations they attributed 'to most kids'. Their accounts did not support HMT, though their disinclination towards higher education (HE) did echo the findings of research on class and masculinity to show that university trajectories were viewed as risky and off limits; this in some ways aided their own HE exclusion.

Chapter 6 moved towards more dynamic data, focusing on current experiences in the labour market, first at ages 18–24, then at ages 25–31. The initial key point is that, contrary to much research, front-line, customer-facing, service work was not antithetical to working-class masculinity; they actually enjoyed the emotional labour required. This though, I argue, is no surprise. Manufacturing, mining and other traditional men's jobs have declined and increasingly been replaced by service sector roles for close to 40 years. Nowadays, large numbers of young men work in what were previously non-traditional men's jobs (Roberts, 2011), indicating, in Bourdieusian terms, that the emotional capital being used is informed by the contemporary working-class masculine habitus; habitus entirely at ease with service sector employment. The (incorrect) idea that great swaths are 'struggling to adjust to a shifting gender order' (Nayak, 2006: 814) seems reliant on studies of young men who openly reject such work – but they are a small minority.

The second point from this chapter is that while very few of the men remained in such work by the end of the research, this was always because they were pursuing better wages, rather than the status of the work troubling masculine norms. Indeed, two men who remained in retail had the most secure lifestyles, despite not having proceeded up the occupational ladder. For the others, with limited social, cultural and economic capitals, almost all their employment biographies were characterised by turbulence (though not chaos). This evidences the limits offered by inclusive masculinity in this setting for working-class young men: despite committing to the required emotional labour of the neoliberal worker, the labour market positions they obtain remain characterised by low pay, low status, relative precariousness and few prospects. In such circumstances, some participants turned to more conventional methods of pursuing self-worth and dignity by engaging in various typically masculine activities and showcasing autonomy.

Chapter 7 followed a similar model of using interviews from the two time points. In their first interviews, it was clear that the participants imagined futures in which, in terms of the division of routine housework, attitudes towards traditional gender ideology were somewhat attenuated. While not illustrative of a full-scale detraditionalisation of gender (Beck, 1992; Giddens, 1991), they showed, at the point of their second interview, that developing an attitude associated with a traditional, and (for working-class men) expected, gendered division of labour is far from ineluctable. Several of the men were primary caregivers, while several more were committed to egalitarian distribution of household tasks in ways that correspond with their imagined futures from when they were seven years younger. The lived egalitarianism on display is a particularly working-class outcome (Lyonette & Crompton, 2015), and one that sits entirely at odds with many academic readings, and also popular discourses, pertaining to working-class men.

A final myth to be busted by the data emerged in Chapter 8. The spectre of the gender performance-policed, non-emoting, working-class man – so evident in older accounts explicating the necessity for men to avoid 'sissy stuff' and to 'remain strong' – was absent. Of course, these discourses remain influential and constraining for some men, and are implicated in a wide range of men's health issues (Fleming et al., 2014), seen as the 'cost of masculinity' (Messner, 1997). Nonetheless, the emotion on display in participants' social media activity and in their interview narratives clarifies that *expressed emotionality is central to their lives*, rather than just at times deemed 'situationally appropriate'. A full range of positive and negative emotions – happiness, sadness, pride, shame, love, vulnerability – were all evident in actions and discussion. I did, however, trace some continuity amongst this change, with homophobia and misogyny sometimes used to fortify male bonds in a world of expanded emotionality. This, though, was complicated by abundant evidence of socio-positive practice reminding us that the intent, context and effect of such behaviours must form part of our analysis.

The transformed working-class habitus

The distinctive social conditions a generation experiences is argued to shape the possibilities of young people's transitions to adulthood, as well as their consciousness *throughout the life course* (Woodman & Wyn, 2015). Therefore, in a context of changes that have been brought about by 40 years of second-wave feminist thought and activism, critical masculinities scholarship and considerable (and somewhat related) social and economic transformation, it should be unsurprising that young working-class men's transitions to adulthood do not look like those of similarly located generations past. Similarly, we also ought not to be surprised that working-class masculinity has been in transition, and that it is young men who are the face of this transformation. First, despite a predilection towards understanding working-class men as being somewhat fixed in their gender performance, scholars *do* recognise that masculinity is 'a constantly changing collection of meanings we construct through our relationships with ourselves, with each other, and with our world'

(Kimmel, 1994: 120). Second, to re-quote MacDonald (2011: 427), '[i]f new social trends emerge it is feasible that they will be seen here first or most obviously, amongst the coming, new generation of young adults'. This is one of the defining understandings in youth sociology.

In all cases, the young working-class men discursively constructed their lives in ways indicating a socio-historical moment characterised by a more inclusive masculinity, with aspects of femininity that once threatened masculine ideals appearing to hold less cultural sway. Their failure to commit to ideals that correspond with working-class masculinity of generations past did not necessarily prevent them from obtaining a culturally validated form of masculinity. As Cottingham (2017: 282) argues, even where men 'must continually reiterate their claim to masculinity ... they can also redefine masculinity to align with the caring practices they enact on a habitual basis'.

The less-than-traditional masculinity espoused by the young men in my study, and by many other men (see Chapter 1, Figure 1.1), can be explained with reference to Bourdieu's concept of habitus, the 'system of durable and transposable dispositions through which we perceive, judge and act in the world' (Wacquant, 2006: 267), and produced by the dialectical relationship with the surrounding ecology of social life – such as the family, community, media, education and employment. A significant influence on that ecology of social life for those men who do not subscribe to traditional masculinity has been declining 'homohysteria' (the fear of being thought gay; see Anderson, 2009), and also falling levels of cultural homophobia. Another has been the transformation of the economy, starting almost 40 years ago, from being industry to service led. Consequently, an expanded repertoire of gender behaviours is now not only possible for working-class young men, but is part of their predispositions – that is, a 'practice'.

Practices emerge 'from bodily dispositions conditioned by a *social context*, which always has *cultural and historical specificity*' (Scheer, 2012: 193, my emphasis). They are, thus, more than agential responses and behaviours, and instead are part of one's habitus. The more 'inclusive' practices displayed and described in education (to a lesser extent), employment and domestic settings, and underpinned by higher levels of emotional capital more generally (as per Chapter 8), characterise 'a shift in the masculine habitus to incorporate compassionate responses to others' (Cottingham, 2017: 278). Given that generations exist as *specific collective* identities (Corsten, 1999), we can confidently suggest that working-class masculinity, not just a few individuals, has undergone a process of transition.

Practical implications

While much of the story has been one with theoretical implications, there are a variety of practical insights to be derived from this book. The first, a more general point that straddles both theory and practice, is that working-class masculinity, and indeed working-class men, should not feature as inherently negative in popular, academic or political rhetoric. The 'tendency to use working-class identity as a repository for anti-social attitudes and attributes' (Walker & Roberts, 2018: 3) has scapegoated communities and individuals. While not the subject of this book, the alienation that occurs as a result of these tendencies is likely to have implications for democracy. Indeed, the scapegoating of working-class people is evident in the narrative that it is they, 'left behind by globalization and resentful of multiculturalism' (Walker & Roberts, 2018: 3), who are responsible for the rise of far-right politics, the election of Trump, the vote for 'Brexit' (Pilkington, 2016). Yet, the clearest trend in class voting patterns has been 'the rise of working-class abstention' from the political process (see Heath, 2016). The widespread discursive construction of working-class masculinity as axiomatically 'in deficit' is an act of symbolic violence, but also functions as a diversionary tactic for middle-class and elite men whose practices are thus more rarely scrutinised. With working-class men positioned as the sole, or even main, bearers of 'bad' masculinity, attention to the oppression of women is only ever a limited enterprise. For all the wrongs that do emerge as a result of masculinity, there's nothing specifically working-class about them at all; orthodox masculinity is problematic and spans the class spectrum, as does inclusive masculinity. Harnessing the latter and tackling the former can only be achieved by acknowledging this and making greater efforts to stop reifying stereotypes and recreating myths. Relatedly, cataloguing more positive practices, highlighting the change that has happened, can present opportunities for greater critical reflection and for disrupting stubborn narratives of toxic masculinity. We should *never minimise* the effects, nor the people who cause them, but we *must minoritise* harmful masculinities. This involves accurately describing how widespread these ideals remain and challenging their supposed normativity.

The data have more specific implications for the formulation of policy related to men and education, men and work, and men and domestic labour. In education, being neither fully compliant nor necessarily disengaged has led these young men to mediocre attainment profiles. The key finding for policy makers, though, is that while masculinity is often implicated in boys' educational disengagement, this applies to a minority rather than the ordinary majority (Brown, 1987). Facilitating even stronger degrees of educational engagement requires more than focusing on masculinity. Class has a bigger impact on attainment than gender, yet receives disproportionate policy attention. This is likely because facing up to the class question is neither cheap nor politically expedient. Limited 'legitimate' cultural and economic resources, and a habitus not quite rewarded, but not necessarily entirely at odds with the educational field, are part of the reason why working-class kids get *less* education than their middle-class peers, even when they go to the same school (Reay, 2017). Tackling this demands better financial and pedagogical investment, and necessitates abandoning the idea that working-class young people mostly need to be 'controlled' (Reay, 2017). Gearing the education system towards incorporating, even celebrating, working-class culture would be a useful start, and more productive than emphasising student drive and aspiration, issues which have an inverse relationship with the amount of years at school (Berrington et al., 2016).

A less nebulous recommendation in the education space relates to the way that higher education is seen as a risky investment and so perceived as declared off limits for many men like those in my study. One approach would be, of course, to focus on getting more such young people to consider university (see Chapter 5). However, a more sensible first step might be to harness their willingness for so-called feminine work and their capacity to develop and utilise emotional capital. This would involve drawing on men's positive experiences of service work as a method for helping disentangle masculinity from certain professions and the presumed femininity of others. Recognising the reality of the shift in the working-class masculine habitus documented in this book could be the start of helping practitioners and parents to encourage students to choose courses at ages 16–18 that lead to career paths more congruent with their more inclusive dispositions. Current workplace learning opportunities in front-line service work jobs in the UK are often seen as 'badges of dishonor' (Roberts, 2013), but accredited college courses with sufficient learning content and recognition by a variety of service providers could prove attractive for employers and individuals, similar to the model used in Germany's vocational system (Brockmann, 2012), and *potentially* facilitate better upward occupational and social mobility.

With regards to men's employment, the data do not directly inform us how to better convince unemployed or labour market-inactive men to consider the possibility of front-line service sector work; yet, the normalisation of service work as palatable, even enjoyable, for young working-class men offers opportunities to trouble the understanding among older men (and/or unemployed men of all ages) that such jobs emasculate. Masculine norms built up in previous generations will be hard to shift, but they were produced in reference to 'what was done' at the time. By making clear that such jobs are no longer considered women's work, and men in such jobs are not so overwhelmingly 'outnumbered', challenging dismissive attitudes becomes possible.

However, the data illuminate another significant problem. Labour market data indicate that, alongside growth in the high skills economy, the bottom echelons are also burgeoning, while mid-skill jobs are continually hollowed out. The type of work that is increasingly available to men like those in my study, or even unemployed men, is often low-paid, poor-quality jobs. Even where relative stability exists, in terms of contract tenure, chances of progression are limited. In a context of low pay, this means such workers often leave the service sector in pursuit of better wages; as for many participants in my study, precarious work and turbulent employment biographies often ensue. Research shows that poor-quality jobs lead to poor health outcomes (Caroli & Godard, 2016). Important here, then, is that rather than implicating the toxicity of masculinity, we might instead consider the toxicity of neoliberalism (Walker & Roberts, 2018). The evidence is clear that men's dispositions are not the problem; even inclusive masculinity cannot inoculate against weak labour markets and poor-quality jobs.

Finally, the working-class men's shifting attitudes towards housework and childcare are emblematic of recent trends towards men's increased contributions in these areas. Unequivocally, though, we know that women still take on an overall highly disproportionate level of the burden. Women also often undertake tasks that are more time bound, with men conducting duties allowing discretion and autonomy in the task's execution. Corresponding with the idea that lived, rather than spoken, egalitarianism is more likely a working-class virtue (Lyonette & Crompton, 2015), the men in my study veer towards more equitable divisions of domestic labour. This echoes Maume's (2016) position that 'especially [men] in the working class, will be increasingly called upon and able to do family care work, irrespective of their motivation to do so'. Relatedly, policy makers must not shy away from recognising 'how necessary paid work [by both] women and men is to the income security of families' (Bianchi et al., 2012: 61) in the neoliberal era. Initiatives promoting this message may foster an increasing understanding of how important it is for all adults to also 'participate in the care work that complements paid work' (ibid.). Gender ideology is implicated in domestic labour iniquity, but it is far from immutable.

My data also speak to very common barriers to men's further contributions to domestic labour that go well beyond attitudes. It's somewhat depressing to note that today's situation demands similar responses to those suggested by scholars for decades. As Messner (1993: 732) noted 25 years ago, 'State social welfare policies, parental leave and childcare programs, workplaces transformed by affirmative action and comparable worth and the creation of democratic workplaces are structural changes that are necessary' to further unsettle the entrenched imbalanced division of labour. Men's jobs and government policy still play a significant role in constraining or facilitating any egalitarian impulses (Maume, 2016). Lip service provision will not suffice. For instance, the UK's 'Shared Parental Leave' scheme, instituted in 2015, offers up to 50 weeks of leave that can be shared by parents. In addition to having complex eligibility requirements,[1] the scheme provides a maximum of £139.50 per week for 37 weeks, with the remainder unpaid. The uptake of this initiative has been dire, at around 2% of eligible families.[2,3] This appears to be an effect of the gender pay gap that, in heterosexual couples, results in men mostly being the main financial breadwinner. To make the most of the willingness towards shifting the balance of roles in the home, policy makers and industry leaders must institute stronger incentives for fathers such that they are entitled to paid paternity leave that corresponds with statutory maternity rights, and the maternity pay offered by many companies.

The history of working-class masculinity is littered with problematic contributions, where working-class men's resistance to a marginalised status have resulted in, and even seemingly necessitated, the marginalisation and subordination of other men and women. We cannot and should not wipe the related injustices from the record; however, we can and must change the tune when talking, writing and thinking about working-class masculinity. The story of this book has not been about working-class men simply changing the style of masculinity in efforts to retain or obscure institutional power (Messner, 1993; Bridges & Pascoe, 2014); such men have always held relatively little institutional power, and arguably even less nowadays. Social and economic change as well as political struggle have transformed the meaning, practice of and possibilities for working-class masculinity. We must harness this and use it in the service of realising a society that is even more inclusive.

Notes

1 See www.gov.uk/shared-parental-leave-and-pay/eligibility.
2 From UK government research published on 12 February 2018; see www.gov.uk/government/news/new-share-the-joy-campaign-promotes-shared-parental-leave-rights-for-parents.
3 Gender disparities remain even when the paid benefit is slightly better. This is evident in Australia, for example, where claimants of parental leave can receive around $700 per fortnight, but are more than 99% women; see www.wgea.gov.au/sites/default/files/Parental-leave-and-gender-equality.pdf.

References

Anderson, E. (2009). *Inclusive masculinity: The changing nature of masculinities*. New York: Routledge.
Anderson, E., & McCormack, M. (2016). Inclusive Masculinity Theory: Overview, reflection and refinement. *Journal of Gender Studies* [online], 1–15.
Beck, U. (1992). *Risk Society: Towards a New Modernity*. London: Sage.
Berrington, A., Roberts, S., & Tammes, P. (2016). Educational aspirations among UK Young Teenagers: Exploring the role of gender, class and ethnicity. *British Educational Research Journal*, 42(5), 729–755.
Bianchi, S., Milkie, A., Sayer, C., & Robinson, J.P. (2000). Is Anyone Doing the Housework? Trends in the Gender Division of Household Labor. *Social Forces*, 79, 191–228.
Bianchi, S.M., Sayer, L.C., Milkie, M.A., & Robinson, J.P. (2012). Housework: Who did, does or will do it, and how much does it matter? *Social Forces*, 91(1), 55–63.
Bridges, T., & Pascoe, C.J. (2014). Hybrid masculinities: New directions in the sociology of men and masculinities. *Sociology Compass*, 8(3), 246–258.
Brockmann, M. (2012). *Learner biographies and learning cultures-identity and apprenticeship in England and Germany*. London: Tufnell Press.
Brown, P. (1987). *Schooling ordinary kids; inequality, unemployment and the new vocationalism*. London: Tavistock.
Caroli, E., & Godard, M. (2016). Does job insecurity deteriorate health? *Health Economics*, 25(2), 131–147.
Connell, R.W. (1996). Teaching the boys: New research on masculinity, and gender strategies for schools. *Teachers College Record*, 98(2), 206–235.
Corsten, M. (1999). The time of generations. *Time & Society*, 8(2–3), 249–272.

Cottingham, M.D. (2017). Caring moments and their men: Masculine emotion practice in nursing. *NORMA*, 12(3–4), 270–285.

de Boise, S. (2015). I'm Not Homophobic, 'I've Got Gay Friends': Evaluating the Validity of Inclusive Masculinity. *Men and Masculinities*, 18(3), 318–339.

Ehrenreich, B. (1983). *The Hearts of Men: American Dreams and the Flight from Commitment*. New York: Anchor.

Fleming, P.J., Lee, J.G., & Dworkin, S.L. (2014). 'Real Men Don't': Constructions of masculinity and inadvertent harm in public health interventions. *American Journal of Public Health*, 104(6), 1029–1035.

Giddens, A. (1991). *Modernity and Self-identity: Self and Society in the Late Modern Age*. Cambridge: Polity.

Hammarén, N., & Johansson, T. (2014). Homosociality: In between power and intimacy. *Sage Open*, 4(1), doi:2158244013518057.

Healy, K. (2017). Fuck nuance. *Sociological Theory*, 35(2), 118–127.

Heath, O. (2016). Policy alienation, social alienation and working-class abstention in Britain, 1964–2010. *British Journal of Political Science*, 1–21.

Kimmel, M.S. (1994). *Consuming manhood: The feminization of American culture and the recreation of the American male body, 1832–1920*. Ann Arbor, MI: University of Michigan.

Lyonette, C., & Crompton, R. (2015). Sharing the load? Partners' relative earnings and the division of domestic labour. *Work, Employment and Society*, 29(1), 23–40.

MacDonald, R. (2011). Youth transitions, unemployment and underemployment: Plus ça change, plus c'est la même chose? *Journal of Sociology*, 47(4), 427–444.

Maume, D.J. (2016). Can men make time for family? Paid work, care work, work-family reconciliation policies, and gender equality. *Social Currents*, 3(1), 43–63.

McCormack, M. (2012). The positive experiences of openly gay, lesbian, bisexual and transgendered students in a Christian sixth form college. *Sociological Research Online*, 17(3), 5.

McDowell, L. (2003). *Redundant masculinities?: Employment change and white working class youth*. London: John Wiley.

Messerschmidt, J. (2012). Engendering gendered knowledge: Assessing the academic appropriation of hegemonic masculinity. *Men and Masculinities*, 15(1), 56–76.

Messner, M. (1993). 'Changing men' and feminist politics in the United States. *Theory and Society*, 22(5), 723–737.

Messner, M.A. (1997). *Politics of masculinities: Men in movements*. Lanham, MD: Altamira Press.

Moller, M. (2007). Exploiting patterns: A critique of hegemonic masculinity. *Journal of Gender Studies*, 16(3), 263–276.

Nayak, A. (2006). Displaced masculinities: Chavs, youth and class in the post-industrial city. *Sociology*, 40(5), 813–831.

Pilkington, H. (2016). *Loud and proud: Passion and politics in the English Defence League*. Manchester: Manchester University Press, p. 328.

Reay, D. (2017). *Miseducation: Inequality, Education and the Working Classes*. Bristol: Policy Press.

Roberts, S. (2011). Beyond 'NEET' and 'tidy' pathways: Considering the 'missing middle' of youth transition studies. *Journal of Youth Studies*, 14(1), 21–39.

Roberts, S. (2013). Boys will be boys … won't they? Change and continuities in contemporary young working-class masculinities. *Sociology*, 47(4), 671–686.

Scheer, M. (2012). Are emotions a kind of practice (and is that what makes them have a history)? A Bourdieuian approach to understanding emotion. *History and Theory*, 51(2), 193–220.

Schmitz, R.M. (2016). Constructing men as fathers: A content analysis of formulations of fatherhood in parenting magazines. *The Journal of Men's Studies*, 24(1), 3–23.

Wacquant, L. (2006). Pierre Bourdieu, in R. Stones (Ed.), *Key Contemporary Thinkers*. London: Macmillan.

Walker, C., & Roberts, S. (Eds.). (2018). *Masculinity, Labour, and Neoliberalism: Working-Class Men in International Perspective*. London: Springer.

Ward, M. (2015). *From labouring to learning: Working-class masculinities, education and de-industrialization*. Basingstoke: Palgrave.

Woodman, D., & Wyn, J. (2015). Class, gender and generation matter: Using the concept of social generation to study inequality and social change. *Journal of Youth Studies*, 18(10), 1402–1410.

Index

Anderson, E. xii, 3–4, 53–61
Arnett, J.J. 8–9; critique of 9
aspiration 92, 100, 107–108, 111–112, 217
Atkinson, W. 62–63, 65–66

Beck, U. 7–8; critique of 9
Becker, G.S. 152, 158, 175
Bourdieu, P. 61–68, 99–114, 125–127, 212–215
Brannon, R. 44
breadwinner/homemaker ideology 7, 22, 29, 46–7, 150–153, 174–175; lessening importance to construction of masculinity 18, 158, 165–168

capitals 63–65
chameleonisation 28–29
classed inequality 20–22, 63, 65,
Coles, T. 66
complicity/complicit masculinity 4, 47–48, 52, 157, 210
Connell, R.W. xii, 3, 44–57, 67–69, 89–91, 113–114
continuity 8–10, 21, 63
conventional transitions paradigm 5–6; critiques of 8
counter-school culture 23–24
crisis of masculinity: cyclical nature of crisis talk 19–21; as a problematic discourse 18; critical understanding of 21–22, 32–34
cultural capital 63–64

de-industrialisation 19–20, 29–31
detraditionalisation of gender 121, 144, 158, 182, 189, 212–215
dignity 22, 28, 121–124, 139, 143, 185

domestic labour: diminishing threat to masculinity 159, 171–175; as feminine terrain 7, 22, 150–159; and the intersection of gender and class 151–153
double domination 66
du Bois-Reymond, M. 9

economic capital 63–64
education, underachievement 17–20, 85–86
education, participation: 18, 107–114
'egalitarian habitus' 68
emasculation 139–141, 152, 175
emerging adulthood 8–10, 131
emotion: as antithetical to masculinity 12, 44, 50, 180–181; on *Facebook* 188–189; in interviews 183–188; in male-to-male interaction 53, 56, 192–194; men's increasing display of 181–183, 213–215
emotion work 120–126, 194, 213
emotional literacy 125, 194
employment 93–95, 120–122; after the GFC 131–132; in the service sector *see* service sector roles 144–146; sources of identity beyond the sphere of 138–144
'erotic capital' 66

fatherhood 153, 156–159, 169
field *see* social fields
field of masculinity 66
'field of power' 63
femininity: subordination of 44–47, 55, 150
feminism 41, 65, 211, 214; and the crisis of masculinity 18–20
'fixing mechanism' 26, 33

'gay capital' 66
gender 1–9, 41–45, 212–218; and domestic labour 150–153, 174–175; and education 85–86; and emotion 180–182; 203–205; as intertwined with economy 32–34; and work 144–146
'gender capital' 65
gender order 3, 33, 45–49, 67, 145, 181, 211
gendered *social surface* 66
generations: and domestic labour 158–159, 168–169, 173–175; and education 113–115; as shaping transitions to adulthood 6–8, 59–61, 115, 214–217; and social change 55, 59–61, 173–175; and the sphere of work 127–128, 145; *see also* intergenerational transfer of knowledge; *see also* social generation theory
'generational units' 59–61, 115, 127–128, 174–175
Gramsci, A. 46, 50–51

habitus 62–70 ; in domestic sphere 175; in education 91, 94, 114; and emotion 194, 205; 213–217; in the sphere of work 125–126, 145
hegemonic masculinity xiii, 3–4, 44–48, 56, 112–114, 210–212; critiques of 48–51, 54–57, 67–69; as deterministic 51–53, 56–57; in family life 151, 169, 171, 185, 189–190; in male friendship 198, 202; in the sphere of work 144, 146
heterosexuality 47–49, 54–55
heterosexual recuperation 127, 197
higher education 85–86, 94, 107–115
Hochschild, A. 150–154, 162
homemaker role *see* breadwinner/homemaker ideology
homohysteria 54–56, 194–195
homophobia: as central to masculinity 46–48, 52, 54, 69; declining significance of 54–58, 70, 145; heterosexism 12, 52; the meaning beyond homophobic slur 60, 182, 193, 194–197; persistent in complex ways 182, 194, 205, 214
homosexualisation 54
homosociality 56; and homophobic language 194–198; and tactility *see* tactility, homosocial; and talk about women 198–205
Howson, R. 48, 50–52

inclusive masculinities 53–57, 212–218; critiques of 57–59; in family life 158, 169, in male friendship 181, 194, 203–205; in sphere of work 121, 127, 144–145
Ingram, N. xiii, 23–25, 63
intergenerational transfer of knowledge 31, 126
intimacy 56, 180–181, 192–194, 198–199, 204–205

Jones, G. 9, 79

Kimmel, M. 55

laddishness 22–29
'Learning to Labour' 22–24
'lived egalitarianism' 153, 175, 214, 218

maleness 41
Mannheim, K. 59–61, 115
marginalised masculinities 47, 205, 211
masculinity/ies: classed portrayals of 3, 17, 58, 113, 211–213; crisis of *see* crisis of masculinity; as a deficit category 53; as economic achievement 7, 28, 120; as homophobia and heterosexism 46–48, 52, 54, 69; intersection with class 17, 20, 25, 86; intersection with place 25–32; as misogyny *see* misogyny; as multiple/plural 32, 41–42, 45–46, 56; as a performance 29–30, 62, 187–196, 214; as positive 3, 175, 216 *see also* inclusive masculinities; as a rejection of the feminine 3, 22–23, 29–32, 44–47, 55, 127, 152, 211; as relational/hierarchical 3, 45–52, 69; and social/economic change 5, 10, 17–22, 25
McCormack, M. 42, 53–61, 68, 196–198
McDowell, L. 27–28, 30–34
meritocracy 23, 104
Messerschmidt, J. 3–4, 45–51, 212
Messner, M. 49, 211, 218–219
misogyny 23, 29, 46, 194–195, 198–205, 214
'missing middle' 4,79

Nayak, A. 25–27, 30–33
newmannishness 154
'new lad' 154

patriarchal gender relations, maintenance of 47–48, 51–52, 152, 203–204
positive hegemony 69
post-compulsory education 6, 95–100
post-structuralism 42–43, 61
power 42–43, 113–115, 210–211; as gendered 44–48, 155, 180–183, 203–205; and class 69–70, 211
precarious labour market 11, 25, 34, 120–121, 131–132

reflexive modernity 7–8
risk society thesis 7
Roberts, K. 5–6

sex role theory, Connell's critique of 44–46
sexual double standard 27–28
service sector roles: and emotional labour *see* emotional labour; growth of 6–7; positive attitudes toward 121–122–128, 138, 144–146, 213, 217–219; as women's work 25–34, 27–31, 120; working-class men's reflections on 128–132
social capital 63–64
social constructionism 42–43, 61
social fields 63–68
social generation theory 59–61, 212
social practice 62
'spoken egalitarianism' 153, 175
'stalled gender revolution' 150
status, masculine 11; through employment 126–127, 130–131, 136, 143–145; and aggression 114, 180; in the domestic sphere 172–173

subordinated masculinity 47–49, 198, 205, 211
symbolic economy 64

tactility, homosocial 68, 181–182, 92–94
time allocation theory 152
toolbox approach 41–42
'traditionally male jobs' 6, 25–34, 144–145
traditional masculinity 27–28, 32–34, 50
transitions approach 5–10
transition to adulthood 4–10, 34, 78, 210–214; 'golden age' of 6; in particular British locales 25–29

un/*under*employment 7, 11, 19–20, 26; case studies of 133–137; and the rejection of service work 31–32, 120–121

Ward, M. 28–33
weak structuralism 42–43
Willis, P. 22–24
women's labour force participation 19–20, 22, 151–152
Woodman, D. 8, 59–63
work on the body 140–141
working-class labour aristocracy 25
working-class masculinities 2–4, 10, 17; negative characterisation of 17, 23, 52, 58, 113–115, 128, 210–216; as incompatible with service sector employment 28, 31; pathologised as static or fixed 24, 33
Wyn, J. 8

youth sociology 5–10
youth transitions *see* transitions to adulthood